D0480382

INSTITUTE OF PSYCHIATRY

Maudsley Monographs

CHILD GUIDANCE AND DELINQUENCY IN A LONDON BOROUGH

INSTITUTE OF PSYCHIATRY

MAUDSLEY MONOGRAPHS

Number Twenty-Four

CHILD GUIDANCE AND DELINQUENCY IN A LONDON BOROUGH

By

DENNIS GATH

M.A., D.M., F.R.C.P., M.R.C.PSYCH.

Clinical Reader in Psychiatry, University of Oxford,
Hon. Consultant Psychiatrist, Warneford Hospital,
Oxford

BRIAN COOPER

M.D., M.R.C.PSYCH.

Professor and Chairman, Department of
Epidemiological Psychiatry, Central Institute
of Mental Health, Mannheim, Federal
Republic of Germany
Formerly Reader in Epidemiological Psychiatry,
Institute of Psychiatry, University of London

FRANK GATTONI

B.SC.(ECON.), M.SC.(STAT.)

Associate Lecturer in Statistics,
Dept. of Humanities, University of Surrey

DOROTHY ROCKETT

Assistant, Institute of Psychiatry,
University of London

OXFORD UNIVERSITY PRESS

1977

Oxford University Press, Walton Street, Oxford OX2 6DP

OXFORD LONDON GLASGOW NEW YORK
TORONTO MELBOURNE WELLINGTON CAPE TOWN
IBADAN NAIROBI DAR ES SALAAM LUSAKA ADDIS ABABA
KUALA LUMPUR SINGAPORE JAKARTA HONG KONG TOKYO
DELHI BOMBAY CALCUTTA MADRAS KARACHI

© Institute of Psychiatry 1977

All rights reserved. No part of this publication may be reproduced,
stored in a retrieval system, or transmitted, in any form or by any means,
electronic, mechanical, photocopying, recording or otherwise, without
the prior permission of Oxford University Press

British Library Cataloguing in Publication Data

Child guidance and delinquency
in a London borough. – (Maudsley
monographs; 24).
Bibl. – Index.
ISBN 0-19-712146-2
1. Title 2. Series 3. Gath, Dennis
364.6
364.36'09421'91   HV9148.C/
Juvenile delinquency – Social aspects,
Croydon (London Borough)

HV
9148
C7C55

*Printed in Great Britain
by Richard Clay (The Chaucer Press), Ltd,
Bungay, Suffolk*

CONTENTS

Acknowledgements   x

Preface   xi

I   Child Psychiatry and Child Guidance   1

II   The Need and the Demand for Child Guidance Services   14

III   Croydon: the Borough and the Clinic   27

IV   Aims and Design of the Investigation   40

V   The Child Guidance Survey   44

VI   The Delinquency Survey   54

VII   The Influence of the Neighbourhood   63

VIII   The Influence of the School   78

IX   Child Guidance and the General Practitioner   93

X   Conclusions   107

APPENDIX A Research Instruments   123

APPENDIX B Statistical Procedures   137

APPENDIX C Tables   157

References   177

Indexes   185

LIST OF FIGURES

1. Child psychiatric services, England and Wales, 1949–72   1
2. Factors influencing child guidance referral   20
3. Schoolchildren treated at child guidance clinics in England and Wales during 1967, by region   24
4. Addition of new wards to the Borough of Croydon in 1965   31
5. Age–sex distribution of child guidance and delinquency samples   57
6. Distribution of child guidance referral rates by electoral ward   64
7. Distribution of delinquency rates by electoral ward   65
8. Electoral ward rates for child guidance referral and delinquency   66
9. Ward rates for child guidance referral and delinquency by percentage of persons in owner-occupied households   67
10. Distribution of enumeration districts constituting one cluster   69
11. Comparison of social class distribution of child guidance attenders and background population, by cluster of enumeration districts   73
12. Social class distribution of child guidance attenders, by enumeration district clusters   74
13. Child guidance referral rates—secondary schools   82
14. Probation/supervision rates—secondary schools   84
15. Secondary school rates for child guidance referral and probation/supervision   85
16. Distribution of child guidance rates by schools and electoral wards   88
17. Distribution of delinquency rates by secondary schools and electoral wards   89
18. Relationship between referral rates and social classes I and II for 22 clusters of enumeration districts   145
19. Relationship between referral rates and social classes IV and V for 22 clusters of enumeration districts   146
20. Relationship between referral rates and proportion of owner-occupiers for 22 clusters of enumeration districts   146
21. Relationship between referral rates and density of population for 22 clusters of enumeration districts   147
22. Relationship between delinquency rates and social classes I and II for 22 clusters of enumeration districts   147
23. Relationship between delinquency rates and social classes IV and V for 22 clusters of enumeration districts   148
24. Relationship between delinquency rates and proportion of owner-occupiers for 22 clusters of enumeration districts   148
25. Relationship between delinquency rates and density of population for 22 clusters of enumeration districts   149

MAUDSLEY MONOGRAPHS

HENRY MAUDSLEY, from whom the series of monographs takes its name, was the founder of The Maudsley Hospital and the most prominent English psychiatrist of his generation. The Maudsley Hospital was united with the Bethlem Royal Hospital in 1948, and its medical school, renamed the Institute of Psychiatry at the same time, became a constituent part of the British Postgraduate Medical Federation. It is entrusted by the University of London with the duty to advance psychiatry by teaching and research.

The monograph series reports work carried out in the Institute and in the associated Hospital. Some of the monographs are directly concerned with clinical problems; others, less obviously relevant, are in scientific fields that are cultivated for the furtherance of psychiatry.

Joint Editors

PROFESSOR SIR DENIS HILL   PROFESSOR G. S. BRINDLEY
F.R.C.P., F.R.C.PSYCH., D.P.M.   M.D., F.R.C.P., F.R.S.

with the assistance of

MISS S. E. HAGUE, B.SC. (ECON.), M.A.

ACKNOWLEDGEMENTS

WE should like to express our warm thanks to a number of people whose help and support made the research possible.

Dr. S. L. Wright, formerly Medical Officer and Principal School Medical Officer of Croydon, Mr. K. J. Revell, Director of Education and Mr. G. Grainge, formerly Assistant Education Officer, authorized the study, facilitated contact with other local authority staff, and supplied confidential information.

Dr. G. Crosse, Director, Croydon Child Guidance Clinic, and the Croydon and Warlingham Park Group Hospital Management Committee gave permission to examine case-notes at the clinic, and Mrs. S. Meadows, secretary to the clinic, helped to locate the case-notes.

Mr. W. Wake, Chief Assistant, Admin. Section, Area Health, and his staff assisted in the survey of school health cards.

The Home Office Research Unit gave permission to inspect the records of juvenile offenders; Mr. A. J. Chislett, formerly Clerk to the Justices, Croydon, gave access to Juvenile Court records, and Mr. H. Dean, formerly Senior Probation Officer, Croydon, made the Probation Service records available.

Mr. D. Lambert, Deputy Director of Social Services (formerly Children's Officer) and Miss J. Wilson, Principal Assistant, Social Services (formerly Chief Clerk, Children's Department) furnished records of Croydon Children's Department.

The Croydon Natural History and Scientific Society provided background information on the history of the borough.

Professor G. Kalton, Dr. R. Maliphant, Mr. M. J. Power, Professor M. L. Rutter, and Dr. P. D. Scott gave their expert advice on various aspects of the study. Professor M. Shepherd and Professor M. G. Gelder provided general support and encouragement.

We are particularly grateful to Dr. H. G. Morgan, who took part in the early stages of the investigation and helped to survey the case-notes of the Child Guidance Clinic.

Finally, though we cannot name them individually, we are grateful to the 107 general practitioners who replied to the postal questionnaire inquiry, and to the eighty-two head teachers whose schools we visited.

London   D.G.
1975   B.C.
                                                                                                   F.G.
                                                                                                   D.R.

x

PREFACE

THIS monograph reports the findings of a survey undertaken in a Greater London Borough, into the relationship between child guidance rates, delinquency rates, and the social environment of the child population. The findings throw no light on questions of diagnosis, prognosis, or treatment in child psychiatry; rather, they are concerned with the patterns of utilization of existing children's services; with factors determining the local level of demand for these services and with the urban distribution of children who are known to be maladjusted or delinquent.

Research of this kind is not easy to categorize. The approach is basically *epidemiological*, in that it seeks to test variation in the rates of reported morbidity against the strength of certain environmental factors. At the same time, being concerned with referral to a specialist service as a process involving a number of medical and social agencies, it can be classed as *operational*, in the sense of 'an attack on problems such as arise in systems embodying a number of interacting parts' (Kendall, 1962). Studies of the delivery and use of medical services, and of factors governing the demand for medical care, have come increasingly to employ both epidemiological and operational techniques (MacLachlan, 1962; Cochrane, 1972). Such inquiries may also be seen as the logical first step in *evaluation* of services, which according to Wing (1973) should be addressed to the questions: 'How many people are in contact with the various services that already exist, what patterns of contact do they make, and what are the temporal trends in contact rate?' Examination of the patterns of service-contact need not be confined to simple descriptive data, but can extend to relatively sophisticated demographic and sociological analyses.

Child psychiatry, until very recently, has suffered from a dearth of such studies: indeed, of empirical research in general. Tizard (1966) attributed the lack of major advances in this field largely to a failure to pose simple, basic questions of a kind which permit scientific answers. Despite some progress in the past decade, his comments remain valid today:

What is the frequency of mental disorder or maladjustment in children? How many children require the services of the child guidance clinic? What kinds of backgrounds do they come from? What kinds of service do they require? What are the effects of these services upon the incidence or prevalence of maladjustment? ... the large literature on child psychiatry is mainly clinical. There is a dearth of sustained, professional research, and a widespread impatience on the part of clinicians to undergo the discipline which research entails.

Our own inquiry represents a step in the direction indicated by Tizard, and currently being explored by Rutter and other British workers (Kolvin, 1973; Rutter *et al.*, 1975). It goes beyond earlier surveys by relating child guidance rates within an urban population to local rates of juvenile delinquency: an index uninfluenced by service provision or referral factors. This strategy finds its justification in the often-reported linkage between 'maladjustment' and 'delinquency' (Min. of Education, 1955). Clinical studies have shown that, while both categories are highly artificial, it may be hard to detect any difference between children placed in each (Asuni, 1963). Longitudinal surveys have traced connections between maladjusted behaviour and delinquency in the life-histories of selected cohorts (Mulligan *et al.*, 1963; Robins, 1966). A controlled study of Glasgow boys showed that disturbed behaviour among the non-delinquent controls was commoner in areas with high delinquency rates (Stott, 1959).

Parallel investigation of child guidance and delinquency samples thus affords a useful technique for identifying high-risk areas or groups of children, as a first step in preventive action. To combine such groups under some such general rubric as 'deviant children' would be less easy to justify, either on theoretical or on pragmatic grounds, and we have avoided doing so in our own analyses.

The term 'maladjustment' is used by educational authorities in a restricted sense, to denote those children who by reason of emotional instability and psychological disturbance require special school-provision. More generally, it covers all types and degrees of psychological and behavioural disturbance in childhood which cannot be related to clearly-defined disease processes. We have employed it throughout the text in this latter sense, but only as a descriptive label for the clientele of a child guidance clinic. In discussing these children, we have not attempted to differentiate between those who were 'maladjusted' and those who had a clear-cut psychiatric illness. No such distinction could be derived from the clinic records, and we doubt if it is possible in epidemiological research at the present state of knowledge. The diagnostic distribution of the sample, together with some information on the children's behavioural disturbances, is presented in CHAPTER V.

Investigation of the children's social environment was restricted to analysis of the available social statistics, and concentrated on two main aspects; namely, the neighbourhood and the school. For purposes of ecological research, the school is a clearly-defined, ready-to-hand unit, although difficult to characterize; the neighbourhood, on the other hand, is a much more elusive concept. One of the main aims of this study has been to refine and clarify techniques of neighbourhood analysis, using much smaller geographical units and more homogeneous socio-demographic groupings than those employed in previous research.

Since the survey was confined to treated cases, problems of case-definition and case-identification did not arise. It is axiomatic that studies restricted to declared cases—that is, to patients making contact with health services—are inadequate as guides to the prevalence, inception, and distribution of any given type of morbidity in the general population. Even where free, comprehensive medical services are provided, a variety of selective processes may operate. The point is discussed in some detail, in relation to child psychiatric services, in CHAPTER II. Investigations of treated patients may be valuable, nonetheless, in helping to formulate working hypotheses and to select contrasting areas for comparative field-surveys. Thus, studies of the residential distribution of patients admitted to Chicago mental hospitals in the 1930s opened up a new vein of ecological research which is still far from exhausted (Faris and Dunham, 1939; Levy and Rowitz, 1970). Surveys of this kind, which rely on the collation and analysis of 'second-hand' data, have the advantage of being relatively cheap and hence feasible in many situations where the resources are insufficient for field surveys. The investigation described in these pages was undertaken with no special research funds and no means other than that amount of the authors' working-time generously agreed by their respective departments.

CHAPTER I

CHILD PSYCHIATRY AND CHILD GUIDANCE

OUR age has witnessed an unprecedented growth of interest both in normal child psychology and in the psychological disorders of childhood. In step with this development has gone a rapid increase in the provision of services for disturbed children. Since the advent of the National Health Service in 1948, the numbers of children referred to psychiatric clinics in England and Wales have increased more than twelve-fold: a trend illustrated by FIGURE I.

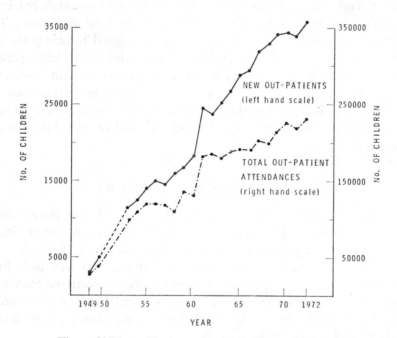

Fig. 1. Child psychiatric services England and Wales 1949–72

This expansion, proportionately greater than for either paediatrics or adult psychiatry during the same period, has in effect created a new medical sub-speciality. In 1971, 250 child psychiatrists working in the National Health Service saw over 34,000 new cases, while total attendances neared the quarter-million mark (Dept. of Health, 1973). These figures appear to indicate a public health problem of major dimensions, yet their significance is not fully understood. There is no firm evidence of an increase in children's disorders that would account for the rising demand; nor is there any clear agreement as to whether most of the children seen in the clinics should be regarded as ill, maladjusted, or, as some critics aver, merely passing through a stage of normal development. The answers to these questions have obvious importance for the rational planning of services. Moreover, a scientific approach to prevention will require much more information about the environmental factors of childhood disorders, and about which groups of children are most exposed to risk. There is thus an outstanding need for investigation of children referred to the psychiatric services and of their social background. In order to mount such research, it is essential first to know something about the existing services and how they work.

The official statistics represented in FIGURE 1 combine children seen in hospital departments with the much larger numbers attending child guidance clinics, and in so doing conceal a division of some importance. The hospital departments correspond roughly to adult out-patient clinics, are administered by the same authorities and for the most part share their medical orientation. Child guidance clinics, in contrast, are situated not in hospitals but in the community, usually in small buildings provided by local authorities. They constitute a unique form of joint-user service, designed to bridge the gaps between medical, educational and social agencies, while in its daily operation remaining largely independent of all three. To understand the differences between hospital and community-based services, and to avoid confusion as to their respective aims and functions, it is necessary to know something about the historical development of child psychiatry and of the child guidance movement.

HISTORICAL BACKGROUND

Fortunately, the subject is well-documented. In particular, the reviews by Keir (1952), Kanner (1959), and Walk (1964), each written from a different standpoint, together provide an account as balanced as it is detailed.

According to Kanner, modern child psychiatry is best seen as 'a fusion of what used to be a collection of more or less loosely scattered fragments'; namely, medical studies of mental retardation and behavioural disorders; remedial education; differential psychology; criminology; psycho-analysis and the mental hygiene movement.

The medical origins must be sought at least as far back as the sixteenth century, when case-descriptions of insomnia, nightmares, bedwetting, and stammering in childhood were already being published and their treatment discussed (Walk, 1964). In the early nineteenth century, the French alienist Felix Voisin, at his private 'Orthophrenic Institution' in Paris, was concerning himself with four categories of children who had special needs: (1) the feeble-minded; (2) those showing character abnormalities from birth; (3) those born normal but become deviant through faulty upbringing; (4) those born of insane parents and hence thought to be predisposed to mental or nervous disorder. The work of Voisin and his contemporary Seguin led to the establishment in a number of countries of institutions for the mentally defective, in the best of which physicians and teachers worked side by side. For the most part, however, medical and pedagogic interests were pursued separately throughout the sixteenth century.

The attention of medical alienists remained focused on mental deficiency, perhaps because their observations were largely restricted to institutional cases. Nevertheless, functional disorders were not entirely ignored. Henry Maudsley (1879) devoted a chapter of his *Pathology of Mind* to insanity in children. Langdon Down (1887) wrote of 'the children intermediate between the idiot and the lunatic, children of neurotic parents who break down under any vital strain'. Works on the subject appeared in Germany (Emminghaus, 1887), France (Moreau de Tours, 1888; Manheimer, 1899), and Great Britain (Ireland, 1898). Meanwhile, both in Europe and in the United States, some physicians working with children recognized the need for more psychological knowledge in their specialty and, finding little guidance in the psychiatric literature, set out to explore the field for themselves (Rachford, 1905; Guthrie, 1907).

The frequency of functional disorders among children indicated an unmet need for treatment facilities outside the institutions. To meet this need, clinics began to be opened. When Fletcher Beach, a former asylum superintendent, was appointed Physician to the West End Hospital for Nervous Disorders, London, his outpatients included children as well as adults (Beach, 1898). In Italy, de Sanctis anticipated by a quarter-century the American model of the child guidance team, bringing together for the first time psychiatrist, psychologist, teacher, and social worker (Unesco, 1956). But the medical profession as a whole was slow to follow these leads. By the turn of the century, the initiative for developing new services rested largely with non-medical workers.

Foremost among these were the pedagogues. The new legislation making school attendance compulsory had opened a Pandora's Box of learning and behavioural problems. In central Europe, the influence of Voisin and Seguin led to the growth of the *Heilpädagogik* movement, which provided special educational facilities for children with physical or mental handicaps. More important, however, for the growth of systematic knowledge was the part played by the new science of psychology. The psychologist's contribution— based, unlike the psychiatrist's, on the study of normal children—received a strong impetus from mid-nineteenth century evolutionary biology. Darwin's *Biographical Sketch of an Infant* (Darwin, 1877) was hailed as pointing the way to a revolutionary science of childhood.

The new field was clearly expected to form part of the domain of biology. 'Mental life,' declared Spencer (1855), 'like all life, consists essentially in the continuous adjustment of internal relations to external relations, of the individual organism to its material and social environment.' Thus was the biological principle of homeostasis extended to the social sphere.

The practical expression of these new ideas was soon visible in many parts of the world. Galton's 'anthropometric laboratory' in South Kensington opened in 1884 and Sully's psychological laboratory at University College in 1896; meanwhile, in Paris, Alfred Binet had begun his psychometric studies of children. A psychological laboratory was founded at Johns Hopkins in 1883, while at Pennsylvania both a chair of psychology and a psychological treatment clinic had been established by 1896.

Witmer at Pennsylvania, like Sully in England and Binet in France, insisted on the need for teamwork between physicians, psychologists, teachers, and social workers. From the outset, psychologists seem to have entertained few doubts about their central position. What was required, wrote Sully, was '. . . a new kind of specialist—a psychological specialist in fact', who would combine a training in general psychology with clinical experience of children's disorders. Gertrude Keir, reviewing progress half-a-century later, restated the claim:

Child guidance sprang from the early work of the British school of 'biological psychology' . . . In this country child guidance has, from the very outset, been regarded not as a branch of medicine but as a branch of psychology, namely as a practical application of the psychology of the individual child. Owing to its biological origin it has conceived its task to be primarily that of adjusting the growing individual to his own immediate environment (and often that of adjusting his environment to him) rather than that of curing a mental illness or treating a psychiatric patient [Keir, 1952].

Support for this viewpoint may be found in the long-standing association between educational psychology and criminology. Juvenile courts had been set up in Australia and the United States in the nineties; the Children's Act of 1908 introduced them to England, and soon magistrates were calling for psychological assessment of young offenders. In 1913 Cyril Burt was appointed clinical psychologist to London County Council and began a series of classic studies. His book, *The Young Delinquent* (1925), graphically portrayed the problems of young people brought before the courts. Burt's influence on British educational psychology would be hard to over-estimate:

The service which he created set a pattern of close co-operation with the schools, of investigation by rigorous scientific methods of the practical problems of education, of the treatment of individual cases and of the integration under the guidance and inspiration of the Psychologist's office of the many special educational facilities of a large authority—a pattern which still dominates the best services in England [Unesco, 1956].

While the problem of juvenile delinquency was just as important for the growth of children's services in the United States, there the emphasis was less on education than on medical treatment. The appointment of a physician, William Healy, as director of the Juvenile Psychopathic Institute in Chicago has been called the beginning of child guidance as we know it. Levy (1968) has given an intriguing account of the circumstances.

A philanthropic lady, a Mrs. Dummer, was appalled by accounts in newspapers about juvenile crime and contributed money to make possible a proper investigation of this malady . . . A committee was formed, a search was made for a 'skilled physician' and there at the appropriate moment William Healy emerged. Why Chicago ? Why Mrs. Dummer ? Why Dr. Healy ?

In attempting to answer his own questions, Levy drew attention to the important part played by wealthy philanthropists, a thread in the skein of child psychiatry missed by Kanner and other writers. The Commonwealth Fund, a private foundation destined to play a major role in the early child guidance movement, was established in 1918 by a Mrs. Harkness of New York, 'for the welfare of mankind'. Mrs. Dummer was a member of the Hull House Group, a Chicago social settlement founded by Jane Addams, later a Nobel prize-winner. Mr. Dummer also took an active part in the enterprise, drawing up the legal terms of the trust fund under which he and his wife donated money for the new institute.

Although Healy was an eclectic physician who fully grasped the need for teamwork, it was his application of Freudian methods to the treatment of delinquency that aroused Mrs. Dummer's admiration, and so secured for him directorship of the clinic. His was an appointment of some consequence. When the first Child Guidance Demonstration Clinics were opened in the early 1920s, Healy's clinics, first in Chicago and later at the Judge Baker Foundation in Boston, were adopted as a model. Thus, from its earliest days the child guidance movement in America was subjected to the pervasive influence of Freud's 'new psychology'. Hailed with enthusiasm by many workers, rejected equally vehemently by others, psycho-analytic theory became the single most important influence on the child guidance movement. In some countries, indeed, child psychiatry remains to this day the stronghold of psycho-analysis.

Meanwhile, the last of Kanner's 'fragments' had been added to the mosaic. In 1909, the former mental patient Clifford Beers, author of *A Mind that Found Itself* (Beers, 1948), set up a National Committee for Mental Hygiene with the support of Adolph Meyer, William Dewey, and other eminent persons. Their initial aim was to gain better conditions in the mental hospitals, but soon they turned their attention to the possibility of preventing insanity and delinquency by social measures. It was this notion that inspired the committee's interest in children's services and its sponsorship of the Child Guidance Demonstration Clinics.

Circumstances now decreed that, despite its stronger tradition of educational psychology, Britain should emulate the American example. Once again, philanthropy took a decisive hand. In 1925, Mrs. St. Loe Strachey, a prominent Juvenile Court magistrate, visited the United States to see the new clinics, and there made contact with the Commonwealth Fund. On her return to England, she called a meeting of interested parties to discuss the establishment of similar clinics in this country. A group of people engaged in social work was dispatched across the Atlantic, with support from the Commonwealth Fund, in order to acquire psychiatric skills; on their return they presented the newly-formed Child Guidance Council with a report advocating the setting up of clinics in conjunction with the school system. Soon afterwards, the Commonwealth Fund gave money for a Demonstration Clinic in North London, the second in the country.[1] A policy based on medical treatment was assured by the appointment as director of a psychiatrist, Dr. William Moodie.

During the inter-war years, a few attempts were made to develop fully co-ordinated services. A children's department was opened by the Tavistock Clinic in 1926 and a child guidance clinic by Guy's Hospital four years later. For the most part, however, hospital- and community-based services grew up separately, child guidance clinics coming increasingly under the aegis of local government. Birmingham opened the first provincial clinic in 1932; other large cities followed, and by 1939 there were over twenty such clinics in England and Wales. Throughout this period only a handful of hospital clinics were in operation.

The split between child guidance and hospital child psychiatry, firmly established by the end of the Second World War (Blacker, 1946), was perpetuated under the N.H.S., which placed hospital clinics under the newly-formed Regional Hospital Boards, but left most child guidance clinics under local authority control. Both types of service now began to multiply: in 1953, there were 150 child guidance clinics and ten years later over 300, while in the same period the number of hospital clinics also doubled, to over 100. More recently, hospital child psychiatry has expanded rapidly with the creation of new in-patient units and a large increase in both consultant and training posts.

CHILD PSYCHIATRY AND CHILD GUIDANCE TODAY

Against this historical background, the scope and function of present-day services become more readily comprehensible. The distinction between child psychiatry as a hospital-based specialty, and child guidance as a community service, has remained an administrative reality and has been accepted as such in official planning. The joint-user schemes whereby health, education, and welfare authorities co-operate in running child guidance clinics have arisen from a concern as much with delinquency and educational problems as with illness in the accepted sense; they represent, in short, an attempt to integrate the work of a number of professions involved in child care.

Unfortunately, a true synthesis either of professional disciplines or of theoretical concepts has proved elusive. Psychiatrists, educational psychologists, teachers, and social workers, however closely they may work together,

[1] The first was the East London Child Guidance Clinic opened by the Jewish Health Organization in 1927, under the directorship of Dr. Emmanuel Miller.

tend to remain identified with their differing professional standpoints. Accepted notions of illness and maladjustment; neurosis and emotional disturbance; delinquency and behaviour disorder; defect and retardation; deviance and handicap; stubbornly refuse either to coincide or to dovetail neatly into a single system of classification. Nowhere in psychiatry has there been a more serious failure to translate concepts into definitions, or to render definitions operational. The result is to be seen in a remarkable dearth of precise information.

In contrast to the wealth of material on their historical development, very little is known about the present-day functioning of child guidance clinics. In the words of one observer:

Our lack of general knowledge about child guidance is striking . . . Ignorance is due partly to the fact that services are provided by different authorities which make returns in different ways, but it is also due to the attitude of those who work in child guidance. It is significant that some of the early clinics were known as 'demonstration' clinics. The terminology is suggestive of a long-standing attitude: the manner in which maladjustment can be treated is already known, it requires demonstration rather than exploration or testing. Admittedly, research activity was one of the stated aims of the early clinics, but few if any research findings are available today on the nature of child guidance clientele, the effectiveness of treatment, or the rationale of different treatment policies (Timms, 1968).

This passage is taken from the report of one of the few British studies to try to remedy the deficiency. Timms examined the records of six clinics in different parts of the country, in the hope that their pooled data would reflect the national scene. From his vignette of each clinic, it is clear that they differed radically in organization, staffing, and treatment policy. One was administered by a psychologist; another by consultant psychiatrists; while in a third the psychiatric social worker dealt with new cases, allocating each and deciding when it should be 'closed'. At one clinic, first interviews lasted as a rule less than half-an-hour; at others up to one-and-a-half hours. Per 100,000 school population, the average number of weekly referrals ranged from 6 to 17; of psychologists' sessions from 0 to 112; of social workers' sessions from 17 to 138 and of psychiatrists' sessions from 10 to 100. Waiting-times also varied greatly, the proportion of children seen within three months of referral falling between 19 and 83 per cent.

These large disparities suggested that the six clinics represented, in effect, a broad cross-section of local services in England and Wales: a conclusion supported by the findings of a contemporary survey of child guidance staffing (Dept. of Education and Science, 1968). Characteristics of the clientele, as revealed by the 1964–5 case-records, thus provided a valuable thumb-nail sketch of British child guidance clinics in action. The main features of the sample can be summarized under the headings of demographic distribution; sources of referral; clinic waiting-times; diagnosis; treatment and disposal.

1. DEMOGRAPHIC DISTRIBUTION

More boys were seen than girls, the proportions of the former ranging from 64 to 76 per cent among the clinics, with a mean of 68 per cent. The male preponderance held good for all age-groups and sources of referral, and was unaffected by the exclusion of court referrals. The numbers were roughly equal for children between 5 and 10, and over 10 years old; at all but one of the clinics, children under 5 comprised only a small fraction of the total. In five of the six clinics, the Registrar-General's Social Classes IV and V were over-represented: a finding which must be treated with some caution because of the large number of children whose fathers' occupations were not recorded.

2. SOURCES OF REFERRAL

The children had been sent from many sources, but educational and medical agencies were the most important. Altogether, the school system (including school medical services) accounted for two-thirds of all referrals. Direct referral by parents had occurred in less than 5 per cent of cases. This figure is probably representative, though a comparable study in Bristol some years earlier had reported direct parental referral in 16 per cent of cases (Barbour and Beedell, 1955). Such findings may in any case under-estimate the importance of parental action. Although details of the paths by which children had reached the six clinics were seldom recorded, it was known that some had been sent by doctors at the parents' instigation, while in other instances referral had been the outcome of a more-or-less protracted 'bargaining process' involving a number of people. In general, it seems that parents' influence on the referral pattern is largely indirect, being mediated through family doctors and other medical agents.

3. CLINIC WAITING-TIMES

Though the average waiting-time varied a good deal between clinics, the overall pattern was one of protracted delays: six months after referral, 17 per cent of the children were either still awaiting appointments or had been withdrawn from the lists. In many instances, further long intervals elapsed between the initial interview and the start of treatment.

Clinic waiting-times have been a recurrent theme in the commentaries of recent years. The Seebohm Committee (1968), noting an average wait of six months and an establishment of trained workers well below the target set a decade earlier in the Underwood Report (Min. of Education, 1955), diagnosed '. . . a dire shortage of skilled staff in child guidance clinics'. Another official inquiry found little prospect of the situation being remedied within the next twenty years (Dept. of Education and Science, 1968). Such assessments suggest that the pattern found for the six clinics' sample was by no means atypical.

4. DIAGNOSIS

Despite poor diagnostic recording, there was little doubt that the majority of children had been sent to the clinics because of their disturbed behaviour. Even excluding known delinquency, conduct disorders accounted for at least half the cases in every clinic except one, which specialized in educational problems.

No diagnostic classification has been generally accepted in child psychiatry, and none of those in use is regarded as wholly satisfactory. Perhaps in consequence, the records of child guidance clinics tend to be unrewarding as sources of diagnostic data. As a rule, however, cases can be allocated to broad diagnostic categories on the basis either of a formal diagnosis or of recorded clinical features.

Neuroses and conduct disorders are usually found to be the biggest groups. The former is customarily taken to include all disorders characterized by anxiety, depression, phobias, obsessions, compulsions, or hysterical symptoms, but without the gross loss of reality-sense typical of the psychoses. The latter covers forms of behaviour which are culturally deviant, socially undesirable and associated with emotional disturbance or impaired personal relationships (Min. of Education, 1955; Rutter et al., 1970).

In the six-clinics sample, conduct disorders (including delinquency) comprised half the case-load, whereas 'nervous' (neurotic) disorders accounted for only 7 per cent. The corresponding proportions in the Bristol survey were 41 and 12 per cent (Barbour and Beedell, 1955). Allowing for overlap and inaccuracy of classification, it does seem that conduct disorders form the biggest single category of child guidance cases.

5. TREATMENT AND DISPOSAL

In three of the six clinics, only 6 per cent of children on average were taken on for psychiatric treatment, while between 45 and 60 per cent received no psychiatric diagnosis. In the remaining three, about one-quarter of the children were recommended for psychiatric treatment, but most of these soon stopped attending or else were discharged. According to Timms (1968):

... the picture of the child guidance clinic as preoccupied with the long-term treatment of children is not confirmed by findings from the clinics studied. Instead we find all clinics engaged in quite a high proportion of diagnostic and short-term work.

These features of the six-clinics sample serve as a useful frame of reference for the findings of the present investigation set out in CHAPTER V. They also provide a basis for comparison between child guidance practice and hospital child psychiatry. Diagnostic data for the Maudsley Hospital Children's Department (Hare, 1968), for example, suggest a clientele not unlike that of a typical child guidance clinic. In the triennium 1964–6, three-fifths of cases were classified as 'habit disorders', while psychoses, organic disorders, and mental retardation together made up less than one-fifth. The sources of referral, however, were markedly different: 62 per cent of the children were sent by medical, and only 5 per cent by educational, agencies. In this instance, therefore, a high preponderance of medical referrals was not reflected in a high proportion of purely 'medical' case-material. The fact that 14 per cent came from child guidance clinics suggests that the hospital was being used as a secondary specialist service for unusually difficult cases.

The most striking difference between child guidance and hospital child psychiatry is to be found in the relative weight placed upon medical treatment. Nearly all children accepted for care by hospital clinics are under the direct supervision of psychiatric consultants and a high proportion are given some form of psychiatric treatment. Most children attending child guidance clinics, on the other hand, are dealt with by psychologists, social workers, lay psychotherapists, or play therapists, and receive little or no formal medical treatment. The disparities probably relate as much to staffing ratios as to differences in policy, or the nature of the clientele. How substantial are the resulting differences in strategy, quality, or intensity of care is unknown.

One feature shared in common by child guidance clinics and hospital departments is the brevity of most spells of treatment. The Maudsley Hospital statistics, for example, show that in the triennium 1964–6 only 43 per cent of children attended more than three times and only 22 per cent more than ten times (Hare, 1968). The figures are not dissimilar from those reported by Timms for his child guidance sample. It appears that, contrary to widely-held belief, both child psychiatric and child guidance practice under the N.H.S. are concerned in the main with short episodes of care, providing little opportunity for the exploration in depth of individual or family psychopathology. There is, indeed, a striking discrepancy between the theoretical basis of child guidance and its day-to-day practice under existing conditions.

THE INTERNATIONAL SCENE

It is tempting to conjecture that the patterns of child guidance practice delineated by Timms and other British investigators are largely a product of the type of service which has evolved in this country during the past half-century. There is, however, insufficient evidence to permit a critical examination of the question. It is undoubtedly true that quite different types of service have developed in other parts of the world, and that some of the contrasts appear to derive as much from prevailing ideologies as from scientific theories. At the same time, there are indications that the major constraints on service provision, in particular shortages of money and skilled manpower, cut across these divisions so as to produce similar problems in all comparably developed nations.

Child guidance services in the United States and Western Europe, having much the same provenance as those of Great Britain, share a number of features in common: a multi-disciplinary teamwork approach; a fairly open system of referral by non-medical as well as medical agencies; a concern as much with educational problems and delinquency as with psychiatric disorders; a reliance on psychological methods of treatment, largely underpinned by psychodynamic theory, and a functional independence, not to say isolation, from psychiatric services for adults. It is not surprising, therefore, that child guidance clientele in these countries have profiles alike in some respects: thus, the age, sex, and diagnostic distributions of American samples are similar to those reported in this country (Witmer, 1933; Anderson and Dean, 1956; Hunt, 1961), as are also the patterns of attendance and disposal (Maas, 1955; Hunt, 1961). The shortage of facilities and preponderance of short-term care in Great Britain do not appear, therefore, to be distinctive features of practice under the N.H.S. Indeed, the United States, despite greater affluence, a vastly bigger corps of practising psychiatrists and a deeper permeation of popular culture by psychodynamic concepts, has proved no more capable than Great Britain of coping with the public health problem of child maladjustment. 'In no State,' declared a mid-century report, 'is there adequate service for children. Three children out of a thousand are now getting care at psychiatric clinics; these usually have large waiting-lists' (Schwarz, 1950).

Clinics in Western Europe have developed largely on the American model (Buckle and Lebovici, 1960). Statistical data are scanty, but an account of a service for the canton of Vaud, Switzerland, presents many familiar aspects despite a scale of provision very generous by British standards (Landoni et al., 1973). The staff comprises child psychiatrists, psychologists, social workers, and speech therapists, who work mainly in the clinic but also act as consultants to local paediatric and educational agencies. In the period 1966–9, the main sources of referral, in descending order of frequency, were (1) medical agencies; (2) families; (3) schools; (4) official recommendations from police courts and social agencies. Boys outnumbered girls, by nearly two to one. Educational problems accounted for 35 per cent of referrals, neurotic symptoms for about one-quarter, and 'difficulties of family adaptation' for one-sixth. Children from well-to-do homes tended to be sent by medical agencies or schools; those from poor homes to come from the courts or from social agencies. From a British viewpoint, perhaps the most striking feature of the clientele of this service is the high proportion of pre-school children, amounting to one-third of the total. Presumably, though this point is not made clear, the large number of very young children in treatment is related to the frequency of direct referral by parents.

Child psychiatry in communist countries presents a number of sharp contrasts with that in the West. To begin with, its theoretical basis is quite different. Following a brief period of acceptance after the 1917 revolution, Freudian psychology was decisively rejected by the new Soviet state. Child psychiatry, like all psychiatric practice in the Soviet Union, came to rely increasingly on biological models and, in particular, on Pavlovian teaching (Rollins, 1973). Secondly, children's services in the U.S.S.R. have developed as part of a comprehensive health programme, with a strong emphasis on preventive care. All children are medically examined at regular intervals from infancy onwards, and at these checks attention is paid to the possibility of brain damage, retarded development, or disturbed personality-functioning (Miller, 1968). Thirdly, links between child psychiatry and paediatrics are very close. Most doctors entering child psychiatry have had special training in child health from their undergraduate days, and are assigned to work in children's polyclinics. Hence, child psychiatric practice has a conspicuously medical and biological orientation.

These aspects of the Soviet system have impressed some Western observers. A group of eminent American specialists, reporting back after a visit to the U.S.S.R. in 1967, stressed the generous scale of provision, comprehensive nature of screening programmes, and undoubted concern for children's welfare and happiness that they had found there. Doubts persist, none the less, as to whether Soviet psychiatry is coping any more successfully than its Western counterparts with the enormous number of maladjusted children who manifest no definite biological abnormality, and for whom no proven methods of prevention are available. The American mission noted, for instance, an imbalance between in-patient and residential facilities for children, which appeared to be much better than those of the United States, and out-patient services, which presented an all-too-familiar spectacle:

The child psychiatrist at Children's Polyclinic 22 seemed unsure of herself and harried. She had cause to be harried: with one nurse to assist her she had an active case-load of 190 children and 3,000 clinic visits each year. At least one day each week was supposed to be spent visiting and counselling at one of the 22 kindergartens or nine elementary schools in the area served by her polyclinic (Miller, 1968).

There is thus a distinct possibility that Soviet child psychiatry would reveal, on closer scrutiny, much of the same sort of discrepancy between its theoretical tenets and its daily practice which is such a prominent feature of the North American and European scenes.

SUMMARY

In step with the modern growth of interest in child psychology has gone a rapid increase in the provision of services for disturbed children. Statistics for child psychiatry under the N.H.S. seem to indicate the existence of a major public health problem; yet there is little information about the true extent and distribution among children of the need for special care; nor about any social and environmental factors with which it may be associated.

Before undertaking research into this subject, one must know something about the complex nature of existing services. Modern child psychiatry has grown up as a collective discipline, representing concerns as much with mental handicap, educational under-achievement, delinquency, and social deviance, as with illness in the accepted sense. While some child psychiatric clinics have been established within the hospital services, the majority have remained part of local authority structure and are direct descendents of the early child guidance demonstration clinics. The child guidance movement from the first was heavily influenced by psycho-analytic and 'mental hygiene' concepts, and has always incorporated pedagogic and welfare interests as well as those of medicine. In consequence, there has been some confusion over the proper scope and function of child guidance clinics, and their place in the administrative framework.

Data on the clientele and mode of operation of child guidance services today are scanty. A survey of six clinics by Timms (1968) found wide divergences between the individual clinics. Over-all, the clientele was characterized by a preponderance of boys; of children from lower social-class homes, and of conduct disorders. Waiting-times were prolonged, and treatment once initiated tended to be of short duration. Comparison with statistics for a hospital child psychiatric service suggested disparities both in the sources of referral and in the relative emphasis given to psychiatric therapy. Neither child guidance nor hospital psychiatric clinics, however, seemed able to provide intensive or long-term care for most of their clients.

Information from other countries suggests that there are a number of valuable lessons to be learned: notably in the closer integration of child psychiatry with child health care, and in the greater emphasis on preventive screening, to be found in the Soviet Union. Nevertheless, there are strong indications that, despite wide international differences both in theoretical standpoint and in the financial basis of provision, many of the practical problems are similar to those encountered in Great Britain. Everywhere one finds a concern with shortages of trained staff; a reliance on short-term treatment; a gap between professional aspirations and the realities of daily practice; an equal gap between the numbers of children under specialist care and the numbers thought to stand in need; an uncertainty as to whether medical, educational, or sociological models offer the best hope for future planning. Nowhere, as yet, does there appear to be a deployment of services based on rational assessment of the needs of the child population.

CHAPTER II

THE NEED AND THE DEMAND FOR CHILD GUIDANCE SERVICES

THE data on child guidance practice presented in the foregoing chapter, scanty though they are, constitute the bulk of what is known about contemporary patterns of service utilization under the N.H.S. They cannot be regarded as a direct measure of the number of maladjusted children in the population, or of the need for specialist care. 'Need,' as Matthew (1971) has remarked, 'is not necessarily expressed as demand and demand is not necessarily followed by utilization, while, on the other hand, there can be demand and utilization without real underlying need for the particular services used.' In child psychiatry, these terms have yet to be clearly defined. Meanwhile, some headway can be made by comparing the prevalence and distribution of childhood maladjustment, as revealed by field-surveys, with the local levels of demand expressed in terms of referral to child guidance services.

MALADJUSTMENT IN THE CHILD POPULATION

All the evidence suggests that far more children are maladjusted than child guidance statistics reveal. Although, largely because of problems of definition and method, survey estimates have varied, most agree that between 5 and 12 per cent of children are disturbed enough to warrant specialist treatment or supervision. The Underwood Committee found the proportion to vary from 6 to 12 per cent among schoolchildren in three areas of England (Min. of Education, 1955). American studies, reviewed by Eisenberg (1961), seem to indicate that at least one child in ten is maladjusted, but that fewer than one in a hundred are under specialist care.

Two British surveys of recent years have examined the question. In the Isle of Wight survey (Rutter et al., 1970), which investigated psychiatric disorder as well as physical health and school progress, all children from 10 to 12 years at school on the island were screened by means of questionnaires, completed independently by parents and teachers. Those picked out as possible cases—13 per cent all told—were then interviewed by psychiatrists. The prevalence of psychiatric disorder, a term excluding educational retardation, mental handicap, and monosymptomatic conditions such as enuresis, was estimated at 6·8 per cent. Only one case in ten was under specialist care, though one-third were thought probably, and a further one-third possibly, to require treatment. In short, the existing services appeared to be meeting only from 15 to 30 per cent of the real need.

Agreement between parents' and teachers' responses was low in this study, implying that the child's behaviour at home may bear little relation to that at school, and that neither alone is an adequate index of maladjustment. The same conclusion could be drawn from the Bucks. Child Health Survey (Shepherd *et al.*, 1971), which also made use of parents' and teachers' questionnaires. Since the investigators' purpose was to chart the distribution of deviant behaviour, rather than to estimate illness-prevalence, they did not proceed to a second stage of clinical interviewing. Instead, they made use of a 'cut-off' score of four deviant responses, which discriminated quite well between child guidance attenders and the normal child population. On this basis, 11 per cent of their sample could be deemed maladjusted: a proportion which, like the 13 per cent in the Isle of Wight survey, would doubtless have been reduced by clinical examination.

The few longitudinal studies in this field have reported high maladjustment rates. Brandon (1960), following up children included in the Newcastle survey of 1,000 families (Spence *et al.*, 1954), reported that one-fifth had shown serious disturbance by the age of 11. Bremer's five-year survey of a Norwegian rural community yielded similar findings (Bremer, 1951). Probably the number of children who become disturbed at some stage is much higher than cross-sectional surveys indicate. On the other hand, the study of case-histories shows that a high proportion of disorders become chronic or recurrent (Rutter *et al.*, 1970).

The underlying causes of maladjustment are still imperfectly understood. That many children are placed at risk by an adverse environment is common ground among psychiatrists, psychologists, and educationists. So far, attention has been concentrated on factors in the home and in the nuclear family. Pringle (1965), for example, has categorized the following high-risk groups:

(i) socially and culturally underprivileged children;
(ii) those from families where there is emotional neglect, and where personal relationships are impaired;
(iii) those from families where there is major physical or mental illness, or disabling handicap;
(iv) those living with one parent only, as a result of illegitimacy, desertion, divorce, or death;
(v) those whose families have been affected by sudden and disrupting crises.

Four of these categories are defined by the family situation, and only one—the first—in more general social terms. Yet we know that there is a close and continuing interaction between family and neighbourhood conditions. Disorganized families tend to congregate in slums or public housing estates; poverty, overcrowding, and bad housing conditions are common to many families in certain districts. Unemployment, lack of cultural and recreational

compare with (19 table.

facilities, and a local prevalence of anti-social behaviour patterns may combine to exert destructive pressures on the cohesion of family life. Intra- and extra-familial risk-factors, though positively associated, may operate to some extent independently. Hence, indices of risk must be derived from the wider environment as well as from the family, neither kind being accepted as merely an indirect measure of the other.

Little is known about the social correlates of maladjustment and child psychiatric disorder. Most field-surveys have been restricted to the basic data on age, sex, and social class, and even here the findings have at times conflicted. Perhaps the most relevant findings are those of the Isle of Wight survey (Rutter *et al.*, 1970), which demonstrated that child psychiatric disorder was linked with evidence of family pathology, but not with socio-economic status.

Pursuing these leads, the same research group later compared maladjustment among ten-year-old children on the Isle of Wight and among their peers in an Inner London Borough (Rutter *et al.*, 1975). Both populations were screened with the aid of a teachers' questionnaire of known reliability, children picked out as possible cases being examined more carefully by means of a home interview. In addition, randomly-selected control groups were interviewed in both areas. Psychiatric disorder was found twice as commonly among the London children as on the island. This striking disparity could be related to the differing social characteristics of the two areas. Overcrowding, large family-size, a history of having children placed in care, of mental illness among the mothers, and of prison sentences among the fathers: all these features were more often present in the disturbed children's families than in control families, and more often in the Inner London Borough than on the Isle of Wight. The schools of the metropolis appeared to be labouring under greater difficulties than those on the island, to judge from such indices as the turnover of teachers and pupils. In short, this study of maladjusted children pointed to the influence of social disorganization in much the same way as had earlier surveys of adult mental disorder.

SOCIOLOGICAL AND ECOLOGICAL SURVEYS

It is now well-established that the incidence of adult mental illness, as well as of suicide, varies with demographic and ecological indices. High rates have been found in areas characterized by high mobility (Faris and Dunham, 1939), low socio-economic status (Hollingshead and Redlich, 1958), social isolation (Sainsbury, 1955; Hare, 1956), and a lack of community organizations (Leighton *et al.*, 1963).

These findings must be viewed with caution, for two reasons. To begin with, associations differ as between the main diagnostic categories: it has been shown repeatedly, for example, that the social and ecological correlates of schizophrenia are not those of affective psychosis (Faris and Dunham, 1939; Hare, 1955; Häfner and Reimann, 1970). The composite pattern may thus be built up from a series of contrasting motifs. Secondly, most published studies have dealt only with *reported* morbidity; that is, with patients known to psychiatric agencies. How far their distribution conforms to that of mental disorder as a whole is far from clear. The probability of hospital admission is known to be influenced by demographic, social, and nosocomial factors (Terris, 1965), so that hospital returns are inaccurate measures of incidence. None the less, field-surveys have tended to confirm that mental disorder as a whole is concentrated among low-status groups and in areas of social disorganization (Langner and Michael, 1963; Leighton *et al.*, 1963).

Ecological surveys of children have focused mainly on the problem of juvenile delinquency. One of the famous series of pre-war social surveys in Chicago revealed a concentration of delinquency in the decaying central areas of that city (Shaw and McKay, 1942). More recently, similar patterns have been observed in San Francisco (Eisner and Tzuyemara, 1960), in Philadelphia (Savitz, 1962), and in a number of British cities (Bagley, 1965). Such studies have shown that urban delinquent areas can be mapped out with some precision, and tend to be characterized by high adult crime rates, overcrowding, poor housing, low rental values, and low owner-occupancy rates; these are also the correlates of high infant mortality, tuberculosis, alcoholism, and suicide. In addition, high rates of delinquency have been found in new housing estates built to rehouse slum populations (Morris, 1957; Bagley, 1965).

The urban ecology of delinquency thus appears to have been clearly depicted; yet doubts persist as to the significance of the findings. Some critics have stressed the 'ecological fallacy' of equating social characteristics of a group with its urban distribution. The conclusion that delinquents come mainly from the lowest socio-economic groups, merely because delinquency rates are highest in areas of poor housing and overcrowding, could be one example of this fallacy. Evidence on the social class distribution of delinquent children is conflicting (Douglas *et al.*, 1966; Palmai *et al.*, 1967) and it may be that incongruity between the social status of the family and that of the neighbourhood is itself a factor of delinquency (Wallis and Maliphant, 1967). Ecological correlates do not necessarily coincide with direct correlates: for a true perspective, both are required.

Another cause of doubt is the difficulty of identifying all cases of delinquency. Most surveys have relied on the records of juvenile courts, probation services, or child care services. How legitimate, in scientific terms, is this approach? The presence of a young person's name on such a list is the end-result of a process in which the nature of the offence, the setting in which it occurs, the identification of the culprit, the police decision to prosecute, and the court's decision regarding disposal, each have a part to play. If juveniles brought before the courts were found to be seriously unrepresentative of the total delinquent population, we should be faced with the familiar epidemiological problem that one cannot extrapolate from reported, or 'declared' morbidity to the great mass of 'undeclared' cases. Studies of delinquents known to the courts would then have the same kinds of limitation as psychiatric surveys restricted to institutional cases.

Fortunately, information about the true frequency and distribution of delinquency is available from 'self-report' surveys of juveniles (Belson, 1968; Gold, 1970). These have shown that, while isolated or occasional delinquent acts are very widespread among juveniles, *persistent* delinquency is much less common and the young person involved mostly known to the authorities. Of special interest here is the Cambridge Study in Delinquent Development (West and Farrington, 1973), which examined a sample of over 400 schoolboys in a London district at the age of 8 to 10 years, and followed them up to nineteen years. The one-fifth who became known delinquents, and especially those who became recidivists, had been in many ways less fortunate in early life than their peers: they tended to be less popular; to have higher 'neuroticism' scores; to come more often from poor families and from broken homes; to be more often illegitimate; to have nervous mothers, and fathers with criminal records. The main features discriminating between the delinquent group and the other boys remained the same when the former was selected on the basis of self-reported acts rather than of officially-known offences. It did not appear that the adverse home and social background of the delinquent boys was an artefact caused by selective bias:

However it comes about, the courts do seem to see and convict the worst-behaved among the juvenile population; the arrest and conviction processes may seem chancy or unfair, but in reality they are far from haphazard (West and Farrington, 1973).

Evidence from field-surveys thus provides support for the use of official data in delinquency research and confirms that a number of psychological and social variables are related to the incidence of delinquency, as distinct from its recognition.

A further question must be asked about any ecological study; namely, how up-to-date are its findings? Socio-economic and demographic indices are usually derived from periodic censuses which cannot be expected to keep pace with rapid change, as, for example, in programmes of slum clearance. Fortunately for research workers, most ecological patterns appear to change only slowly. It has been found, for example, that suicide rates for the London Boroughs have changed little in their rank-order over the decades, despite large inter-borough differences (Sainsbury, 1955; Whitlock, 1973). Patterns of delinquency in London have also remained consistent for forty years (Wallis and Maliphant, 1967). However much the pace of urban change may accelerate in future, ecological findings to date can hardly be dismissed on these grounds.

Equally significant for child psychiatry are studies relating the risk of delinquency to the child's school. Educationists have long suspected that the individual school can modify the effect of adverse home and neighbourhood conditions. Attention has been drawn to the fact that:

... certain schools serving social areas which might be expected to produce difficult and even delinquent children manage somehow to prevent this happening, or at least greatly reduce the incidence by comparison with other schools serving similar areas (Clegg and Megson, 1968).

The school's influence on delinquency was examined by a Medical Research Council team, which found widely varying rates among secondary schools in the London Borough of Tower Hamlets (Power et al., 1967). Having separated the effects of neighbourhood and of school, they concluded that each exercised an effect independently of the other. No school characteristic was found to explain the pattern. Neither school size, nor the educational achievement of the pupils, appeared to be directly relevant. The research workers suggested that the crucial factor may be the school's 'ethos', a term difficult to define and even more difficult to employ in operational research.

If the school can modify the risk of children becoming delinquent, presumably it can influence other aspects of their behaviour. Moreover, the detection and treatment of maladjustment may depend partly on school conditions, many forms of behaviour disorder being recognized more easily at school than in the home environment (Min. of Education, 1955; Shepherd et al., 1971; Rutter et al., 1970). Differences between schools must, therefore, be borne in mind when trying to interpret area differences, either of child guidance referral or of total maladjustment rates. The relationship between the latter can be understood only in terms of selective factors governing the decision to refer.

DETERMINANTS OF CHILD GUIDANCE REFERRAL

A number of British studies of adult psychiatric referral have been published over the past twenty years. The factors influencing referral by general practitioners and other physicians have proved complex and difficult to untangle. Relevant variables include the patient's age and the duration of his illness (Shepherd et al., 1966); the presence of disturbed behaviour (Mowbray et al., 1961); the attitudes of relatives (Rawnsley and Loudon, 1962) and of the patients themselves (Hopkins and Cooper, 1969); the effectiveness of the doctor's own treatment (Mowbray et al., 1961; Cooper, 1964) and the distance of his practice from the psychiatric clinic (Hare, 1968). One can thus safely concur with Kessel (1963) that 'the processes by which people obtain psychiatric treatment are devious and often arbitrary'.

Similar factors operate in child psychiatry. Here, a stronger bias may be introduced in selection for treatment, since child guidance clinics are often over-subscribed and have long waiting-lists. Stevens (1955), for instance, reported that of children given diagnostic examination in the State of Illinois in 1950, only one-quarter was taken on for treatment, and that the social characteristics of this group differed from those of the majority who were not accepted. Ideally, one would like to have social profiles for the maladjusted group as a whole, for all cases referred to specialists and for that sub-group which eventually receives treatment. Comprehensive information of this kind is nowhere available.

Analysis of the factors of child guidance utilization requires, as well as epidemiological data, studies both of case-identification by doctors, teachers, and other professional workers, and of the decision-making process once the child's disturbance has been recognized. FIGURE 2 is a simple interactional model of the referral system.

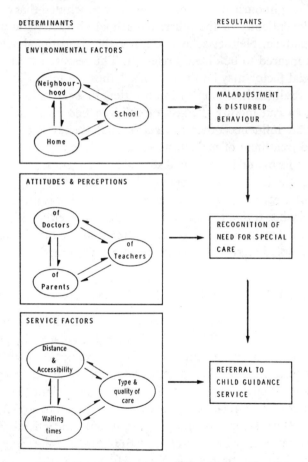

Fig. 2. Factors influencing child guidance referral

Earlier research has demonstrated some of the forces schematized in FIGURE 2; others, still to be investigated, may be inferred from the differing profiles of clinic attenders and other maladjusted children. For convenience, the principal factors can be grouped as clinical, demographic, attitudinal, and nosocomial.

1. CLINICAL FACTORS

A fundamental question, but one until recently neglected, is whether or not child guidance attenders are really more disturbed than average children from a similar background. Since no British survey has systematically examined all children in a service area, we cannot relate the clientele of any child guidance clinic to its background population. Some indirect evidence has been provided by the Isle of Wight survey (Rutter et al., 1970), which found that children aged 10–12 who were under specialist care had handicaps fully justifying their treatment. The Bucks. Child Health Survey (Shepherd et al., 1971) reported a much higher frequency of items of deviant behaviour among local child guidance patients than in a 10 per cent sample of schoolchildren in the county. More directly, a study in Edinburgh (Wolff, 1967) compared 100 primary school children seen at a psychiatric clinic with a control group matched for age, sex, and social class, and found clear differences: the clinic children showed more anti-social behaviour, soiling and wetting; were more discontented and anxious, and got on less well with their peers.

Less is known about differences between child guidance patients and other *maladjusted* children. Both severity and duration of symptoms are of importance in assessing the need for specialist care. All children show psychological disturbance at some stage of development, and most forms of deviant behaviour require to be taken seriously only if they persist or recur. Logically, therefore, one would expect clinic cases to be on average both more severe and more chronic than those identified in the community.

What little evidence we have does not bear out this expectation. The Bucks. Child Health Survey discovered no significant difference in clinical severity between a child guidance sample and a matched group of maladjusted schoolchildren (Shepherd et al., 1971). In view of the small sample-size, this finding was not conclusive. The Isle of Wight survey assessed severity in terms both of functional impairment and of chronicity. Two-fifths of the neurotic children, and one-third of those with conduct disorders, were seriously disturbed or handicapped. Three-quarters of the neurotic children, and two-thirds of those with conduct disorders, had had symptoms for at least three years (Rutter et al., 1970). Thus it appeared that the problems of many children who had not been referred were just as severe as those of the small group under child guidance.

Apart from the question of severity, the *type* of disturbance may be an important selective factor. The Isle of Wight team reported that neurotic disorders were relatively more common, and conduct disorders relatively less common, than one might suppose from examining only child guidance cases (Rutter et al., 1970). Neurotic syndromes comprised 34 per cent of cases on the island, compared with only 7 per cent in Timms' six-clinics sample (Timms, 1968). The corresponding figures for conduct disorder were 34 and 49 per cent respectively. Such comparisons must be viewed with caution because of the lack of any standard classification, the unreliability of diagnosis and the moderating effect of age on the clinical picture.

In summary, the evidence to hand suggests that child guidance patients *are* drawn from among the more disturbed members of the child population; that in terms of severity and duration of symptoms they are roughly comparable to a much larger group of children who are not referred, and that the most important selective factor in referral is the presence of disturbed behaviour, as distinct from neurotic symptoms. This last point may have a bearing on the age–sex distribution of the child guidance clientele.

2. DEMOGRAPHIC FACTORS

The relative excess of boys among child guidance attenders is probably due to their greater propensity for conduct disorders. Neurotic symptoms, on the other hand, are equally common among girls (Mulligan, 1964; Rutter et al., 1970) and are more often a reason for sending girls to child psychiatrists.

The only pronounced effect of age on referral appears to be an increase at the age of 5, when most children start school. Thus, fewer than 5 per cent of Timms' sample were under school age (Timms, 1968). While little is known about maladjustment in this age-group, evidence from family health visitors suggests that neurotic traits are not infrequent (Douglas and Blomfield, 1958). No doubt many pre-existing cases of maladjustment first become conspicuous in the early school years and are brought to child guidance as a result of school pressures.

Within the school age-range, no direct effect of age has been demonstrated. In most reported studies, the proportions of child guidance attenders have been roughly equal for the age-groups 5–10 and over 10 years. This equal ratio cannot be checked against field-survey findings; indeed, if we accept the view that maladjustment should be defined in relation to developmental norms, the proportion of children classed as deviant will presumably remain constant with age (Lapouse and Monk, 1964; Shepherd et al., 1971).

The influence of social class is still unclear. Field-surveys have not shown any clear association between social class and the prevalence of maladjustment (Lapouse and Monk, 1964; Mulligan, 1964; Rutter et al., 1970). There is some evidence, though unreliable, that children from poor homes are more likely than those from upper- or middle-class homes to be sent to child guidance clinics (Timms, 1968). It is possible that selection by diagnosis and by social class are interrelated, conduct disorders being relatively more frequent, and neurotic syndromes relatively less frequent, among children in the lower socio-economic groups.

Any reported social class gradient may be a function of the type of service under scrutiny; fee-paying clinics in the United States, for example, have shown a different pattern of utilization from those under the N.H.S. (Roach et al., 1958; Ginot and Lebo, 1963; Rabkin and Lyttle, 1966). More research is needed into the relationship between diagnosis, social class, and use of specialist services.

3. ATTITUDINAL FACTORS

One reason for the apparently poor clinical discrimination between referred and non-referred cases is to be found in differences of parental attitude, which in turn are bound up with differing perceptions and levels of tolerance (Kanner, 1959; Eisenberg, 1961). Parents may require help in dealing with normal developmental patterns because they can neither cope with the child's behaviour nor accept it as a temporary phase; conversely, they may fail to seek treatment for a severe disorder because of failure to grasp its significance, mistrust of the available services or their own neurotic conflicts.

The former types of mechanism could be discerned among families in the Bucks. Child Health Survey (Shepherd et al., 1971). What chiefly distinguished a sample of clinic children from a control group matched for age, sex, and behavioural profile were the mental health of the parents and their reactions to the children's conduct. 'Clearly,' commented the authors, 'the tolerance of disturbed behaviour takes its place alongside the nature of that behaviour as key factors in deciding for or against referral' (Shepherd et al., 1966a).

A study of fifty children referred to the Maudsley Hospital by general practitioners provided complementary findings (Gath, 1968). To avoid possible bias, each practitioner was seen before he had received a hospital report. The family situation appeared to have been at least as important as the child's symptoms in deciding the doctor to refer. In most instances, the child's condition was not thought to be serious; indeed, the doctors had regarded some of the children as normal and had referred them to hospital simply to placate anxious or over-protective parents.

That parental attitudes may have the opposite effect was demonstrated in the Isle of Wight, where fewer than half the parents of disturbed children were aware that anything was amiss, and fewer still wanted medical intervention. Many did not know that appropriate services were available, or else considered their problems outside the scope of medical care (Rutter et al., 1970). One might say that those children are most likely to be sent for treatment whose parents are both anxious and well-informed.

The decision to refer to a specialist often results from an interaction between the parents' attitudes and those of the family doctor. Large differences have been noted in the numbers of adults sent to psychiatric clinics by individual doctors, and it seems that subjective opinions play an important role (Shepherd et al., 1966; Kaeser and Cooper, 1971). Doctors' attitudes can exert influence on child guidance statistics. Gath (1968), for example, reported that most of the practitioners in his study preferred not to undertake the treatment of seriously disturbed children, regarding themselves as insufficiently trained and equipped for the purpose. Probably this is a majority view. Few general practitioners maintain a special interest in psychiatric problems or undertake systematic treatment of neurotic disorders, either in adults or in children. If the average family doctor is less clear about the clinical indications for referral to child psychiatrists than, say, to paediatricians, he will be correspondingly more open to parental influence.

Central to the doctor's decision will be his relationship with local consultants, and his previous experience with the local specialist services (Kaeser and Cooper, 1971; Kellett and Mezey, 1970). The practitioner who enjoys access to a wide range of treatment facilities can make a selective choice. In most parts of the country, where no such choice is possible, the doctor's views are more likely to find expression in a higher or lower over-all rate of referral.

4. NOSOCOMIAL FACTORS

Nosocomial factors are those appertaining to the nature and delivery of medical care. Most research on this subject has been focused on hospitals, but the basic principles are the same for any form of health care and can be readily applied to child guidance services. The fundamental principle—often neglected in research—is that the numbers and types of patient making contact with any given service will depend upon its nature, quality, and accessibility. Hence, local variations in reported morbidity may be due as much to inequalities of service provision as to differences in prevalence.

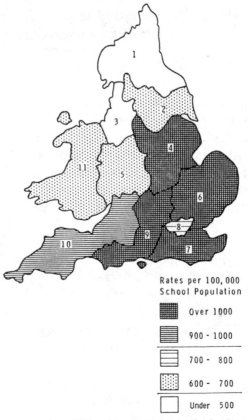

Rates per 100,000
School Population

▓	Over 1000
▤	900 - 1000
▭	700 - 800
▒	600 - 700
□	Under 500

Fig. 3. Schoolchildren treated at child guidance clinics in England and Wales during 1967, by region

Child guidance statistics provide a striking case in point. FIGURE 3 illustrates the wide variation in regional rates for England and Wales, exemplified by the 1967 figures (Dept. of Education, 1969).

The ratio of schoolchildren seen in the clinics to total school population ranged from 1:87 for the Southern Region to 1:238 for the Northern Region: almost a threefold difference. Differences within regions were much greater, even as between adjacent areas: 1:54 in Liverpool and 1:1,078 in Birkenhead; 1:343 in Cheshire and 1:2,108 in Chester; 1:68 in Derbyshire and 1:368 in Leicestershire. Among the Greater London Boroughs, the figures ranged from 1:35 for Waltham Forest to 1:510 for Kingston-upon-Thames. Such disparities are hardly to be explained in terms of differential rates of maladjustment. A report of the National Child Development Study, noting a similar range of variation, commented:

There is no evidence that the *need* for child guidance varies greatly between areas in Britain, and one cannot but attribute most of the marked variation in attendance rates to the local level of concern and provision, and ability to attract staff (Davie *et al.*, 1972).

In TABLE 2.1, the regional child guidance ratios have been set alongside the levels of professional staffing revealed by a national survey (Dept. of Education, 1968). It can be seen that referral rates tended to be higher in the better-staffed regions, though this trend by no means fully explains the observed variation.

TABLE 2.1

REGIONAL CHILD GUIDANCE RATES IN ENGLAND AND
WALES BY RATES OF PROFESSIONAL STAFFING

REGION OF E. & W.	PROFESSIONAL STAFF PER 100,000 SCHOOL POPULATION AT END OF 1966 (FULL-TIME EQUIVALENTS)*			TREATED AT C.G.C.S IN 1967
	Psychiatrists	Educational Psychologists	Social Workers	(Rate per 1,000 school-children)
South-east	2·7 (1)	5·7 (4)	5·8 (2)	9·8 (5)
South	2·6 (2)	5·0 (6)	5·3 (3)	11·5 (1)
Greater London	2·3 (3)	6·2 (1)	6·1 (1)	7·8 (6)
South-west	2·2 (4)	5·7 (3)	5·0 (4)	10·2 (4)
Wales	2·1 (5)	4·1 (7)	2·4 (9)	7·8 (6)
East	1·7 (6)	5·9 (2)	4·2 (5)	11·4 (2)
N. Midlands	1·4 (7)	3·6 (9)	2·6 (8)	10·4 (3)
E. & W. Ridings	1·2 (8)	3·6 (10)	3·2 (7)	7·4 (8)
Midlands	1·1 (9)	3·6 (11)	3·6 (6)	6·3 (9)
North-west	1·0 (10)	3·9 (8)	2·1 (11)	5·4 (10)
North	0·8 (11)	5·6 (5)	2·2 (10)	4·2 (11)

* In rank order of psychiatrist rates
Source: Department of Education and Science (1968; 1969)

Apart from the question of staff provision, utilization of a clinic may be influenced by the size of its catchment area, its proximity to other services, its standard of communication with local schools and doctors, and other less tangible factors. The probability of any individual child being referred and accepted for specialist treatment thus depends, not only on the nature and severity of his disturbance and the attitudes of his parents and teachers, but also on the area in which he happens to live.

SUMMARY

The findings of a number of field-surveys have indicated that between 5 and 12 per cent of children in the general population are so disturbed as to require specialist care. In assessing the individual child's risk of psychiatric disorder or maladjustment, the weight of emphasis has been placed upon his family situation and home environment. There is, however, evidence that family pathology and adverse home conditions tend to be concentrated in areas of social disorganization, and that local rates of maladjustment vary accordingly. This observation, which serves to bring childhood maladjustment into line with juvenile delinquency, and also with many forms of mental disorder in adult life, has important implications for future research and, ultimately, for prevention.

A closely related issue concerns the variation in rates of psychiatric disorder and maladjustment among schools. If the risk of maladjustment, like that of delinquency, depends to some extent on the child's school environment, differences in school rates must be taken into account in epidemiological and ecological research.

Regional or local differences in child guidance rates cannot be assumed to reflect differences in the prevalence of maladjustment, since the frequency of referral may be influenced by various factors which can be categorized as clinical, demographic, attitudinal, and nosocomial. The main causes of selective bias appear to be the following:

(a) children with behaviour disorders are more likely to be referred than those with neurotic syndromes;

(b) boys are more likely to be referred than girls;

(c) children with anxious, over-protective parents are more likely to be referred than others whose symptoms may be equally severe;

(d) children in areas with a high level of service provision are more likely to be referred than equally disturbed children in other areas.

These tendencies must be borne in mind when patterns of child guidance utilization are under review.

CHAPTER III

CROYDON: THE BOROUGH AND THE CLINIC

THE issues discussed in CHAPTER II suggested that an ecological study of child psychiatric referral could be undertaken most successfully on an urban population for which demographic and social statistics were available, and which was covered by a single health and a single educational authority. More precisely, we required an administrative area with a clearly defined population served by a local child guidance clinic with a near monopoly of referral; also, preferably, a local juvenile court taking cases from the whole of the area.

The thirty-two Greater London Boroughs lend themselves to research of this type, since a good deal of statistical information is available and can be analysed for quite small sub-populations. The Inner London Boroughs, however, each have a number of over-lapping medical services provided by local teaching hospitals and postgraduate medical institutes; those grouped around the London postal districts W.1, N.W.1, and N.W.3 also provide convenient access to a wide variety of private specialist consultation and treatment for residents who can afford the fees. These considerations made the choice of an Outer London Borough seem more appropriate and, in the event, we decided on Croydon.

Croydon is in several respects highly suitable for such an investigation. Its distance from the London teaching hospitals is sufficient to ensure that most patients in need of specialist care are referred to the local hospital services. In particular, we expected to find the single, centrally-situated Child Guidance Clinic taking the great bulk of child psychiatric referrals from the borough: a point later confirmed by a survey of Croydon practitioners (see CHAPTER IX). The present study formed one of a series being carried out on problems of community mental health in Croydon, and we already knew the local authority officers to be helpful and co-operative. With a population of over 300,000 and a total of some 140 doctors in practice, Croydon provided ample scope for the type of statistical survey we planned. Its wide range of social conditions, from the decaying tenements and overcrowded dwellings of the old, central zone to the affluent 'stockbroker belt' in the south, offered distinct advantages for ecological research. This social heterogeneity was ideal for a study of neighbourhood effects on child guidance and delinquency rates. Indeed, it would have been hard to find a metropolitan area better suited to the research requirements.

HISTORY OF THE BOROUGH

The emergence of Croydon as a Greater London Borough in 1965 set the official seal on a process of assimilation into the metropolis which had begun with the Industrial Revolution. At that time, Croydon had already been in existence, first as a village and then as a small market town, for a thousand years. Originally one of a chain of villages that grew up where chalk springs emerged from the Surrey Downs to run down to the Thames, it grew to importance as a halting-place on one of the main roads to the south coast, and as a manor of the Archbishops of Canterbury. In the Domesday Book, Croydon boasted a church, a mill, and a population of over 300. The presence of the Archbishop's seat, the Old Palace, brought meetings of the Privy Council and visits by several monarchs, including Henry VIII and Elizabeth. Six Archbishops were buried in the parish church, among them John Whitgift, whose sixteenth-century almshouses still stand in the centre of the borough.

Until the latter half of the nineteenth century, Croydon remained a market town, separated from London by farms and woodland, and preserving much of its old character. 'It is evident to me in retrospect,' wrote John Ruskin in late life, 'that the personal feeling and native instinct of me had been fastened irrevocably long before to things modest, humble and pure in peace, under the low red roofs of Croydon, and by the cress rivulets in which the sand danced, and minnows darted above the springs of Wandel' (Ruskin, 1899). But already the Croydon he recalled with nostalgia was disappearing beneath the tide of industrialism and speculative building that swept over London's outskirts with the coming of the railways.[1]

The growth of Croydon had been heralded, early in the nineteenth century, by the city merchants who settled in Norwood, building their own versions of the country houses of the landed gentry. Thus began a period of rapid expansion: the population quadrupled in the first half of the century, from 5,000 to 20,000, and increased six-fold in the second half as Croydon became a dormitory suburb for workers commuting to London.

The proliferation of new suburbs followed closely on the spread of railways and canals. The Surrey Iron Railway, built to carry limestone and builder's stone from the quarries of Merstham to the fast-growing London suburbs, was already in operation by 1803. The London and Croydon passenger line, opened in 1839, at that time ran for most of its length through fields and countryside. New lines were opened to Brighton and Epsom in the 1840s, and by 1890 no fewer than fourteen stations had been built in Croydon to meet the rising demand for cheap daily transport.

Industrial and urban growth combined, in Croydon as throughout Victorian England, to produce major problems of sanitation. Until 1850, the River Wandle (Ruskin's 'Wandel') had flowed through Croydon's Old Town,

[1] A graphic account of this epoch, and its effects on the near-by town of Bromley, can be found in H. G. Wells' novel, *The New Machiavelli*.

fed by small springs where formerly trout had been caught. Now the water was fouled with sewage, and outbreaks of cholera and typhus grew frequent. A new era commenced in 1851, when Croydon became one of the first towns to implement the recent public health legislation. Once the streams had been covered over, a pumping station installed, and main drainage laid, the epidemics diminished. By the 1880s, when the Wandle was becoming another of London's lost rivers, it could be claimed that '. . . the increase in population in Croydon is due to the salubrity of its position on a substratum of gravel and chalk at the foot of the North Downs, the beauty of the neighbourhood and a constant supply of water of unsurpassed purity' (Anderson, 1882). Mortality rates, and especially infant mortality, were to remain high for some years more; but by the turn of the century they had begun to fall steadily. Since then, the local patterns of mortality and morbidity have remained typical of modern urban communities with no mining or other heavy industry.

The whole machinery of English local government developed largely out of the Public Health Act of 1848 and the need to control urban sanitation. The Croydon Local Health Board, created in 1849 to look after drainage, sewage disposal, and water supplies, formed the nucleus of the new Borough Council thirty-four years later, when Croydon received its official Charter. The Borough's hospitals were also founded in the mid-nineteenth century, one as an infirmary for the poor and the other to replace the old Parish Workhouse infirmary.

Poverty is a constant theme in the annals of Victorian England, and Croydon was no exception. In 1872, the School Board recommended that the police should stop children under 13 from begging and sweeping street-crossings. To prevent the local townspeople being troubled by beggars, a Croydon branch was formed of the 'Charitable Society for the Suppression of Mendicity and the Relief of Temporary Distress' (the fore-runner of today's Family Welfare Association). Among the Society's activities were the issuing of bread tickets, the maintenance of soup kitchens during severe winters, and the doling out of benefits to the 'deserving poor', a form of charity widely considered to be less shameful, and perhaps less uncertain, than dependence on parish relief.

What happened to those not considered deserving? A commentary on the age is provided by a tombstone which exists in Mitcham Road cemetery. It commemorates a girl of 18 who, with her newly-born child, died in a shed one winter's night, of exposure and starvation. There were several charities run by the ladies of the parish to provide for the confinements of respectable married women (Smither, 1970).

Against sickness and loss of earnings, working men paid their weekly coppers to Sick Clubs or Benefit Societies. Croydon Dispensary was opened to serve the poor people of the borough, and in 1900 was charging one penny a week to meet the costs of doctors and medicines. In 1907 a Guild of Help was founded to co-ordinate existing charities, to bring pressure on officialdom and to arouse public opinion against the continuing evils of poverty. This body, still in existence as the Croydon Guild of Social Service, was the first secular agency for social work in Croydon.

Civic responsibility for education, as for public health, grew from a recognition of the needs created by industrialism and the densely-populated new towns. The founding after the early Industrial Revolution of many kinds of voluntary school was superseded by compulsory attendance following the Education Acts of 1870 and 1880. Prior to 1870, Croydon had six national or church schools, one Roman Catholic school, a so-called British school, two Schools of Industry, and a Ragged School, together with various private establishments and 'Dame Schools'. Now, the newly-formed School Board took over responsibility for child education, opening its own schools and instituting its own examinations. In the 1890s, a series of Parliamentary Acts made primary education free and laid down provision for the education of blind, deaf, physically-handicapped, mentally defective, and epileptic children. In 1908, the creation of a School Health Service linked education and public health departments.

At the turn of the century, Croydon with a population of 134,000 was the largest town in Surrey. By 1914, Croydon and Metropolitan London, once separated by miles of open country, had fused as a result of large-scale speculative building. This rapid growth continued hardly abated between the two world wars, a plentiful supply of light industry protecting Croydon from the worst consequences of the economic depression. Private estates and the grounds of country houses were purchased for building land, and whole districts such as Addington, where the Archbishop's Palace had stood, were transformed within a few years. Further west at Waddon, rapid industrial development followed the opening of Croydon aerodrome, for some years Britain's largest airport.

After the Second World War, Croydon continued to expand. By 1951, the population had reached the quarter-million mark, making it one of the biggest County Boroughs in England. The social ecology of Croydon at that time was depicted by Morris (1957), who described it as a metropolitan dormitory, an important business centre for its own well-defined hinterland, and a growing industrial centre, chiefly for electrically-powered engineering and manufactures. Tabulating socio-economic indices of the electoral wards, he compared the middle-class residential districts of Addiscombe and Shirley with the poorer wards such as Whitehorse Manor, Broad Green, and Central: contrasts still largely in evidence today.

THE MODERN BOROUGH OF CROYDON

Within the past fifteen years, central Croydon has undergone another major transformation. The overcrowded areas have been partially cleared and a new commercial centre has been built. At a time in the mid-1950s when office space in London was at a premium, the Croydon Borough Council formulated ambitious plans to promote local business development. Roads were widened, an underpass constructed, and over fifty large office blocks erected. A 1968 business survey rated Croydon the fifth commercial centre in England, after London, Manchester, Birmingham, and Liverpool.

The London Borough of Croydon made its appearance in 1965, as a result of local government re-organization. The addition of five new wards to the

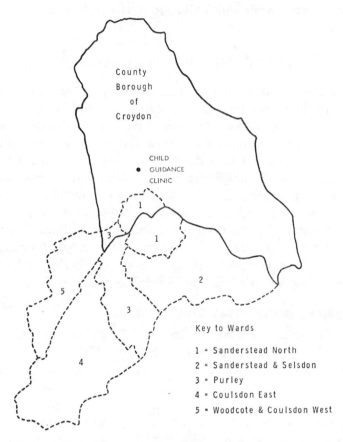

County
Borough
of
Croydon

CHILD
GUIDANCE
CLINIC

Key to Wards

1 = Sanderstead North
2 = Sanderstead & Selsdon
3 = Purley
4 = Coulsdon East
5 = Woodcote & Coulsdon West

Fig. 4. Addition of new wards to the borough of Croydon in 1965

south meant a large expansion of borough boundaries and a corresponding enlargement of the health authority's area of responsibility (see FIGURE 4).

Croydon today covers 24,000 acres, or about thirty-three square miles, divided for administrative purposes into twenty wards. Of the thirty-two Greater London Boroughs, it is the largest in area and fifth-largest in population. The housing estate of New Addington, which provides over 6,000 homes, has been used to rehouse many former inhabitants of the old, necrotic central zone, and has encountered many of the social problems associated with such developments. To foster local employment, a small industrial estate with places for 2,000 workers has been built near by.

The present-day Borough may thus be thought of as a modern creation.

Yet much of it retains a nineteenth-century aura. So many of its houses, shops, pubs, churches, and parks date back to Victorian times that whole neighbourhoods continue to bear the unmistakable stamp of that epoch. What existed before then has been obliterated; what changes have followed since have been mostly superficial. It was in Victorian and Edwardian days that the basic structure of today's Croydon was laid down; and it was then that the social and ecological patterns, with which this study is largely concerned, were first delineated.

STATISTICS FOR THE BOROUGH

Administrative statistics for Greater London, collated from the annual returns of the Boroughs, contain information on health, welfare, and education as well as on population. The official reports provide some data for the thirty-two Boroughs individually, some for the two main groups of Inner and Outer London Boroughs and some only for Greater London as a whole. The twelve Inner London Boroughs are distinct both in their demography and in the organization of their services. The twenty Outer London Boroughs, representing a vast suburbia of nearly five million inhabitants, constitute a much fairer basis of comparison for the Croydon findings. The following summary draws on the official statistics for the year 1967 (Greater London Council, 1969) to give a profile of the demography, health, and educational standards of Croydon in relation to its neighbours.

I. DEMOGRAPHIC AND VITAL STATISTICS

TABLE 3.1 shows that Croydon had slightly higher proportions both of children and of old people than the average for Greater London. The *dependency ratio*, or combined numbers of children (0–14) and old persons (men

TABLE 3.1

AGE–SEX STRUCTURE OF CROYDON POPULATION
COMPARED WITH THAT OF GREATER LONDON
1967 DATA

AGE GROUP	CROYDON	GREATER LONDON
years	%	%
0–4	8·2	7·7
5–14	13·7	12·4
Male:		
15–44	18·8	20·3
45–64	12·7	12·9
65+	4·4	4·4
Female:		
15–44	19·8	20·4
45–59	11·1	10·9
60+	11·3	11·0
Total	100·0	100·0
Size of population	328,290	7,880,760

over 65 and women over 60) per 1,000 persons of working age, was 603 for
Croydon compared with 551 for Greater London: the second-highest ratio
among the London Boroughs.

The distribution shown in TABLE 3.1 suggests a typical residential area,
with many family households, large numbers of elderly persons but relatively
low numbers of young, single adults. This impression was supported by the
marital status index, based on the proportion of women in the 15–44 age-group
who were married: the number per 1,000 was 649 for Croydon, compared
with 613 for Greater London.

The birth statistics for Croydon, set out in TABLE 3.2, were unremarkable.
In the rank order of London Boroughs, Croydon was placed fourteenth for

TABLE 3.2

BIRTH STATISTICS FOR CROYDON COMPARED
WITH THOSE FOR GREATER LONDON, 1967
(RATES PER 1,000 POPULATION)

	CROYDON	GREATER LONDON
Live births (crude rate)	17·0	17·0
Adjusted birth rate (standardized by area comparability factor)	17·3	15·8
Stillbirths	15·3	13·3
Illegitimacy rate	9·9	11·4

live births, sixth for stillbirths and sixteenth for illegitimate births. Adjustment of the live birth rate by a standard weighting factor raised Croydon to
eleventh place, a change of little significance.

The borough's mortality statistics, summarized in TABLE 3.3, were also

TABLE 3.3

MORTALITY STATISTICS FOR CROYDON COMPARED WITH
THOSE FOR GREATER LONDON, 1967
(RATES PER 1,000 POPULATION)

	CROYDON	GREATER LONDON
Crude death rate	12·2	10·8
Adjusted death rate	10·6	10·9
Infant deaths (under one year)	19·7	18·4
Perinatal mortality (infant deaths plus stillbirths)	27·6	24·2

unremarkable except for a rather high perinatal mortality, which placed
Croydon third among the London Boroughs. The relatively high crude death
rate could be explained by the age-structure of the population: application of
a weighting factor gave an adjusted rate very close to the London average.

2. CHILD HEALTH STATISTICS

Fifty-three per cent of Croydon children under 5 were seen at Child Welfare Centres in 1967, compared with an average of 57 per cent for Greater London. The proportions referred for special investigation or treatment as a result of this routine screening were 4·2 per cent in Croydon and 3·9 per cent in Greater London as a whole. The proportions placed on 'At Risk Registers' (which cover such abnormalities as premature or difficult birth, haemolytic disease of the newborn, congenital deformities, etc.) were 5·1 per cent in Croydon and 9·4 per cent in Greater London.

These statistics are not easy to interpret. The finding that relatively few children were judged to be 'at risk' might suggest a health status better than average for the child population if we could be sure that the screening procedure was reliable. An alternative explanation is that the case-finding procedure differed among the boroughs; a possibility which must certainly be considered in relation to school medical examinations. TABLE 3.4, for example, shows an apparent trend for increasing ill-health among schoolchildren, from the Inner to the Outer London Boroughs, and thence to Croydon. The explanation probably lies in higher rates of ascertainment among the outer residential areas.

TABLE 3.4

INDICES OF ILL-HEALTH AMONG LONDON SCHOOL CHILDREN: COMPARISON OF INNER AND OUTER LONDON BOROUGHS WITH CROYDON, 1967 (RATES PER 1,000)

	INNER LONDON	OUTER LONDON	CROYDON
'Unsatisfactory physical health'	4·6	2·6	1·1
Defective vision	74·0	85·0	103·0
Ear, nose and throat defects	15·2	26·2	37·1
Orthopaedic and postural defects	7·4	21·8	28·3
Speech defects	3·8	7·0	8·6
Psychological defects	3·5	6·1	8·2

Two related welfare statistics are worthy of note: in 1967, Croydon had only 3·6 per 1,000 children in care, compared with an average London rate of 7·9 per 1,000; secondly, the number of applications for accommodation of homeless families in that year was only 0·2 per 1,000 population, compared with the London average of 0·8 per 1,000. These figures again suggest that, at the time of the survey, Croydon was a settled residential area, with little of the conspicuous social pathology of the central metropolitan zone.

3. EDUCATIONAL STATISTICS

Comparison of Croydon's educational statistics with those of the other Boroughs was complicated by the fact that, by 1967, the Inner London Education Authority had moved some way towards comprehensive secondary education, whereas the Outer London Boroughs were still mostly in favour of selective schools. TABLE 3.5 shows the distribution of secondary school children among the different types of Local Authority school.

TABLE 3.5

DISTRIBUTION OF SECONDARY SCHOOL CHILDREN AMONG MAIN TYPES OF LOCAL AUTHORITY SCHOOL IN 1967: COMPARISON OF CROYDON WITH INNER AND OUTER LONDON BOROUGHS

	INNER LONDON	OUTER LONDON	CROYDON
	%	%	%
Secondary selective	22·2	27·2	31·6
Grammar	21·7	23·3	27·8
Technical	0·5	3·9	3·8
Secondary modern	7·5	49·2	65·9
Comprehensive	55·3	15·8	–
Other	15·0	7·8	2·5
Total	100·0	100·0	100·0
Number of children	163,534	260,976	18,392

The proportion of children attending comprehensive schools was 55·3 per cent in Inner London as against only 15·8 per cent in Outer London. Croydon Education Authority had maintained a policy of selective education and had no children at comprehensive schools, a fact which accounts for the relatively high proportion attending grammar schools. Compared with other boroughs which had no comprehensive schools, Croydon did not show up so favourably, ranking equal ninth out of thirteen for the proportion of children in selective schools.

Pupil–teacher ratios in the Croydon schools were fairly typical of Greater London as a whole. Figures for primary schools were 26·8:1 in Inner London, 28·1:1 for the whole of Outer London, and 27·6:1 in Croydon. The corresponding ratios for secondary schools were 16·3:1 in Inner London, 17·6:1 for Outer London, and 17·7:1 for Croydon. The proportion of immigrant pupils in 1967 was 13·9 per cent in Inner London, 6·2 per cent in Outer London generally, and 6·1 per cent in Croydon.

These bald administrative statistics cannot provide a distinctive picture of Croydon during, or immediately after, the survey period. Rather, their usefulness lies in helping to put the Croydon findings into perspective. They suggest that many features of the Croydon population, and particularly of its children, are shared in common with the Outer London Boroughs, and, to a lesser degree, with Greater London as a whole. It follows both that data for the metropolitan area could fairly be applied to Croydon and, conversely, that the findings of the Croydon survey could be extrapolated to other Outer London Boroughs.

The former point is relevant to the broad profile of child health in the borough. A century of universal primary education has coincided with an enormous improvement in the health of the nation's children. The mortality rate for children aged 5–9 years fell to less than one-twentieth of its pre-1870 rate, and that for children aged 10–14 almost as much. Instrumental in this dramatic change were improved standards of sanitation, nutrition, and housing, the development of immunisation and other personal preventive measures, advances in scientific treatment, and the opportunities for screening and early diagnosis provided by the School Health Service. During this century, the focus of attention shifted with changing patterns of morbidity: from cholera and typhoid to diphtheria, tuberculosis, scarlet fever, and acute rheumatism; thence to poliomyelitis and meningitis, and more recently to non-infectious disorders such as asthma, congenital malformations, speech and language defects, and mental handicaps. In 1966, over 100,000 handicapped children in England and Wales received special education or were awaiting admission to special schools; 65,000 were treated for defective speech; 57,000 attended child guidance clinics; from 10 to 15 per cent of those in ordinary schools were in need of remedial teaching; about 30,000 were considered to be unsuitable for education at school because of severe subnormality. In the words of Henderson (1968):

The improved physical health of schoolchildren in the past 50 years, and the expansion of medical services for them, have thrown into sharp relief the large number with emotional, behaviour and learning difficulties who need skilled help and guidance.

Croydon statistics followed the national trend. Of Croydon children attending special schools at the end of 1967, 52·8 per cent were classed as educationally subnormal, maladjusted, or speech defective, compared with 31·2 per cent who were physically handicapped and 12·7 per cent who had defective vision or hearing. At school medical examinations, 140 children were found to have 'psychological defects', compared with only nineteen judged to be in unsatisfactory physical health. In the same year, 380 children were seen at Croydon Child Guidance Clinic and 563 were dealt with by the School Psychological Service. These figures reflect latter-day concern with the emotional and mental health of the schoolchild and the consequent expansion of post-war psychiatric and psychological services outlined in CHAPTER I.

CROYDON CHILD GUIDANCE AND SCHOOL PSYCHOLOGICAL SERVICE

Croydon's single Child Guidance Clinic was opened in 1943 by the Local Education Department. Initially, medical cover was provided informally by the psychiatric hospital service based on Warlingham Park Hospital. In due course the Medical Superintendent of Warlingham Park, the late Dr. T. P. Rees, assumed the post of consultant to the clinic, while the Hospital Management Committee by providing new premises assumed greater responsibility. In 1965, however, the new local government structure ensured that in future this responsibility would be more equally shared between the hospital, representing the National Health Service, and the Borough of Croydon.

The administrative situation remained fluid for some time, and then slowly crystallized in its present form (early 1974), in which social workers and educational psychologists are provided by the Local Education Authority, while medical staff employed under the National Health Service work in the clinic on a sessional basis. Essentially, therefore, the clinic began as an educational venture, was transferred to the hospital service and then gradually developed into a truly joint service. Important milestones were the appointment of a consultant child psychiatrist and an educational psychologist in 1960, and the opening four years later of a day unit with facilities for severely disturbed children (Crosse, 1972).

By 1972, the clinic personnel comprised the following:

(i) a consultant child psychiatrist, senior registrar, and part-time registrar, the latter based on the near-by children's hospital;

(ii) five educational psychologists under a Senior Psychologist, based on their own centre adjacent to the clinic;

(iii) four psychiatric social workers, appointed by the Education Authority and seconded to the clinic;

(iv) a teacher seconded to the day unit of the clinic by the Inner London Education Authority;

(v) nursing staff supplied by the Regional Hospital Board;

(vi) secretarial staff employed by the Education Department.

At the time of our survey, the staff was smaller, consisting of a consultant child psychiatrist and two junior psychiatrists, a psychiatric social worker, play therapists, and a secretary, in addition to the attached educational psychologists. The clinic was situated in a large, semi-detached house about half a mile from the centre of Croydon. It contained rooms for consultation and testing, offices, and a play room, all pleasantly furnished. Children were seen in an informal, relaxed atmosphere, with none of the characteristic features of a hospital.

The official catchment area of the clinic coincided with the borough boundaries. The policy of the School Health Service was to refer all serious cases of maladjustment to the Croydon Clinic, either directly or via the School Psychological Service, and none to outside agencies. Most of the children seen at the Clinic came from Croydon homes, only about 3 per cent being from addresses outside the borough.[1]

Croydon School Psychological Service was established in 1960, its purpose

---

[1] The 100 or so adolescent girls referred each year from the local Remand Home for Court Reports were excluded from the inquiry, since their referral to the clinic was a direct consequence of delinquent behaviour.

being 'the giving of advice to parents, to teachers and to the children themselves in those cases where doubt has arisen as to the direction or redirection
of the child's mental development' (Reid, 1968). Clearly, the functions of such
a service must overlap with those of a child guidance clinic, and this fact has
been firmly recognized in Croydon as in most local authority areas. Each
educational psychologist works for one session weekly in the Child Guidance
Clinic; maladjusted children seen in the schools by psychologists are sent to
the clinic for treatment; conversely, the child psychiatrists may recommend
children attending the clinic for special remedial classes in the schools.

The largest number of referrals to the School Psychological Service are
made by head-teachers, but many other groups are represented: school medical officers, youth employment officers, parents, and general practitioners. The
common reasons for referral are unsatisfactory school progress (notably in
reading), school refusal, and behavioural problems. Often the management of
disturbed children calls for co-operation not only with psychiatrists but also
with social workers, Education Welfare Officers, and Probation Officers. In
short, the work of the service is closely co-ordinated with that of the Child
Guidance Clinic and can be seen as an integral part of the wider concept of
child guidance.

The nearest neighbouring Child Guidance Clinic was at Mitcham, about four
miles from central Croydon. Clinics at Sutton and Carshalton were some five
miles distant; those at Chipstead and Bromley about six miles; while Brixton
Child Guidance Clinic and Maudsley Hospital stood approximately seven
miles from central Croydon. Finally, the main London teaching hospitals
were situated ten to twelve miles distant. It thus seemed probable that most
referrals from general practitioners, as well as those from Local Authority
agencies, would be directed to the Croydon clinic: a point subsequently
checked by a survey of the local practitioners' referral habits.

SUMMARY

The thirty-two Greater London Boroughs, and more especially the twenty
Outer London Boroughs, are suitable for ecological surveys of the kind
described here. In the event, we selected Croydon as being highly suitable for
our investigation.

Although the Borough of Croydon has a thousand-year history, its modern
structure was created, and its character moulded, by the rapid industrial and
suburban growth of the nineteenth century. It was during this period that
most of the Borough was built and that its educational, social, and public
health services were established.

Modern Croydon can be seen as part of the enormous suburbia of Outer
London. In terms of its demographic, vital, child health, and educational
statistics, it appears to be closely comparable with the other Outer London
Boroughs. Changes in the patterns of childhood morbidity in the Borough

have reflected national trends during this century and have led to an increasing concern with emotional, behavioural, and learning difficulties as these problems have gained in relative importance.

Since 1943, Croydon has had a single, centrally-placed Child Guidance Clinic to which all referrals from Local Authority sources have been directed, and which is closely linked with the School Psychological Service. The child guidance team, comprising psychiatrists, educational psychologists, social workers, a teacher, nursing, and secretarial staff, is based on the multi-disciplinary approach outlined in CHAPTER I, and is in most respects typical of this kind of service throughout the country.

The geographical situation of Croydon, and the absence of alternative facilities, encouraged the belief that most medical, as well as Local Authority, referrals would be made to the local Child Guidance Clinic.

CHAPTER IV

AIMS AND DESIGN OF THE INVESTIGATION

THE first three chapters have covered the historical, sociological, and local background of the present inquiry. Its purpose and aims can now be formulated more precisely, in terms of three sets of hypotheses to be tested:

(i) Child guidance rates differ widely between local neighbourhoods. Neighbourhood delinquency rates likewise manifest a broad range of variation. The two sets of rates are inter-related and have similar patterns of association with neighbourhood demographic and socio-economic indices.

(ii) Child guidance rates differ widely as between schools. School delinquency rates likewise show a broad range of variation. The two sets of rates are inter-related and have similar patterns of association with school demographic and social indices.

(iii) In addition to the effects of neighbourhood and school, child psychiatric referral rates vary among individual physicians and can be related to defined characteristics of the doctors and of their practices.

To test these hypotheses, we decided to analyse a large sample of referrals to Croydon Child Guidance Clinic, together with a corresponding sample of children appearing before the courts during the same period of time. Child guidance and delinquency rates could then be computed for individual neighbourhoods and schools within the borough. At the same time, information could be obtained about environmental factors, represented by social indices of the neighbourhoods and of the schools, as well as about the practitioners whose referral habits had helped to determine the composition of the child guidance sample.

Essentially, therefore, the inquiry comprised a series of linked sub-studies, as follows:

1. Selection of a child guidance sample, based on the case-records of Croydon Child Guidance Clinic. In view of the problems of multivariate analysis, a sample-size of not less than about 1,000 was thought to be required. The annual number of new referrals to the clinic was known to be about 200, so that a five-year retrospective survey was indicated. The margin of choice proved small, since when the survey began in 1967, clinic records were available only for the six preceding years. The fact that the quinquennium 1962–6 was bounded by two national censuses suggested this as the most opportune period for the survey.

2. Selection of two samples of delinquent children, based on official records for the same time-period. The need for two samples arose from purely practical considerations: information on all Croydon juveniles appearing before the courts in the quinquennium 1962–6 was available from the Borough Children's Department; the records, however, were scanty in detail and, in particular, the child's school was seldom recorded. The records of the Probation Service proved more suitable for research purposes but represented only about one-quarter of known delinquents. Accordingly, we decided that data on all delinquents, taken from the Children's Department, should be used in the main analysis, but that a probation sample should also be drawn for the analysis of schools. We therefore selected two samples:

(a) a one-in-two sample of children known to Croydon Children's Department as having come before the courts in the period 1962–6;
(b) all children placed on probation or supervision orders by Croydon Juvenile Court during the same period.

Since (b) would be in effect a sub-sample of (a), its accuracy could be checked by comparing the number of children known to the Probation Service with the number known by the Children's Department to have been placed on probation or supervision orders during the same period.

3. Compilation of data for classifying electoral areas and schools. For this purpose, information had to be obtained from a number of sources:

(a) from Census data, both published tables and special extractions;
(b) from the Chief Education Officer for Croydon, information about school populations, and about educational and social statistics appertaining to schools;
(c) from the Medical Officer of Health for Croydon, who was also Principal School Medical Officer, information on the health statistics of the borough and its schools;
(d) from the Local Executive Council responsible for general medical services in the area, information on the practitioners in the borough.

4. A survey of Croydon School Health Cards, to ascertain the proportion of children at each school who were registered with each local practitioner and residing in each enumeration district of the borough. For this purpose, a one-in-four sample of the school health cards was drawn and the basic data extracted. The aim of the sub-study was to provide the necessary denominators for calculating rates by neighbourhood, school, and general practitioners.

5. As the Local Executive Council was prepared to supply current lists of doctors practising in the area, but no further information about their practices, a postal questionnaire survey was planned of all general practitioners who had been working in Croydon during the period 1962–6 and who were still in the borough in 1968. The aims of this sub-study were twofold: first,

to gather information about the doctor's practice, such as his approximate list-size and his use of local psychiatric agencies (in particular, of Croydon Child Guidance Clinic); secondly, to give some indication of his attitudes and opinions on the management of child psychiatric disorder.

Each of these sub-studies presented its own distinct problems of method, and it seems better to discuss these in relation to the various stages of the research as they are set out in CHAPTERS V–IX, rather than to catalogue them here. Collection of the various types of data, though laborious, was essentially a simple matter. More difficult and complex were the subsequent manipulations of the data, aimed at defining the effects of different variables, either singly or in combination.

In order to examine carefully the influence of neighbourhood factors, we had to make use of small, homogeneous population units. Such units are provided by the enumeration districts of the official Census, and their grouping by means of a cluster analysis of demographic and socio-economic indices is described in CHAPTER VII and APPENDIX B2. We consider that the application of cluster analysis technique represents a significant advance in ecological survey research.

Neither for the schools, nor for the doctors and their practices, did we have ready-to-hand indices which could serve as the basis of an objective classification, in the way that demographic and socio-economic indices did for the electoral areas of the borough. In attempting to establish a useful classification of schools, we analysed various statistics supplied by the Chief Education Officer, including average class-size, pupil/teacher ratio, rate of teacher turnover, and proportion of immigrant children, as well as indices of scholastic achievement appropriate for the different types of school. In no instance did we have good reason *a priori* to consider a given index relevant to the child guidance rates. The schools analysis, indeed, suffered from the lack of any theoretical model such as earlier ecological surveys of mental illness and delinquency had supplied for the neighbourhoods analysis.

The same comment holds true for the analysis of general practitioner referral rates. Here, we had no basis for classifying the doctors and their practices, other than the data obtained by our own postal questionnaire survey. Given the inevitable limitations of such an inquiry, in terms of its return rate and the validity and reliability of the questionnaire responses, it is clear that any attempt to explain differences of referral pattern between individual doctors and practices could be no more than tentative.

In order to estimate the individual contribution of neighbourhood and school effects, and of selective medical referral, to the observed patterns of child guidance utilisation, we planned to carry out multivariate analyses of the survey data. The technique of *analysis of variance* provides such a quantitative assessment; that of *multiple regression analysis* goes a stage further in that it offers an explanation of the observed pattern in terms of defined characteristics: in the present instance of neighbourhoods, schools, and doctors. These questions are discussed in detail in CHAPTERS VIII and IX and in APPENDICES B3 and B4.

In summary, the broad aims of the investigation can be stated thus: to examine the variation in child guidance and delinquency rates among the neighbourhoods and schools of Croydon; to seek an explanation for any geographical differences in the demographic and socio-economic features of the neighbourhoods; to examine some possible reasons for variation among the schools, and, finally, to see to what extent the over-all pattern was modified by the diagnostic and referral habits of local medical practitioners.

CHAPTER V

THE CHILD GUIDANCE SURVEY

HAVING chosen Croydon as the survey area, we sought the co-operation of the local medical and educational authorities. A memorandum outlining the research proposals was submitted, first to the Director of Croydon Child Guidance Clinic; then to the Medical Advisory Committee of the local hospital group and to the Chief Education Officer. In each instance we received a favourable response and an assurance of future co-operation. The Clinic Director gave permission for the medical records to be examined, thus enabling the research team to draw a representative sample and to extract the basic information on each child.

MATERIAL AND METHOD

The first step was to undertake a pilot study, in which the records for one year, 1966, were inspected. Since all the accession cards for children who had attended in that year were successfully located, and the recording of basic data was found to be of high standard, the prospects for a full-scale inquiry appeared to be good. As an additional check, we also inspected the cards for the latter half of 1962; here again the findings were encouraging and helped confirm the feasibility of the proposed survey.

The definitive sample was based on referrals to the clinic in the five-year period, 1962–6. We took the names of all children referred during these years from the clinic diaries, and then located the corresponding case-files for all those who had attended.[1] Partly because the files were stored separately for current cases, terminated cases still under 16 years, and terminated cases over 16 years, the work of abstraction proved laborious, requiring some thirty visits to the clinic by two research workers over a four-month period.

Data from the case-files were transcribed onto a pre-coded item-sheet with a standard format (see APPENDIX AI). The items we abstracted were: the child's sex; age at first attendance; home address; school (if any); occupation of father or chief wage-earner; name of general practitioner; referring agency; diagnostic category. Only the first four items could be derived from the front case-sheet; for the rest we had to search the clinical and social work notes, school reports, referral letters, and other correspondence. Eventually, all the data were fairly complete except for parental occupation, which was missing in nearly one-quarter of cases.

[1] Excluding the delinquent girls from a remand home, mentioned in CHAPTER III.

A special problem was posed by the eighty-seven children who had been referred in the survey period but had failed to attend. To have excluded this group would have meant a danger of possible bias; hence we decided to include them in the sample, even though the available information might be scanty. Fortunately, the clinic staff, very commendably, had kept a separate file of all correspondence dealing with non-attenders, and the referral letters were traced in every case. The referring agency could be identified from these letters in 97·7 per cent, the child's school in 85·1 per cent, the general practitioner in 55·2 per cent, and the parental occupation in 24·1 per cent. Presumptive diagnoses were made on the basis of symptoms and deviant behaviour noted in the letters: obviously an inaccurate method, but one which permitted a crude comparison of the children who had attended with those who had failed to do so.

During one part of the survey period, because the clinic waiting-list had grown, a small branch clinic had been set up in a day hospital, situated on the housing estate at New Addington. We visited this clinic, examined the case-files of all children seen in the relevant years and extracted the data as for the main sample.

THE DIAGNOSTIC CLASSIFICATION

Special mention must be made of the problem of diagnosis, and the diagnostic coding used in the inquiry. Diagnostic classification is still a contentious issue in child psychiatry. The child psychiatry section of the International Classification of Diseases was criticized by Cameron (1955) for its 'woeful inadequacy', and a number of more elaborate systems have since been promulgated (Cameron, 1955; Langford, 1964; Rutter, 1965; Rutter, Shaffer, and Shepherd, 1973). For the present study, based on a retrospective analysis of clinical case-notes, a simple method was essential. The one we adopted was modified from an earlier study of child psychiatric referral (Gath, 1968) and comprised the following broad categories:

1. Organic mental disorders (organic psychoses; brain syndromes);
2. Mental handicap (subnormality; retardation);
3. Functional psychoses (childhood schizophrenia; early autism);
4. Neuroses (anxiety; phobic and obsessional–compulsive states; abnormally withdrawn or inhibited behaviour);
5. Conduct disorders (truancy; stealing; disobedience; aggressive and destructive behaviour);
6. Mixed neurotic and conduct disorders;
7. Other (including educational retardation, reading backwardness, or other specific handicaps or habit disorders in isolation);
8. No diagnosis or diagnostic formulation recorded.

Whenever possible, we used the diagnostic formulation entered in the clinical notes to categorize the patient. Where more than one diagnosis had been recorded, the more serious or important was accepted, the categories listed above being treated as mutually exclusive. Cases with no formal diagnosis were classified by the research psychiatrists if enough information was given; otherwise they were placed in category 8 above.

FINDINGS OF THE SURVEY

1. REFERRAL RATE IN THE SURVEY PERIOD

During the five-year period covered by the survey, the number of referrals to the clinic totalled 1,061.[1] Nearly all these appeared to be first referrals, though fifteen children were referred twice during the period, and a few others had been seen initially before 1962. The number was difficult to convert into an exact population rate because of the change in the Borough boundaries which took place early in 1965. For the period as a whole, the approximate mean annual rate was 7·9 per 10,000 population. More accurate estimates could be made for 1966 because a national 10 per cent Census was carried out in that year. The rates of 8·2 per 10,000 population, and 32·9 per 10,000 children under 16, compare with national rates for the same year of 6·2 per 10,000 population and 25·4 per 10,000 children under 16.

The number of new cases year by year, set out in TABLE 5.1, shows an overall increase but no consistent trend.

TABLE 5.1
YEAR OF INDEX REFERRAL, BY SEX
CHILD GUIDANCE SAMPLE

YEAR OF REFERRAL	BOYS	GIRLS	BOTH SEXES
1962	117	61	178
1963	129	79	208
1964	136	72	208
1965	122	80	202
1966	146	119	265
Total	650	411	1,061

Making due allowance for the 1965 boundary changes, there was no convincing evidence of a rising referral rate. This finding is not altogether surprising: the national trend outlined in FIGURE 1 could hardly be reflected, at least in the short term, in every separate local authority area. It seems more probable that the fairly steady increase in national referral rates was made up of irregular increases in local rates corresponding to the opening of new clinics and increases in the establishment of trained personnel. Beyond a certain point, increased demand on a clinic with a fixed establishment of staff would

[1] Addition of the remand home cases referred for diagnostic court reports would have increased the total to 1,482.

be more likely to result in longer waiting-times, and a higher proportion of non-contacts, than in a steadily increasing case-load.

2. AGE–SEX DISTRIBUTION OF THE SAMPLE

TABLE 5.2, which summarizes the age–sex distribution of the sample, shows an overall preponderance of boys, with a male:female ratio of just over 3:2.

TABLE 5.2

AGE-SEX DISTRIBUTION OF THE CHILD GUIDANCE SAMPLE

AGE IN YEARS	BOYS	GIRLS	BOTH SEXES
	%	%	%
Under 5	14·4	16·0	15·0
5–10	52·1	41·5	48·0
11–15	32·3	39·0	35·0
Over 15	1·2	3·5	2·0
Total	100·0	100·0	100·0
No. of children	642	405	1,047
Age not known	8	6	14
Total	650	411	1,061

Similar findings have been reported from child guidance clinics in many areas; for example, Bristol (Barbour and Beedell, 1955); London (Hare, 1968); Aberdeen (Baldwin, 1968); Oxford (Oxford Education Committee, 1969) and Nottingham (Department of Health, 1971). Timms (1968), in his study of six clinics, found proportions of boys ranging from 64 to 76 per cent. This relative excess of boys may be due partly to selective referral, deviant behaviour among boys being more conspicuous and troublesome than among girls (Howells, 1965). At the same time, field-survey findings suggest that psychiatric disturbance really is commoner among boys (Ullman, 1952; Lapouse and Monk, 1958; Rutter, 1965).

The sex-ratio for the present sample was highest in the 5–10 year age-group, a finding similar to those reported by Howells (1965) and Hare (1968). There was, however, no overall difference of age-distribution as between the sexes (Chi-sq. $= 3·29$; d.f. $= 3$; $p > 0·05$).

One striking feature of the age-distribution was the relatively high proportion of children under 5 in the sample. This group accounted for 15 per cent of the referrals, compared with 9 per cent in the Oxford sample and less than 5 per cent in Timms' six-clinic sample. The explanation of this finding is by no means clear but presumably resides to some extent in a high use of the Croydon clinic by agencies dealing with pre-school children.

3. SOURCES OF REFERRAL

Certainly, a high proportion of all referrals came from medical agencies. TABLE 5.3, which sets out the principal sources of referral, shows that the majority of children were sent either by general practitioners (43 per cent) or by school medical officers (25 per cent).

TABLE 5.3
SOURCES OF REFERRAL BY SEX, CHILD GUIDANCE SAMPLE

SOURCE OF REFERRAL	BOYS	GIRLS	BOTH SEXES
	%	%	%
General practitioners	42·3	45·5	43·5
School medical service	27·7	21·4	25·2
Hospital physicians	7·2	11·2	8·8
Infant welfare clinics	4·9	4·4	4·7
Teachers	6·2	6·8	6·4
Parents	4·2	3·4	3·9
Children's Department	3·4	3·7	3·5
Other	3·8	3·4	3·7
Not known	0·3	0·2	0·3
Total	100·0	100·0	100·0
No. of children	650	411	1,061

By way of contrast, only 11·3 per cent of Timms' sample had been referred by general practitioners; whereas 42·7 per cent had come from school medical officers and 19·0 per cent from other school sources. The inference may be drawn that the Croydon clinic had established a better-than-average liaison

TABLE 5.4
SOURCE OF REFERRAL BY AGE-GROUP,
CHILD GUIDANCE SAMPLE

SOURCE OF REFERRAL	AGE-GROUP					TOTAL
	1–4	5–8	9–12	13+	NOT KNOWN	
	%	%	%	%	%	%
MEDICAL	93·7	90·3	80·6	79·9	64·3	85·1
General Practitioners	39·9	42·3	39·9	54·6	28·6	43·6
School Doctors	1·9	39·5	30·2	13·5	21·4	25·1
Hospital Physicians inc. Psychiatrists	20·3	7·2	9·1	10·9	14·3	10·7
Other	31·6	1·3	1·4	0·9	–	5·7
NON-MEDICAL	6·3	9·7	19·4	20·1	35·7	14·9
Parents	4·4	2·5	5·6	3·5	7·1	4·1
Teachers and School Psychologists	0·6	4·1	8·5	10·9	14·3	6·6
Other or Not known	1·3	3·1	5·3	5·7	14·3	4·2
Total	100·0	100·0	100·0	100·0	100·0	100·0
No. of children	158	319	341	229	14	1,061

with local medical agencies, and in consequence tended to receive a higher-than-average proportion of medical referrals.

Although the great majority of pre-school children had been referred by doctors, this group alone did not account for the over-all distribution of the sample. TABLE 5.4 shows that, even in the highest age-group, most of the children had been sent by medical agencies. Unexpectedly, general practitioner referrals were even more strongly represented in this age-group than among the pre-school children.

4. DIAGNOSTIC DISTRIBUTION

Diagnostic assessment had to be limited to the 974 children who had attended the clinic and undergone at least one clinical interview: the eighty-seven children who had failed to attend could not be reliably diagnosed on the strength of their referral letters. Using the simple diagnostic classification outlined on p. 45, we grouped the children as shown in TABLE 5.5.

TABLE 5.5

DIAGNOSTIC DISTRIBUTION BY SEX, CHILD GUIDANCE
ATTENDERS

DIAGNOSIS	BOYS	GIRLS	BOTH SEXES
	%	%	%
Organic disorder	3·4	2·0	2·8
Mental subnormality	6·6	7·3	6·9
Psychosis	1·5	1·8	1·6
Neurosis	32·0	36·5	33·8
Conduct disorder	30·4	27·8	29·4
Mixed neurosis and conduct disorder	5·9	3·1	4·8
Other	19·2	20·5	19·7
Not known	1·0	1·0	1·0
Total	100·0	100·0	100·0
No. of attenders	593	381	974

Because of the lack of a generally-accepted classification, comparison with other child guidance or child psychiatric populations is difficult. Broadly speaking, the proportion of neurotic disorders appeared to be higher, and that of conduct disorders lower, for the present sample than for most of those reported. Timms (1968), for example, found that an average of 49 per cent of children seen at six clinics had presented with conduct disorders (including delinquency) and only 7 per cent with 'nervous disorders'. The high proportion of medical referrals in the Croydon sample did not appear to explain this discrepancy: of children sent by medical agencies, 35·9 per cent were diagnosed as neurotic and 29·9 per cent as conduct disorders—proportions corresponding closely to those for the sample as a whole.

It may be that the statistics of some clinics, unrelated as they are to defined populations, are weighted by specialized referrals from neighbouring institutions. The distribution of the present sample, for instance, would have been radically altered by inclusion of 421 remand home cases referred for court reports during the survey period. Since, however, the great majority of these girls came from home addresses outside Croydon, their inclusion in the sample would have seriously distorted the population rates. It is thus important to distinguish carefully between the total case-load of a clinic and that proportion representing a defined service population.

5. SOCIAL CLASS DISTRIBUTION

The social class distribution of the sample closely resembled that of the male population of Croydon, as can be seen from TABLE 5.6. Unfortunately, the social class data were of limited value because, as has been stated, we could not ascertain the parental occupation for 23 per cent of the sample. In a further 7 per cent, the father's occupation was an unreliable guide to family social status, since either the child was in care; or the parents were separated; or the father was unemployed, disabled, retired, in prison, or dead. Moreover, though the age-distribution of the fathers was unknown, it could be assumed that they were a relatively young group; hence direct comparison with the social class distribution of the general population might be misleading.

TABLE 5.6

SOCIAL CLASS DISTRIBUTION OF CHILD GUIDANCE SAMPLE BY SEX: COMPARISON WITH GENERAL POPULATION OF THE BOROUGH

REG. GEN. SOCIAL CLASS 1966	BOYS	GIRLS	BOTH SEXES	POPN. OF CROYDON 1966[1]
	%	%	%	%
I	5·4	4·0	4·9	7·4
II	17·6	21·5	19·1	20·9
III	54·6	53·7	54·2	52·7
IV	14·8	14·2	14·6	13·8
V	7·6	6·6	7·2	5·2
Total	100·0	100·0	100·0	100·0
No. of persons	460	274	734	105,270
Social class not known	190	137	327	3,290
	650	411	1,061	108,560

[1] Economically active males.

All that can be safely deduced is that the child guidance sample showed no evidence of social class skewing. This does not preclude the possibility that social conditions were relevant to its composition: a point of central importance to the ecological analysis discussed in CHAPTER VII.

Other child guidance surveys have encountered comparable difficulties in examining social class data. Timms (1968), for example, could allocate a social class to only between 20 and 40 per cent of his six-clinics sample, even after the staff had been asked to supply additional information. It is thus not possible to say how far the Croydon sample was representative of the social class distribution of child guidance clients as a whole.

6. DIAGNOSIS IN RELATION TO REFERRING AGENCY AND SOCIAL CLASS

The two principal diagnostic categories, neurosis and conduct disorder, each accounted for about one-third of the sample. Tabulation of diagnosis against social class showed a significant difference between these two categories, children in Social Class II being more often grouped under neurosis and children in Social Classes IV and V under conduct disorder. The distribution is shown in TABLE 5.7.

TABLE 5.7
SOCIAL CLASS OF CHILD GUIDANCE ATTENDERS, BY DIAGNOSTIC CATEGORY

SOCIAL CLASS	NEUROSIS	CONDUCT DISORDER	OTHER DIAGNOSES	TOTAL
	%	%	%	%
I	3·3	5·2	5·9	4·8
II	23·7	12·2	19·9	18·9
III	57·5	55·9	50·8	54·6
IV	10·6	18·3	15·2	14·6
V	4·9	8·4	8·2	7·1
Total	100·0	100·0	100·0	100·0
No. of children	245	213	256	714
Social class not known	84	73	103	260
	329	286	359	974

For neurosis v. conduct disorder, Chi sq. = 16·17, d.f. = 4, p < 0·01.)

This finding suggested that maladjusted children from middle-class families might be more often taken to medical agencies, and thence referred to child guidance with 'neurotic' symptoms; whereas those from lower-class families might be more often referred by the schools, the courts, or social agencies,

TABLE 5.8
SOCIAL CLASS OF CHILD GUIDANCE SAMPLE, BY REFERRING AGENCY

REFERRING AGENCY	SOCIAL CLASS				
	I & II	III	IV & V	NOT KNOWN	TOTAL
	%	%	%	%	%
General Practitioners	48·9	42·2	44·4	42·2	43·6
School doctors	23·9	28·2	28·1	20·8	25·2
Hospital physicians	6·8	8·8	5·6	11·3	8·8
Teachers	9·1	6·5	6·9	4·6	6·4
Others	11·3	14·3	15·0	21·1	16·0
Total	100·0	100·0	100·0	100·0	100·0
No. of children	176	398	160	327	1,061

because of anti-social or delinquent behaviour. Tabulation of diagnosis by social class and by type of referral agency failed to support this hypothesis, the proportion of children referred by medical agencies being very similar for the different social classes and the main diagnostic categories, as shown in TABLES 5.8 and 5.9.

TABLE 5.9

DIAGNOSTIC CATEGORIES OF CHILD GUIDANCE SAMPLE, BY REFERRING AGENCY

REFERRING AGENCY	NEUROSIS	CONDUCT DISORDER	OTHER DIAGNOSES	TOTAL
	%	%	%	%
General practitioners	50·0	39·8	40·9	43·6
School doctors	22·5	30·7	22·8	25·2
Hospital physicians	9·5	4·3	12·1	8·8
Teachers	5·8	7·0	6·5	6·4
Others	12·2	18·2	17·7	16·0
Total	100·0	100·0	100·0	100·0
No. of children	360	329	372	1,061

On the whole, the evidence failed to show any useful dichotomy of the sample into 'medical' and 'non-medical' types of referral. The findings were more consistent with the notion of a continuum of disturbance, extending from purely neurotic disorders at one extreme to formal juvenile delinquency at the other. There appeared to be no obvious or natural threshold on this continuum that could be used to demarcate the activities and legitimate sphere of interest of different types of services. This point can perhaps be seen more clearly if the characteristics of the child guidance sample are compared with those of the corresponding delinquency sample.

SUMMARY

The survey sample comprised all cases, other than those from a local remand home, referred to Croydon Child Guidance Clinic over a five-year period, 1962–6. The total number of referrals was 1,061, corresponding to an estimated annual rate of 8·2 per 10,000 population, or 32·9 per 10,000 children under 16 years. As in other child guidance surveys, boys outnumbered girls; the M:F ratio for the sample was approximately 3:2.

The Croydon sample was unlike those reported from other areas in a number of respects: it contained relatively more children of pre-school age, more cases referred by medical agencies and a higher proportion diagnosed as neurotic. These characteristics appeared to be largely independent of one another, the preponderance of medical referrals extending through all age-groups and diagnostic categories. No clear dichotomy into 'medical' and 'non-medical' types of case was detected; rather the findings suggested a continuum ranging from purely neurotic disorders at one extreme to juvenile delinquency at the other.

On the basis of these findings, social and ecological correlates of delinquency appeared to have less obvious relevance to child guidance practice in Croydon, during the survey period, than in many other areas of the country.

CHAPTER VI

THE DELINQUENCY SURVEY

THE reasons for examining local patterns of juvenile delinquency, as well as those of child guidance referral, have been indicated in the opening chapters. To recapitulate briefly, we postulated that maladjustment and psychiatric disturbance in childhood are linked, both causally and in distribution, with those forms of deviant behaviour classed as delinquent. Since delinquency rates are known to be influenced by neighbourhood and school factors, we formed the hypothesis that child guidance rates are affected by the same factors, and co-vary with delinquency rates. To test this hypothesis, we decided to compare rates of child guidance referral and of known delinquency, and to establish how far they showed similar patterns of variation with neighbourhood and with school.

The immediate aim was to draw a representative sample of juvenile delinquents in Croydon and to record their home addresses and schools, so that delinquency rates could be computed for each ward and each school. A juvenile delinquent was defined, for the purpose of the inquiry, as any young person or child brought before a juvenile court and dealt with by any court action other than absolute discharge. Children brought before the courts as in need of care and protection were included under the rubric.

Such a definition automatically excludes all offenders not detected or not brought to court: in the present study, as in most research on delinquency, it would have been wholly impracticable to have tried to include the large mass of unreported cases. What evidence we have suggests that cases brought to court provide a fair representation, at least of repeated acts of delinquent behaviour: a point discussed in CHAPTER II.

SELECTION OF SAMPLES

Because of the possible difficulties of data-collection in this field, a number of different sampling-frames were considered. First, we explored the possibility of using the local Juvenile Court records. With the permission of the Home Office, the court diaries were searched for all offenders who had appeared in the first half of 1966; names were abstracted from the diaries and the corresponding files located. The results showed that data collected in this way would be seriously incomplete, the child's school in particular being seldom recorded. Hence, a sample based solely on the court records would have been unsatisfactory.

A second possibility was to draw a sample of children and young persons on probation. About one-quarter of all those coming before juvenile courts had been placed on probation or supervision orders, and in consequence were known to Croydon Probation Officers. The Probation Service records proved more fruitful than those of the court, information being more detailed and more complete; children put on probation during the survey period thus comprised a potentially valuable sampling-frame. Such a group, however, could not be taken to represent juvenile delinquency as a whole, because of the special grounds for probation and supervision orders.

A representative sample was obtainable from Croydon Children's Department,[1] which kept records of all known delinquent children living in the Borough. By permission of the Children's Officer, we inspected the Department's files. Although the case-records proved less detailed than those of the Probation Service (school data, in particular, being less consistently recorded), the basic data were complete. The files were more comprehensive than those of the Juvenile Court, since they included all children and young persons, resident in Croydon, who had appeared in courts outside the Borough.

It thus appeared that no one source could provide a wholly satisfactory sampling-frame: the Children's Department possessed basic data of a representative sample, while the Probation Service could supply more detailed information on a selected sub-sample. In the event, we decided to draw on both these sources.

THE MAIN DELINQUENCY SAMPLE: ALL JUVENILE COURT APPEARANCES

The Children's Department kept an alphabetical card-index of all Croydon children who had come before the courts during the past fifteen years. The card gave in each case the child's home address and details of all court appearances. A hand-sort of every *second* child who had appeared in court during the survey period, 1962–6, yielded a total of 912 boys and 182 girls. For each child, the home address, together with details of all offences and court disposals during the relevant period, was copied on to an item-sheet designed for the purpose (see APPENDIX A2).

We also attempted to record in each case the name of the child's school, information which was not recorded on the index card but had to be sought in the individual case-files. As the school was named in only 70 per cent of the first 300 case-records examined, the attempt was abandoned. Hence, analysis of the school distribution of delinquency was undertaken only for the probation sample.

[1] In 1971, the Children's Department became part of the new Social Services Department.

THE SUBSIDIARY SAMPLE: PROBATION AND SUPERVISION CASES

The second sample, though drawn independently, was in effect a sub-sample of the first; that is to say, all children on probation or supervision orders were automatically included in the Children's Department files. The sub-sample was, however, unrepresentative of the parent sample in two ways: first; it contained only children brought before the Croydon courts and dealt with by the Croydon Probation Service. Secondly, it excluded all children dealt with by any form of disposal other than probation or supervision orders.

The procedure we adopted was to work through the Croydon court diaries, in which all disposals were recorded, and to extract any cases which had been placed on probation or supervision orders. We then located corresponding files of the Probation Service and extracted the data as for the main delinquency sample.

A total of 526 children had been referred to Croydon Probation Service in the survey period, of whom 364 were on probation and 162 on supervision orders.[1] In each instance, the home address was recorded, while for the 453 children who had been attending school, the school name was invariably given.

To avoid confusion, the main sample will be referred to henceforth simply as the *delinquency sample* and the sub-sample of Probation Service cases as the *probation sample*. The former provides the main basis of comparison with the child guidance sample; in relation to the schools analysis in CHAPTER VIII, however, only the probation sample could be utilized.

FEATURES OF THE DELINQUENCY SAMPLE

1. AGE AND SEX DISTRIBUTION

Most of the delinquent children had been in the upper age-range at the time of their first court appearance during the survey period (hereafter called the *index* appearance). One-third had been over the age of 16 years, and no less than two-thirds over 14 years. TABLE 6.1 summarizes the data.

In theory, all young persons appearing before the juvenile courts are under 17 years of age; however, the time-lag between offence and court appearance means that a small number may be over the age-limit. Of the present delinquency sample, nine were 17 years old at the time of appearance.

Both age and sex distribution of the sample differed markedly from that of

---

[1] The number of children in the 1-in-2 delinquency sample who had been put on probation during the survey period was 184. Doubling this figure gives an estimated total of 368, which corresponds closely to the Probation Service records.

TABLE 6.1
DELINQUENCY SAMPLE: AGE AT FIRST OFFENCE IN THE SURVEY PERIOD

AGE AT FIRST OFFENCE	BOYS	GIRLS	BOTH SEXES
	%	%	%
Under 11	6·9	11·5	7·7
11–13	22·3	23·5	22·5
14–16	31·2	46·9	33·8
Over 16	39·2	17·5	35·5
Not known	0·4	0·6	0·5
Total	100·0	100·0	100·0
No. of children	912	182	1,094

the child guidance sample: a point illustrated by FIGURE 5. As a generalization, one can say that the child guidance sample had a broad age–sex distribution, whereas the delinquency sample consisted mainly of male teenagers.

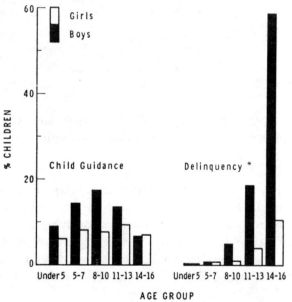

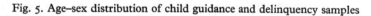

Fig. 5. Age–sex distribution of child guidance and delinquency samples

2. NUMBER OF OFFENCES

Few of the children had been known as persistent offenders before the survey period. Of the 1,094 offenders, 86·4 per cent had committed no known previous offence; 9·0 per cent had committed one, and 4·6 per cent more than one. The findings are set out in TABLE 6.2.

The proportion of children who appeared in court repeatedly during the

TABLE 6.2

DELINQUENCY SAMPLE: NUMBER OF KNOWN OFFENCES
BEFORE SURVEY PERIOD

NO. OF OFFENCES	BOYS	GIRLS	BOTH SEXES
	%	%	%
0	85·1	92·9	86·4
1	9·8	5·5	9·0
2	2·9	1·1	2·5
3–6	2·2	0·5	2·1
Total	100·0	100·0	100·0
No. of children	912	182	1,094

TABLE 6.3

DELINQUENCY SAMPLE: NUMBER OF KNOWN OFFENCES
DURING SURVEY PERIOD

NO. OF OFFENCES	BOYS	GIRLS	BOTH SEXES
	%	%	%
1	72·6	81·9	74·1
2	16·8	13·8	16·3
3	6·5	2·7	5·8
4–8	4·1	1·6	3·8
Total	100·0	100·0	100·0
No. of children	912	182	1,094

survey period was also small. TABLE 6.3 shows that only one-quarter committed two or more known offences, and only one-tenth three or more.

3. TYPES OF OFFENCE

Among the boys, offences against property predominated, comprising nearly half the total. Driving offences formed the next most frequent group: including 'taking and driving away', offences involving motor vehicles accounted for nearly two-fifths of the male cases. Property offences were also the commonest type among the girls; but here the second-largest group comprised 'care and protection' cases, while offences involving motor vehicles were very infrequent.

The distribution set out in TABLE 6.4 conforms to the typical pattern of juvenile delinquency in our society (West, 1967). The distribution for first offences in the survey period is closely similar to that for all offences (see APPENDIX C, TABLE 6a).

Court action and disposal for these offences is summarized in TABLE 6.5. Apart from conditional discharge, the rank order of penalties for boys was fine, probation order, and supervision order; for girls, supervision order, fine, and probation order.

The penalties for subsequent offences showed that, as might be expected,

TABLE 6.4

DELINQUENCY SAMPLE: NATURE OF FIRST OFFENCE IN SURVEY PERIOD

NATURE OF OFFENCE	BOYS	GIRLS	BOTH SEXES
	%	%	%
Offence against property	46·8	40·6	45·8
Taking and driving away	10·4	1·1	8·9
Driving offence	28·7	1·1	24·1
Offence against person—sexual	0·7	1·1	0·7
Offence against person—other than sexual	3·9	0·6	3·4
Education Act offences—(school attendance)	4·3	16·5	6·3
Care and protection cases	3·4	34·1	8·5
Breach of probation or supervision order	1·1	3·3	1·5
Other	0·7	1·6	0·8
Total	100·0	100·0	100·0
No. of children	912	182	1,094

the tendency to resort to custodial measures increased with the number of court appearances. Thus, the proportion of offenders sent to a detention centre, approved school or Borstal was 3·2 per cent for first offences in the

TABLE 6.5

DELINQUENCY SAMPLE: COURT ACTION AT FIRST OFFENCE IN SURVEY PERIOD

COURT ACTION	BOYS	GIRLS	BOTH SEXES
	%	%	%
Conditional discharge	20·7	13·8	19·6
Fine	50·8	20·3	45·7
Probation Order	13·4	17·0	14·0
Supervision or Fit Person Order	6·4	45·6	12·8
Attendance Centre	4·8	—	4·0
Detention Centre or Approved School	3·3	2·7	3·2
Other	0·6	0·6	0·7
Total	100·0	100·0	100·0
No. of children	912	182	1,094

survey period, 13·1 per cent for second offences, and 31·4 per cent for third or subsequent offences. (See APPENDIX C, TABLE 6b.)

RELATIONSHIP BETWEEN THE CHILD GUIDANCE AND DELINQUENCY SAMPLES

On checking the names of individual children, we found that only thirty-seven appeared both in the child guidance and in the delinquency samples. Since the latter comprised a random half of Croydon children appearing before the courts during the survey period, it is safe to assume that the true total of children appearing in both groups would have been about seventy-four. Each sample consisted of over 1,000 children, so that the amount of overlap seems relatively small.[1]

As the age–sex distribution of the two samples differed so widely, it is hardly surprising that no clear association was revealed in terms of individual membership. A prospective study of a child guidance sample over a five-year period or longer could be expected to show an increased risk of court appearance, at least among the boys (Douglas *et al.*, 1966; Robins, 1966).

The point can be examined more closely by comparing the offences of the delinquent children with the forms of deviant behaviour reported for the child guidance sample. Among the latter, 329 had been categorized, on the strength of the clinical records, as cases of 'conduct disorder' and a further forty-eight as 'mixed neurosis and conduct disorder'. Obviously, much of the recorded behaviour of these children could not be equated with delinquency: among the younger ones especially, restlessness, aggressiveness, temper outbursts, and disobedience were the most frequent items. Even so, 145 of these children were noted to have committed actions directly comparable with the offences of the delinquent children. Similar delinquent-type behaviour had been reported for thirty-seven other children, of whom six were mentally handicapped, twenty-nine placed in the 'other' category of diagnosis, and two given no diagnosis. The distribution of types of misconduct among these children appeared to be broadly similar to that among the delinquents, with the notable exception of offences involving motor vehicles. TABLE 6.6 provides a direct comparison of the 'delinquent' behaviour of the child guidance

TABLE 6.6

TYPES OF OFFENCE AMONG CHILD GUIDANCE SAMPLE AND DELINQUENCY SAMPLE

TYPE OF OFFENCE	CHILD GUIDANCE SAMPLE*	DELINQUENCY SAMPLE (first offences)
	%	%
Offence against property	70·2	45·8
Taking and driving away	—	8·9
Driving offence	—	24·1
Offence against person—sexual	3·4	0·7
Offence against person—other than sexual	2·4	3·4
Education Act offences—(school attendance)	16·8	6·3
Care and protection cases	7·2	8·5
Breach of probation or supervision order	—	1·5
Other	—	0·8
Total	100·0	100·0
No. of offences	208	1,094

* Based on 182 children with reported delinquent-type behaviour.

[1] Of 440 children in the child guidance sample aged 10–17 years, thirty-three appeared before the courts in the survey period. This compares with an expected number of 28·3 based on the average population in this age-group during the same period. The calculation is, however, at best approximate because the age-distribution for child guidance and delinquency did not coincide, even within this age-range.

sample with that of the officially delinquent sample based on court appearance.

Among the child guidance sub-sample, stealing was by far the commonest type of offence: ninety-eight boys and thirty-six girls had shown this kind of behaviour, although only a handful of them were known to have been before the courts prior to child guidance referral. In addition, seven children were reported to have started fires, and one to have broken windows. Sexual offences included interference by teenage boys with a sister or younger girls, and one case of overt homosexual acts by a boy of 14. Other offences against the person included serious violence to a younger brother, threats with a knife, and several more or less serious physical assaults. Seven girls and one boy were said to have been in moral danger such as would have justified placing them on supervision orders; two of the girls had been referred to the Child Guidance Clinic when the question of termination of pregnancy was under consideration.

The most conspicuous difference between the two samples, in terms of their delinquency 'profiles', was the absence of motor vehicle offences among the child guidance group: presumably because such offences are nearly always committed by older children. In the delinquency sample, 71·5 per cent of the driving offences and taking of vehicles was done by young persons of 16 or 17 years. If such offences were to be discarded from the sample, the distribution of the remainder would be quite closely in line with the offences of the child guidance group, the proportion of offences against property becoming 68·7 and 70·2 per cent for the two groups respectively.

These findings suggest that delinquency has its analogues in the child guidance population. Among teenage children—especially boys—it seems that the same types of deviant behaviour may lead either to child guidance referral or to court appearance, according to circumstances. Many of the younger child guidance children had manifested conduct of a type which, if persisted in, would seem destined to bring them before the courts a little later in life.

In studying the ecology of child guidance referral, we have to remember the possibility that any resemblance to that of delinquency may be due to a distinct sub-group of children whose diagnosis may vary, but whose abnormality of behaviour is essentially delinquent in nature. Such a sub-group would appear to consist largely of children diagnosed as cases of 'conduct disorder', though it might well overlap with other diagnostic categories. The contribution of this sub-group to the ecological picture will be examined in CHAPTERS VII and VIII.

SUMMARY

Two samples of delinquent children were drawn: a primary sample from the records of Croydon Children's Department, and a subsidiary sample from the Probation Service records. The second of these was required for the schools analysis reported in CHAPTER VIII.

The main delinquency sample, which represented one-half of Croydon children coming before the courts in the survey period, showed a heavy predominance of youths aged 14–17 years. The principal category of offence was against property, notably stealing; offences involving motor vehicles were also common among the boys. Most of the young people had had no police record before the survey period, and the great majority committed only one known offence during the five years of the survey. Court action and disposal usually consisted in fines, probation, and supervision orders, though recurrent court appearances were more often dealt with by custodial action. In all these respects, the delinquency sample appeared to be thoroughly typical of its kind.

Comparison of the types of offence committed by the delinquent children with the conduct disorders of the child guidance sample showed some striking similarities, offences against property comprising much the largest class of offence for both groups. The major disparities—notably in the proportion of motor vehicle offences—could be explained in terms of differing age and sex distributions.

These findings underline the need, when studying the correlates of child guidance referral, to examine separately those children presenting with anti-social behaviour.

CHAPTER VII

THE INFLUENCE OF THE NEIGHBOURHOOD

IN order to assess the influence of the home neighbourhood, we had to compare rates of child guidance referral and delinquency for localized areas of the borough. At first, we decided to take the electoral ward as the basic unit of analysis. Though surprisingly little used in ecological research, the electoral ward has definite advantages. Individual streets and houses are easily allocated to wards, so that the coding of home addresses for statistical purposes becomes feasible even for large samples. Moreover, demographic and socio-economic indices for each ward can be derived from the official census returns. The electoral ward is, however, a relatively large unit and may be so uneven in its characteristics that smaller divisions are required. This point will be taken up later.

WARD RATES FOR CHILD GUIDANCE

On the basis of the child's home address, we allocated child guidance referrals for the quinquennium 1962–6 among the twenty wards of Croydon, with the exception of forty-two cases from outside the borough and fourteen from unknown addresses. A mean annual rate was then computed for each ward, the denominator being the number of children under 16 years resident at the time of the 1966 Census. This age-range corresponded most closely to the child guidance sample, 15 per cent of whose members were under school age. The at-risk population was estimated by modifying the 10 per cent Census numbers published for the age-groups 0–4, 5–14, and 15–19 years. In calculating ward referral rates, we had to adjust for the 1965 changes in the Borough boundaries mentioned in CHAPTER III (see APPENDIX B 1.1).

The mean annual rates thus computed varied from 15 to 45 per 10,000 children at risk (see APPENDIX C, TABLE 7a). The pattern of distribution within the Borough is shown in FIGURE 6.

The highest rates were found in the densely-populated inner wards (Central, Broad Green, Whitehorse Manor), together with the outlying housing estate of New Addington, where many families from the decaying parts of the borough had been rehoused. Those with the lowest rates were mostly the residential suburbs to the south (Purley, Sanderstead North, Coulsdon East, Woodcote, and Coulsdon West). Since the referral rates for boys and girls co-varied quite closely (see APPENDIX C, TABLE 7a), the referral pattern

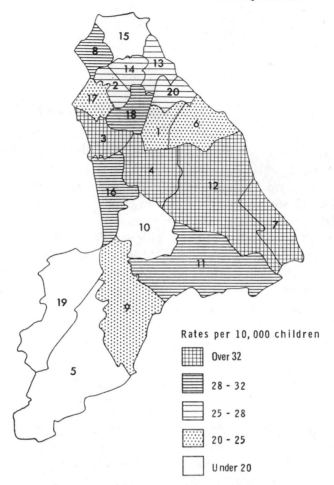

Rates per 10,000 children

▦	Over 32
▤	28 - 32
☰	25 - 28
⠿	20 - 25
☐	Under 20

Fig. 6. Distribution of child guidance referral rates by electoral ward

as a whole was not to be explained simply by a selective referral of boys to the Child Guidance Clinic.

The observed distribution raises a question as to whether geographical or social factors were the more important determinants of referral. Broadly speaking, the parts of Croydon surrounding the Child Guidance Clinic were the older, more densely populated wards; those further away the middle-class suburbs. Distance from a medical facility being one of the major factors influencing its utilization, we had to try to assess the effect of distance from the clinic. This problem was resolved with the aid of a cluster analysis of enumeration districts, undertaken to strengthen the ecological findings (see p. 68).

WARD RATES FOR DELINQUENCY

The next step was to compare ward rates for child guidance referral with those for delinquency. When we allocated the 1,094 children in the delinquency sample to electoral wards on the basis of their home addresses, the numbers ranged from 7 in Sanderstead and Selsdon and in Coulsdon East to 194 in New Addington. Annual delinquency rates for children under 16 years were computed for each electoral ward, as for the child guidance sample. Here again we found a wide range of variation, from 7 to 102 for

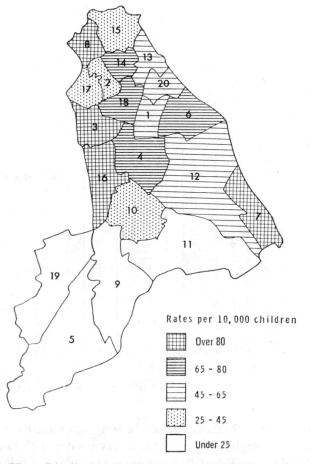

Rates per 10,000 children

Over 80

65 - 80

45 - 65

25 - 45

Under 25

Fig. 7. Distribution of delinquency rates by electoral ward

offenders and from 8 to 154 for offences, per 10,000 children at risk (see APPENDIX C, TABLE 7b). The distribution is shown in FIGURE 7.

The pattern is similar to that for child guidance referral, with high rates in the old, central wards and low rates in the suburban zone. The similarity becomes more apparent when child guidance and delinquency rates are juxtaposed as in FIGURE 8. Here, the wards have been grouped in rank order of child guidance rate. The ranking by delinquency rates can be seen to follow that by child guidance rates, wards with high rates for the one having high rates for the other and vice-versa. The rank order of child guidance rates was indeed positively correlated with that of delinquency rates, whether based on numbers of offenders (tau = +0·52**), or on numbers of offences (tau = +0·56***).[1]

To find characteristics of the wards that might help to explain this pattern, we compared both child guidance and delinquency rates with a number of ward socio-demographic indices derived from the 1966 Census data for Croydon. The results, set out in TABLE 7.1, showed that the association of

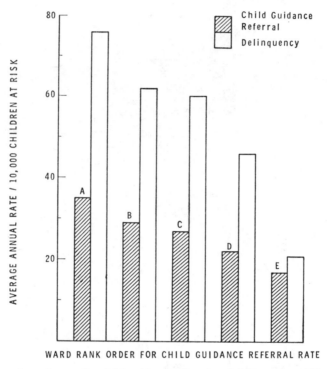

Fig. 8. Electoral ward rates for child guidance referral and delinquency. (Wards in groups of four from highest rates (A) to lowest rates (E).)

child guidance rate with these indices broadly resembled that shown by delinquency rate, though it appeared to be less strong. Both rates were significantly related to social class distribution and to type of housing. The most closely related index was the proportion of persons living in owner-occupied houses.

The rank correlations shown in TABLE 7.1 suggested that child guidance and delinquency rates would reveal similar trends when plotted against the main

[1] All correlations cited in this monograph, other than those given in CHAPTER IX and in APPENDIX B 3.3, were calculated by three methods: that of Pearson for product-moment correlations, and those of Spearman and Kendall for rank correlations. Except where otherwise indicated, the values given in the text and tables are for Kendall's tau. In nearly all instances, the three techniques gave the same levels of significance. The patterns are exemplified by TABLES 7 f, g, and h in APPENDIX C.

Wherever correlation coefficients are cited, in tables or in the text, we have used the convention that * denotes a probability of less than 0·05, ** of less than 0·01, and *** of less than 0·001.

TABLE 7.1
CHILD GUIDANCE AND DELINQUENCY RATES: CORRELATION WITH WARD SOCIO-DEMOGRAPHIC INDICES
(No. of Wards = 20)

SOCIO-DEMOGRAPHIC INDICES	CORRELATION WITH CHILD GUIDANCE RATES†	CORRELATION WITH DELINQUENCY RATES†	
		Offenders	Offences
Proportion in Social Classes I and II	−0·33*	−0·54***	−0·52**
Proportion in Social Classes IV and V	+0·33*	+0·53**	+0·50**
Percent persons in owner-occupied houses	−0·48**	−0·54***	−0·53**
Proportion renting from Local Authority	+0·34*	+0·37*	+0·40*
Proportion sharing households	+0·03	+0·10	+0·07
Density of population[1]	+0·21	+0·21	+0·17
Proportion of foreign born	+0·01	+0·12	+0·09
Rate of migration[2]	−0·09	−0·25	−0·24

† Kendall's τ. For significance levels, see footnote, p. 66. For Pearson's r and Spearman's ρ, see APPENDIX C, TABLE 7f.

[1] Percentage of persons in private households living more than one to a room.

[2] Number of persons entering or leaving during survey period, as a proportion of at-risk population.

social indices. This proved to be the case, a point illustrated by FIGURE 9 in which the electoral wards have been grouped in rank order by the proportion of persons living in owner-occupied houses.

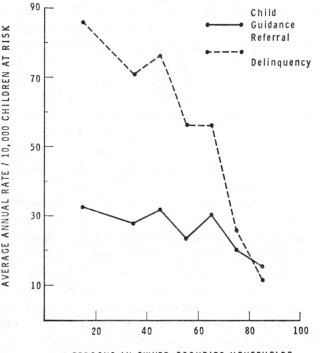

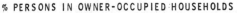

Fig. 9. Ward rates for child guidance referral and delinquency by percentage of persons in owner-occupied households. (Electoral wards grouped by percentage of persons in owner occupied households: 10–20, 30–40, 40–50, 50–60, 60–70, 70–80, 80–90.)

THE ENUMERATION DISTRICT: A CLUSTER ANALYSIS

The true picture may have been partially obscured by the use of electoral wards as units of analysis. The disadvantages of the ward for this purpose have been recognized by other research workers. Hare (1956), for example, wrote of his survey of mental illness and social conditions in Bristol:

In any investigation which attempts to relate the distribution of a disorder to social factors, the choice of geographical unit is of primary importance. In the present study, however, the choice was limited by the necessity of having readily accessible social and demographic data for the units, and in practice this left the city wards as the only possible units. Nevertheless, because of variation in size of the wards and in some instances a marked lack of social homogeneity, their use for this purpose is somewhat unsatisfactory.

Almost anywhere in Greater London, wide differences of social milieu may be observed within the space of a short walk. Of Croydon, in particular, it has been remarked that '. . . there are very few wards which can be said to constitute natural areas in a cultural sense' (Morris, 1957). There were thus good grounds for trying to sharpen the focus of inquiry by utilizing smaller, more homogeneous population units.

The only small unit for which demographic and social data were available was the enumeration district, which typically contains about 400 households. Croydon was divided into some 450 such districts, with an average of twenty-two to an electoral ward. The Census Office was able to supply the required data by means of a special extraction from the 1966 Census tables. Information relating to population size, age and sex composition, social class distribution, housing conditions, and household amenities was obtained in this way.

A preliminary analysis of two electoral wards showed that the numbers of children referred from single enumeration districts were too small to yield reliable rates. We decided, therefore, to combine the districts into groups based, not on spatial proximity but on socio-demographic profiles. Each such group would represent a constellation of social characteristics rather than a geographical area; that is to say, it would be homogeneous in terms of social features, even though its constituent parts might be widely dispersed throughout the borough.

The preliminary analysis also demonstrated that the rank order of enumeration districts within the wards, like that of the wards themselves, differed from one socio-demographic index to another. No one index was consistently of greatest significance for child guidance or delinquency rates. We decided, therefore, to group the districts, not on the basis of any single index, but rather by means of a cluster analysis in which all the socio-demographic indices shown in TABLE 7.1 should be represented. The chief advantage of this strategy was that it could provide a relatively small number of population units, each big enough to give reliable rates, but at the same time much more homogeneous in composition than the average electoral ward. For the kind of multivariate analysis we had in mind, such a population unit appeared eminently suitable.

The statistical technique we employed for this purpose is outlined in APPENDIX B2. The best solution, both in mathematical and in practical terms, proved to be one yielding twenty-two clusters: demographic and social inter-correlations were therefore based on this grouping. An alternative solution,

Fig. 10. Distribution of enumeration districts constituting one cluster (7 cluster grouping)

which gave seven large clusters, was employed for the multiple regression analysis described later (see CHAPTER VIII), because this procedure required each cluster to be further sub-divided.

FIGURE 10 illustrates the spatial distribution of one of the seven large clusters; the dispersion shown was fairly typical and also similar in extent to those of many of the twenty-two smaller clusters.

Mean annual child guidance and delinquency rates now had to be computed for each cluster of enumeration districts. First, we derived the at-risk population of children for each cluster,[1] using data from the 1966 Census extraction. Here again, the lowest age-group was included because many children under five had been referred to child guidance. Next, we allocated to enumeration districts all children in the child guidance and delinquency samples with known addresses in the borough. Total offences, as distinct from offenders, were also allocated to the twenty-two district-clusters.

The child guidance rates for the twenty-two clusters ranged from 12 to 37 per 10,000 children at risk, a variation similar to that found earlier among the electoral wards. The corresponding range of delinquency rates was from 13 to 120 for offenders, and from 17 to 193 for offences (see APPENDIX C, TABLES 7C and 7d). The association between the rank order of child guidance rates and that of delinquency (offences) was positive (tau = +0·46**) and only slightly lower than that revealed by the electoral ward analysis, suggesting that both were related more closely to socio-demographic than to spatial factors.

TABLE 7.2 sets out the rank correlations between child guidance rate and social indices, both for the twenty electoral wards and for the twenty-two clusters of enumeration districts; it can be seen that the latter demonstrated the association more convincingly.

TABLE 7.2

CORRELATION OF CHILD GUIDANCE RATES WITH SOCIO-DEMOGRAPHIC INDICES FOR (a) TWENTY ELECTORAL WARDS AND (b) TWENTY-TWO CLUSTERS OF ENUMERATION DISTRICTS

SOCIO-DEMOGRAPHIC INDICES	CORRELATION WITH CHILD GUIDANCE RATES†	
	20 Electoral Wards	22 Clusters of E.D.s
Proportion in Social Classes I and II	−0·33*	−0·43**
Proportion in Social Classes IV and V	+0·33*	+0·50**
Proportion of owner-occupiers	−0·48**	−0·36**
Proportion renting from Local Authority	+0·34*	+0·32
Proportion sharing households	+0·03	+0·07
Density of population[2]	+0·21	+0·44**
Proportion of foreign born	+0·01	−0·04
Rate of migration[2]	−0·09	−0·03

† Kendall's τ. For significance levels see footnote, p. 66. For Pearson's r and Spearman's ρ, see APPENDIX C, TABLE 7g.
[2] As for TABLE 7.1.

Correlations with social-class distribution and with density of population were higher for enumeration-district clusters than for electoral wards. Overall, the effect of the cluster-analysis was to increase the number of significant associations; it thus provided stronger evidence of a linkage between child guidance rate and socio-demographic indices than had the earlier analysis based on electoral wards. The fact that approximately the same number of population units went into each cluster as into an electoral ward diminishes the possibility of a mathematical artefact.

[1] The rate was based on the population aged 0–19 years given in the Census tables, the numbers involved being too small for any adjustment to be made.

The findings indicated that social-class composition and density of population were the environmental variables most closely linked to the child guidance
rate. Next in importance came the type of housing, as reflected by the proportions of persons living in owner-occupied and in local-authority houses,
respectively. Neither mobility of population nor proportion of foreign-born
residents appeared to be relevant.

We next made a similar analysis of delinquency rates for the twenty-two
clusters. TABLE 7.3 shows the relationship between total delinquency rate
(persons) and the main socio-demographic indices. Corresponding figures for
the twenty-two district clusters and the twenty electoral wards are again given
for comparison.

TABLE 7.3

CORRELATION OF DELINQUENCY RATES WITH SOCIO-DEMO-
GRAPHIC INDICES FOR (a) TWENTY ELECTORAL WARDS AND
(b) TWENTY-TWO CLUSTERS OF ENUMERATION DISTRICTS

SOCIO-DEMOGRAPHIC INDICES	CORRELATION WITH DELINQUENCY RATE†	
	20 Electoral Wards	22 Clusters of E.D.s
Proportion in Social Classes I and II	−0·54***	−0·61***
Proportion in Social Classes IV and V	+0·53**	+0·44**
Proportion of owner-occupiers	−0·54***	−0·56***
Proportion renting from Local Authority	+0·37*	+0·42**
Proportion sharing households	+0·10	−0·10
Density of population[1]	+0·21	+0·55***
Proportion of foreign born	+0·12	−0·12
Rate of migration[1]	−0·25	−0·13

† Kendall's τ. For significance levels see footnote, p. 66. For Pearson's r and Spearman's ρ
see APPENDIX C, TABLE 7h.
[1] As for TABLE 7.1.

Comparison of TABLES 7.2 and 7.3 shows that strengthening of the apparent
association with socio-demographic indices, as a result of using district clusters
instead of wards, was similar for child guidance rates and for delinquency
rates.

The results of the cluster analysis thus broadly confirmed those of the
previous ward analysis; namely, that child guidance rates were related to the
social characteristics of the child's neighbourhood, and that the ecological
pattern of referral was markedly similar to that of delinquency.

The relationships of both child guidance and delinquency rates to socio-
demographic indices of the clusters were also examined by means of a multiple
regression analysis, the results of which are set out in APPENDIX B3.

The next step was to correct the ecological findings for the effect of certain
possibly related variables; namely, distance from the Child Guidance Clinic,
the social class of the child's family, and the diagnostic category or nature of
the child's disturbance.

1. Effect of Distance from the Clinic

The analysis by enumeration district permitted the effect of distance from the clinic to be examined. To measure this distance for the home address of each individual child would have been impracticable. Individual enumeration districts, however, are quite small and their approximate distance from a central point can be measured. The technique we used was to draw two concentric circles, with radii representing one and two miles respectively, centred on the Child Guidance Clinic. In this way, the borough was divided into three concentric zones (see FIGURE 10) and each enumeration district could then be classified as less than one mile, between one and two miles, or more than two miles, distant from the clinic. Mean child guidance rates were then computed for the enumeration districts grouped within each zone. The results were as follows (expressed as mean annual rates per 10,000 children):

Inner zone (within one mile of clinic)   28·1
Intermediate zone (from one to two miles)   20·4
Outer zone (over two miles from clinic)   20·0

These findings suggested that there was a distance effect, but that it was restricted to the inner zone immediately surrounding the clinic. The possibility remained that this effect might be dependent on socio-demographic factors, since the areas of poorer housing and higher population-density were known to be mostly central, whereas the better residential areas were mostly on the periphery of the borough.

This question was examined by looking at the spatial distribution of each of the seven large clusters. Any decrease in referral rate with increasing distance from the clinic, occurring *within a cluster*, could be ascribed to geographical, as against socio-demographic, influences, since the effect of the latter would be held constant. The findings are summarized in TABLE 7.4, in which the seven clusters have been placed in socio-demographic rank order (see APPENDIX B2.3).

TABLE 7.4
RATES OF CHILD GUIDANCE REFERRAL BY ENUMERATION CLUSTER AND BY DISTANCE FROM THE CHILD GUIDANCE CLINIC

E.D. CLUSTER (in socio-demographic rank order)	CHILD GUIDANCE MEAN REFERRAL RATES		
	Within 1 mile of clinic	1–2 miles from clinic	Over 2 miles from clinic
Cluster 2	39·0	13·9	13·6
,, 6	29·3	22·1	18·6
,, 3	32·4	26·5	23·4
,, 5	24·4	28·4	19·3
,, 7	21·6	13·7	23·0
,, 1	21·7	61·5[1]	25·6
,, 4	20·0[1]	21·2[1]	33·7

[1] Based on fewer than five enumeration districts.

TABLE 7.4 shows that only in the three highest-ranking clusters (Nos. 2, 6, and 3) was there a clear gradient in child guidance rates with increasing distance from the clinic. For three of the remaining clusters, the intermediate-zone rates were actually higher than those for the inner zone.

Why a definite trend should have been found only in the highest-ranking clusters is unclear. The reverse might have been expected, since poorer families are more likely to be dependent on public transport, and hence to be more easily deterred by distance from using a facility. Possibly children from middle-class homes in the outer suburbs were more often taken for private treatment, and so lost to the survey. If so, the discrepancy between the social-class and spatial distributions of the child guidance sample becomes more difficult to explain.

2. EFFECT OF SOCIAL CLASS

An incongruity has already been noted between the social-class distribution of the child guidance sample and its ecological characteristics. On the one hand, TABLE 5.6 shows only a small, non-significant difference between the social-class composition of the sample and that of the Croydon population as a whole. On the other hand, both electoral-ward and enumeration-district analyses pointed to a link between child guidance rates and the socio-demographic characteristics of the neighbourhood. To account for this seeming anomaly, we examined the social-class distribution of each of the seven large clusters of enumeration districts. The result, illustrated by FIGURE 11, showed that within each cluster the child guidance attenders were representative, in this respect, of the background population from which they had been drawn.

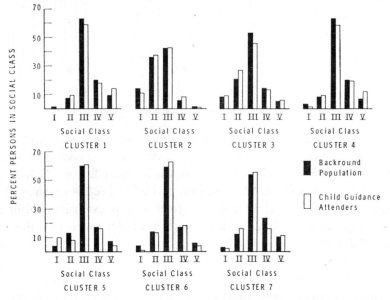

Fig. 11. Comparison of social class distribution of child guidance attenders and background population, by cluster of enumeration districts

The data outlined in FIGURE 11 provided no support for the hypothesis that incongruity between family social status and district of residence is a characteristic of child guidance attenders. In terms of social class, the children in our sample appeared to be closely representative of the neighbourhoods in which they lived. The tendency for enumeration-district clusters with high proportions of Social Class I and II inhabitants to produce fewer cases than expected, and for those with high proportions of Social Class IV and V inhabitants to produce more than expected, could not be explained as a direct effect of social-class distribution, nor as the result of an interaction between social class and district of residence. The findings suggested that social class was not the crucial variable for child guidance referral, although its distribution within the borough was probably linked with that of the crucial variable, or variables. Such a conclusion must, however, be regarded as tentative because of the large number of children in the sample who could not be allocated to a social-class group.

An alternative approach to the data on which FIGURE 11 is based is to

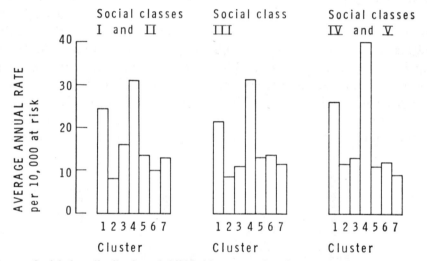

Fig. 12. Social class distribution of child guidance attenders, by enumeration district clusters

examine the child guidance rates for enumeration-district clusters within each broad social-class category. By so doing, one can get some idea as to whether neighbourhood effects continue to operate when family factors are held constant. The results of such an analysis, summarized in FIGURE 12, showed that inter-cluster variation in child guidance rates was as extensive within each social-class group as within the sample as a whole; moreover, the rank-ordering of the clusters by child guidance rate was broadly similar for each social-class group. We may conclude, therefore, that district of residence exercised an influence independent of the social class of the child's family.

One cannot generalize from this finding to argue that the child's neighbourhood exercises an influence independent of family factors in general. The child may be subjected to influences arising out of the home environment, which are either unrelated to socio-economic status or at any rate not reflected in the necessarily crude measures of socio-economic status employed here. To examine the question further, we should need information about the children's family background that was not available in our survey. Meanwhile, the ecological correlations remain to be explained.

3. DIAGNOSIS AND SOCIAL INDICES

A possible explanation of the similarity of ecological patterns for child guidance and delinquency might be simply that many children with delinquent or socially-disturbing behaviour were referred to child guidance. Any obvious tautology of this kind had been avoided by excluding from the sample all remand home cases. The findings in CHAPTERS V and VI demonstrated, none the less, that the conduct disorders of young children were often analogous to the delinquent behaviour of older children. Hence, it could be argued that conduct disorders alone had been responsible for the ecological picture.

We tested this possibility by examining the rates for each major diagnostic category separately. The two principal categories of neurosis and conduct disorder (together comprising 70 per cent of the sample) were defined within each of the twenty-two enumeration-district clusters, and their rates correlated with the various social indices. The results, set out in TABLE 7.5, showed

TABLE 7.5

CORRELATION OF RATES FOR NEUROSIS AND CONDUCT DISORDER WITH SOCIO-DEMOGRAPHIC INDICES OF THE TWENTY-TWO CLUSTERS OF ENUMERATION DISTRICTS

SOCIO-DEMOGRAPHIC INDICES	CORRELATION† WITH	
	Rates for Neurosis	Rates for Conduct Disorder
Proportion in Social Classes I and II	−0·22	−0·44*
Proportion in Social Classes IV and V	+0·33*	+0·37**
Proportion of owner-occupiers	−0·29	−0·23
Proportion renting from Local Authority	+0·33*	+0·18
Proportion sharing households	+0·04	+0·04
Density of population[1]	+0·29	+0·24
Proportion of foreign born	−0·05	+0·00
Rate of migration[1]	+0·03	+0·07

† Kendall's τ. For significance levels, see footnote p. 66.
[1] As in Table 7·1.

that the rates both for neurosis and for conduct disorder varied with the main socio-demographic indices much as did the overall child guidance rate. The neurosis rate was more closely correlated with type of housing; that for conduct disorder with social class. No single diagnostic category appeared to account for the observed ecological distribution. In short, there was no firm evidence that neuroses were associated with more favourable, or conduct disorders with less favourable, social conditions.

COMPARISON WITH ADULT REFERRAL RATES

Some time after the child guidance survey had been completed, we were able to undertake a complementary study of adult psychiatric referral in Croydon. For technical reasons, the same survey period could not be covered; instead, all contacts with Croydon psychiatric services during the two-year period 1967–8 were analysed. As with the child guidance and delinquency surveys, the findings were compared against social data from the 1966 Census. The results showed a distribution similar to that for child guidance referral, with high rates in the old, central wards and the main housing estate; low rates in the residential suburbs. The cluster analysis of enumeration districts also yielded similar patterns for adult and for child services, with a positive correlation of rates for the twenty-two clusters (tau = +0·53***).

The adult referral data were derived from a wide range of in-patient, day-patient, out-patient, and domiciliary services, scattered throughout the borough: in this context, the question of distance from a single, centrally-placed clinic did not arise. The observed co-variance of adult and child referral rates thus lent support to the hypothesis that the latter had been partly determined by neighbourhood factors, and reflected a general trend towards high utilization of psychiatric services in areas of low socio-economic status and high population-density. How far this pattern corresponds to differential prevalence or inception rates remains to be explored.

SUMMARY

The series of studies presented in this chapter were designed to test the first set of hypotheses outlined in CHAPTER IV (p. 52), which dealt with expected variation in child guidance and delinquency rates as between different neighbourhoods.

A wide range of variation was found among the twenty electoral wards of Croydon, both in child guidance rates (from 15 to 45 per 10,000 children at risk) and in delinquency rates (from 7 to 102 offenders, and from 8 to 154 offences, per 10,000 at risk). The child guidance rates, which co-varied for the two sexes, were low in the residential suburbs and high in the central wards, which were on the whole the poorest and most dilapidated. Child guidance rates showed a strong positive association with those for delinquency.

Both child guidance and delinquency rates were related to a number of social indices of the wards; in particular, to social-class composition, type of housing, and density of population. The most sensitive index was the proportion of persons living in owner-occupied houses.

To sharpen the focus, we made use of enumeration districts, the smaller units of which electoral wards are composed. When these were amalgamated into twenty-two clusters, homogeneous for social and demographic characteristics, wide variation was found between the clusters both in child guidance rates (12–37) and in delinquency rates (13–120) per 10,000 children at risk. Rank correlation of the two sets of rates for the individual clusters showed a strong positive association. The associations of both sets of rates with such social indices as social-class composition, type of housing, and density of population were also confirmed.

The cluster analysis was further employed to examine the relationship between child guidance rate and three other variables; namely, distance of the child's home from the clinic, the social class of the child's family, and the child's own diagnostic grouping. On dividing Croydon into three concentric zones, centred on the Child Guidance Clinic, we found a higher rate of referral for the innermost than for the surrounding zones. The effect of distance appeared to be partly dependent on socio-economic factors, a clear trend being apparent in only three of the seven large enumeration-district clusters.

The social-class distribution of child guidance clients within each cluster of districts did not differ significantly from that for the surrounding population; children referred to child guidance appeared to reflect accurately the social-class structure of their neighbourhoods. A similar range of variation in child guidance rates among the clusters of districts was found within each broad social-class grouping.

When rates for neurosis and conduct disorder were examined separately, their correlations with socio-demographic indices proved to be similar: the ecological pattern could not be ascribed simply to a higher prevalence of delinquent or anti-social behaviour among children in some neighbourhoods.

Finally, the ecological correlates of adult psychiatric referral, as revealed by a survey of Croydon psychiatric services for the period 1967–8, proved broadly similar to those for child guidance referral and for delinquency, suggesting the possibility of common underlying factors.

CHAPTER VIII

THE INFLUENCE OF THE SCHOOL

THE next step in the investigation was to examine child guidance and delinquency rates for the individual schools of Croydon. For this purpose, we required information on the number and location of schools in the borough; the number of children attending each school year by year; the teaching conditions in each school and the educational standards of its pupils. Relevant data were available for all schools under the Local Education Authority but not for private establishments; hence the latter were omitted from the inquiry.

MATERIAL AND METHODS

During the survey period, 1962–6, Croydon had a total of 121 schools (excluding nursery schools), comprised as follows:

(a) fifty-eight primary schools, containing eighty-six separate departments (infants, junior boys, junior girls, and junior mixed schools);

(b) thirty-nine secondary schools, of which twelve were selective and twenty-seven non-selective;

(c) three special schools: one for the educationally subnormal (E.S.N.), one for the physically handicapped, and one for partially-sighted children;

(d) twenty-one private, independent, or direct grant schools.

We collected data for all except the last-named group. In addition to the numbers of children on each school-roll, the Chief Education Officer[1] was able to supply, in confidence, the following information:

1. Annual pupil–teacher ratios for each school;
2. Annual teacher-turnover for each school;
3. Number of immigrant children attending each school annually;
4. Examination and formal test results:
    (a) numbers of 'O' and 'A' level passes;
    (b) numbers obtaining Certificate of Secondary Education;
    (c) scores on Moray House Verbal Reasoning Test;
5. Number of children referred annually to the School Psychological Service from each school.

The Chief Education Officer also supplied a list of schools with exceptionally difficult problems, compiled at the request of the Department of Educa-

[1] Now Director of Education.

tion and Science at a time when the possibility of special grants for such schools was under consideration. Ten schools, all secondary non-selective, had been so designated.

The next stage of the inquiry was a survey of school health cards. This, strictly speaking, was a part of the general practitioner survey described in the next chapter rather than of the schools inquiry; it arose because of our need to estimate the number of children registered with each general practitioner in Croydon. Since, however, the health card survey entailed visits to many schools, and thus provided a supplement to the statistical information, it deserves a mention at this point.

The Croydon School Health Service maintained health cards for all children attending local authority schools in the borough: a total of about 45,000 at the time of the survey. Of this total, a one-in-four sample, corresponding to 11–12,000 cards, was the most that could be handled with our resources. The information to be collected was restricted to the child's name, age, sex, home address, and family doctor.

At the time we undertook this survey, the health cards were in process of being transferred to a central file. Those for forty-one school departments had already been moved to the School Health Department, while the remainder were still held in the individual schools. After a letter of introduction from the Chief Education Officer had been sent to the head teachers, we visited the eighty-four school departments in which health cards were still stored.[1] Each head teacher was interviewed personally by a member of the research team, to ensure that he understood the purpose of the inquiry and had an opportunity to raise questions. In every case, we received full co-operation from the teaching staff.

We took every fourth name on the school-roll, and located the corresponding cards either in the school files or in the central index. All 8,500 cards held in the schools were traced, and the family doctor identified in 96·9 per cent. Of the cards held in the School Health Department, 96·3 per cent were found, and the family doctor's name established in 92·5 per cent. From this viewpoint, the health card survey could be deemed highly successful.

The visits paid in the course of this work provided us with a valuable glimpse of each school in action. A wide range of variation was observed, both in material conditions and in the less tangible aspects of school life. At one end of the spectrum was a small handful of modern, open-plan buildings: spacious, well-lit, and surrounded by broad playing-fields. At the other was to be found the familiar Victorian legacy of the redbrick schoolhouse, with its high windows, drab paintwork, poky offices, outside lavatories, and bare playground. Such were the surroundings recalled by a Croydon pupil of an earlier generation as:

[1] Two non-selective secondary schools had closed before the School Health Card Survey was undertaken, and one special school was not visited in view of the small number of children attending.

... those solid, ungainly edifices which successive Education Acts spread over the country. There was an asphalt playground into which we charged at playtime, setting up a curious animal din, still to be heard whenever the inmates of State primary schools are briefly released for recreation. The classrooms were divided by wooden partitions, which could be opened to provide an assembly hall ...

With our morning devotions over, the partitions were closed, and we began our studies. Classes were fifty or sixty strong, but usually included some who withdrew themselves from the proceedings and remained in a condition of blessed and total illiteracy (Muggeridge, 1966).

By the time these words were written, the classes had become smaller and illiteracy less commonplace, but the surroundings were often little changed. Under such conditions, the high morale of many of the teachers was all the more striking.

A notable feature of the Croydon school at this time was the existence of a distinct sub-group of schools whose proportion of immigrant children had risen to over 50 per cent; in this difficult situation, staff responses appeared to range from the frankly authoritarian and pessimistic to the inspiringly dedicated.

Educational statistics for Greater London, some of which have been cited in CHAPTER III, lend support to the belief that this picture of widely varying standards, and of teachers struggling to give of their best often under adverse conditions, was fairly typical of many London Boroughs at the time: and, indeed, remains so to the present day. In this sense, one could fairly regard the Croydon findings as representative for large parts of the metropolis.

FINDINGS OF THE SCHOOL INQUIRY

Since the survey was primarily statistical, and because all the information was given in strict confidence, no further comments will be made about individual schools; nor will any school be identified by name.

The distribution of children by type of school, towards the end of the survey period,[1] was as follows:

Type of School	No. of Children in Jan. 1966
Primary	27,018
Secondary selective	6,345
Secondary non-selective	11,634
Special	414
All Local Authority schools	45,411

[1] The 1966 figures have been taken because a number of schools came under Croydon Local Education Authority for the first time with the re-arrangement of the boundaries in 1965. The rates for these individual schools were weighted accordingly (see APPENDIX B1.2)

The distribution of children among the individual schools provided a basis for computing both child guidance and delinquency rates for the schools and hence for the analysis of school rates by various indices. These relationships will be considered under four headings:

1. school child guidance rates;
2. school delinquency rates;
3. the relationship between these two rates and the school characteristics;
4. the relationship between school rates and the ecological pattern.

1. SCHOOL CHILD GUIDANCE RATES

The distribution of the child guidance sample of 1,061 children by type of school is shown in TABLE 8.1, which includes all schools, both Local Authority and private.

TABLE 8.1

REFERRALS TO CROYDON CHILD GUIDANCE CLINIC, 1962–6, BY SEX AND TYPE OF SCHOOL ATTENDED

TYPE OF SCHOOL ATTENDED	REFERRAL TO CHILD GUIDANCE CLINIC					
	Boys		Girls		Total	
	%		%		%	
Local Authority:	73·6		67·6		71·2	
Primary		47·7		38·7		44·2
Secondary selective		4·5		5·6		4·9
Secondary non-selective		17·6		22·1		19·3
Special		3·8		1·2		2·8
Private and independent	5·1		7·3		5·9	
School out of area	5·2		5·4		5·3	
Pre-school	13·8		14·6		14·2	
Post-school	0·3		2·2		1·0	
Not known	2·0		2·9		2·4	
Total	100·0		100·0		100·0	
No. of referrals	650		411		1,061	

In summary, 14 per cent of the children were under school age at the time of referral; 1 per cent had left school; 6 per cent were attending private schools, and 5 per cent schools outside the borough; in 2 per cent, the child's school could not be ascertained. In the following pages, school referral rates have been based on the remaining 71 per cent of children known to have been attending schools under the Local Education Authority.

We computed mean annual child guidance rates for each school by taking as denominator the size of school-roll at the mid-point of the survey period. The change in borough boundaries early in 1965 meant that some schools had begun to refer children to Croydon Child Guidance Clinic after that time; hence we had to estimate their rates from the numbers for only two years instead of five.

As anticipated, school child guidance rates per 10,000 children at risk showed a wide range of variation: for primary schools from 0 to 153, with a mean of 37; for secondary selective schools from 6 to 39, with a mean of 17; for secondary non-selective schools from 0 to 82, with a mean of 36 (see APPENDIX C, TABLE 8a).

Direct comparison between primary and secondary schools is invalid because of their different age-structures; more meaningful is a comparison of secondary selective and non-selective schools. FIGURE 13 shows that the former for the most part had much lower child guidance rates than the latter.

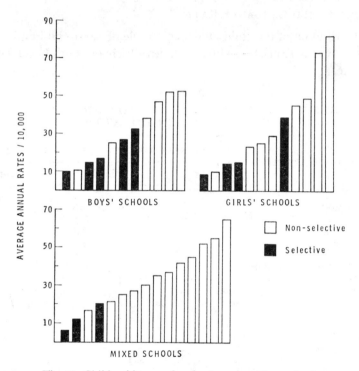

Fig. 13. Child guidance referral rates—secondary schools

A high child guidance rate could mean either that a school had many disturbed children, or that it had a high referral policy, or both. We were unable to assess the relative importance of these factors without information on the behaviour of all the children. Some indication was given, however, by the sources of referral: it was possible to examine whether children had been sent from the schools (by the teachers, the school medical officers, or the school psychologists) or had been referred independently of the schools (by general practitioners, the courts, or other non-educational agencies). In TABLE 8.2, this point was examined by means of a simple division of the schools into those with high, medium, and low child guidance rates. No significant differences were found between these groups in the proportions of children referred by different agencies. In other words, it seems unlikely that

TABLE 8.2
SOURCES OF REFERRAL TO CHILD GUIDANCE, BY REFERRAL
RATE FOR SCHOOL

SOURCES OF REFERRAL	REFERRAL RATE OF SCHOOL		
	High	Medium	Low
	%	%	%
Primary schools			
from the school	41·7	49·4	41·0
from other sources	58·3	50·6	59·0
	100·0	100·0	100·0
No. of referrals	264	166	39
Secondary Selective			
from the school	—	28·0	25·9
from other sources	—	72·0	74·1
	—	100·0	100·0
No. of referrals	—	25	27
Secondary Non-Selective			
from the school	33·7	33·3	34·3
from other sources	66·3	66·7	65·7
	100·0	100·0	100·0
No. of referrals	92	78	35

the differing child guidance rates of the schools could be explained simply in terms of differing policies or habits.

2. DELINQUENCY RATES FOR SCHOOLS

As was explained in CHAPTER III, we could not use the main delinquency sample in the schools analysis, because in many instances the child's school was unknown. Since, however, this item was normally recorded by the Probation Service, we drew a sub-sample of children placed on probation or supervision orders during the survey period.[1]

To ascertain how closely the distribution of the probation sample corresponded to that of the main delinquency sample, we compared the two by electoral ward. The numbers of children in the probation sample varied widely as between electoral wards, from none in four of the southern wards to 108 in New Addington. When we calculated annual probation rates for the wards, the resulting distribution closely resembled that already observed for the main delinquency sample (see APPENDIX C, TABLE 7b). The rank order for ward probation rates correlated positively both with that for rates of all offenders (tau = +0·75***) and with that for rates of all offences (tau =

---

[1] The sample was drawn from the records of the Probation Service and did not correspond exactly with the number of children in the total delinquency sample who had been placed on probation or supervision orders (526 compared with 296 × 2, or 592). The difference was accounted for by children on Fit Person Orders.

+0·78***). Furthermore, each set of rankings showed similar correlations with the principal socio-demographic indices, as TABLE 8.3 demonstrates.

TABLE 8.3

TOTAL DELINQUENCY AND PROBATION/SUPERVISION RATES:
CORRELATION WITH WARD SOCIO-DEMOGRAPHIC INDICES
(No. of Wards = 20)

SOCIO-DEMOGRAPHIC INDICES	CORRELATION WITH DELINQUENCY RATES†		
	Total Persons	Total Offences	Probation/ Supervision
Proportion in Social Classes I and II	−0·54***	−0·52**	−0·52**
Proportion in Social Classes IV and V	+0·53**	+0·50**	+0·48**
Proportion of owner-occupiers	−0·54***	−0·53**	−0·53**
Proportion renting from Local Authority	+0·37*	+0·40**	+0·30
Proportion sharing households	+0·10	+0·07	+0·10
Density of population	+0·21	+0·17	+0·31
Proportion of foreign born	+0·12	+0·09	+0·14
Rate of migration	−0·25	−0·24	−0·12

† Kendall's τ.

Finally, the rank correlation of ward child guidance rates with probation rates (tau = +0·57***) was closely similar to those with rates for all offences (tau = +0·56***) and for all offenders (tau = +0·53**).

From these findings, we concluded that the probation sample was distributed in very much the same way as the whole delinquency sample, and could safely

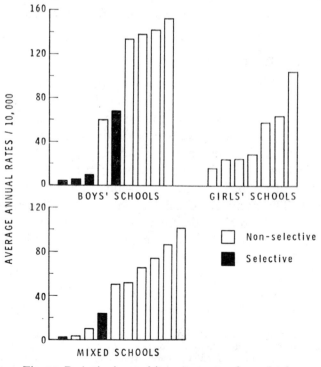

Fig. 14. Probation/supervision rates—secondary schools

be taken as representative for the purpose of calculating school delinquency rates.

The distribution of probation rates showed a wide range of variation among individual schools: mean annual rates for primary schools ranged from 0 to 38 per 10,000 children, with a mean of 3·4; for secondary selective schools, from 0 to 68, with a mean of 6·5, and for secondary non-selective schools, from 4 to 152, with a mean of 57·4. FIGURE 14 illustrates the range of variation for secondary schools.

3. CHILD GUIDANCE RATES, DELINQUENCY RATES, AND SCHOOL
   CHARACTERISTICS

Thus, when the schools were grouped into their principal types, they showed wide differences in child guidance and delinquency rates. Because of

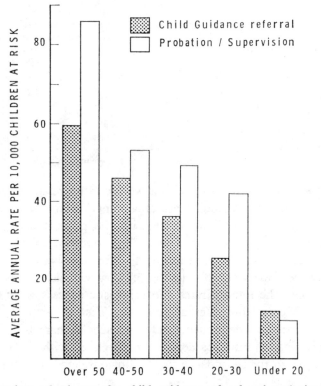

Fig. 15. Secondary school rates for child guidance referral and probation/supervision. (Schools grouped by child guidance referral rates.)

the different age ranges of children at primary and secondary schools, their rates were not properly comparable; among the secondary schools, however, both rates were higher for non-selective than for selective schools.

In FIGURE 15, child guidance and probation rates for individual secondary schools have been grouped and placed in rank order of child guidance rate. As with the electoral ward data outlined in CHAPTER VII, the two sets of rates follow parallel trends, schools with high rates for the one having high rates for the other, and vice-versa. Statistical testing confirmed the positive association (tau = +0·31**).

In seeking an explanation for this pattern of variation, we examined a number of characteristics of the schools. TABLE 8.4 shows wide differences between the principal types of school in relation to some of these features. The larger average class-size, higher proportion of immigrant children, and higher staff-turnover of the secondary non-selective schools all suggest that their apparent excess of deviant children may have been related to unfavourable teaching conditions.

TABLE 8.4

CHILD GUIDANCE RATES, PROBATION RATES, AND SELECTED SCHOOL CHARACTERISTICS, BY TYPE OF LOCAL AUTHORITY SCHOOL

TYPE OF SCHOOL	CHILD GUIDANCE†	PROBATION AND SUPERVISION†	PROPN. OF CLASSES WITH OVER 35 PUPILS	PROPN. OF IMMIGRANT PUPILS	ANNUAL TEACHER TURN-OVER
			%	%	%
Primary	36·6	3·4	48·3	5·9	17·6
Secondary selective	17·4	6·5	1·7	0·8	11·8
Secondary non-selective	36·4	57·4	13·3	5·9	14·8
Special (handicapped)	143·5	67·0	0·0	9·5	—

† Mean annual rate per 10,000 children, based on five-year cumulative totals.

Within the principal types of school, we found no relation between child guidance rates and known school features, a point demonstrated by TABLE 8.5. Here, the only associations are those with the proportions of immigrant children in secondary schools, and with the proportion of 'O' level passes. Both factors can be explained in terms of differences between selective and non-selective secondary schools. In the primary schools, no association was present between the referral rates and scholastic success as judged by the results of the Moray House Verbal Reasoning Test.

Association between delinquency rate and school characteristics was also small. The probation rate was negatively correlated with the proportion of 'O' level passes in the secondary schools, but unrelated to scholastic attainment in the primary schools.

On the available information, therefore, we could discover no index to explain the differences between individual schools. A clue may be given by the designation 'school of exceptional difficulty', used by the Education Authority as a guide to priorities of need. The secondary non-selective schools so designated had a mean annual child guidance rate of 51·0 per 10,000 children, compared with 29·2 for the remaining secondary non-selective schools: a significant difference. The corresponding school probation rates were 93·5 for the 'exceptional difficulty' schools and 48·8 for the remainder.

TABLE 8.5
CHILD GUIDANCE AND PROBATION RATES FOR SCHOOLS:
CORRELATION WITH SELECTED SCHOOL CHARACTERISTICS

SCHOOL CHARACTERISTICS	CORRELATION WITH CHILD GUIDANCE RATES		CORRELATION WITH PROBATION RATES	
	Primary Schools (n = 58)	Secondary Schools (n = 39)	Primary Schools (n = 58)	Secondary Schools (n = 39)
Average class size	+0·11	−0·13	+0·15	−0·03
Teacher turn-over rate	+0·16	0·00	−0·06	+0·20
Proportion of immigrant pupils	+0·16	+0·25*	+0·01	+0·23*
Proportion achieving 'O' level pass	—	−0·38***	—	−0·37***

4. RELATIONSHIP BETWEEN SCHOOL RATES AND THE ECOLOGICAL PATTERN

The findings outlined above might be due simply to the varying distance of schools from the Child Guidance Clinic (though obviously this factor was irrelevant to the probation rates). An alternative explanation could be sought in the neighbourhood effect demonstrated in the preceding chapter; namely, some schools might have had high rates merely because they were situated in wards with high rates. Each of these possibilities was examined in turn.

The effect of distance from the Child Guidance Clinic could be examined more readily for schools than for electoral wards, since it was possible to correlate the child guidance rate for each school with its distance in miles from the clinic. When this was done, no significant association was revealed (tau = −0·08). The probability of referral for the individual child appeared to be no more dependent on the distance of the clinic from his school than on that from his home.

In FIGURE 16, the distribution of schools with high, medium, and low child guidance rates has been superimposed on the ward pattern for child guidance referral, showing little correspondence.

No relationship was apparent between the rank order of the wards and that of the individual schools situated within them. Thus, of the ten secondary non-selective schools with the highest child guidance rates, six were located in low-rate wards, three in medium-rate wards, and only one in a high-rate ward. Rank correlation of the school rates with those of the wards in which they were situated confirmed this impression (tau = +0·07).

Because of the possibility that different patterns might exist among the different types of school, we examined the question separately for primary, secondary selective, and secondary non-selective schools. For no group did we find a significant association with ward rates, the highest correlation being that for the primary schools (tau = +0·23). Child guidance rates for individual schools could not, therefore, be explained in terms of their geographical location.

Next, we analysed the relationship between school delinquency rates and

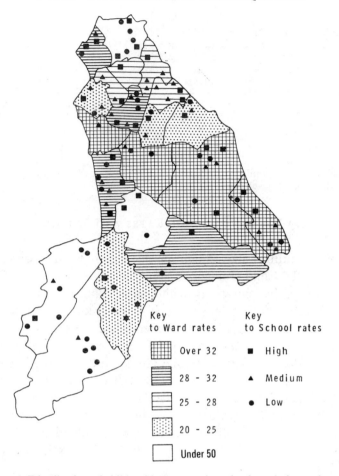

Key
to Ward rates

Key
to School rates

Over 32   ■ High

28 - 32   ▲ Medium

25 - 28   ● Low

20 - 25

Under 50

Fig. 16. Distribution of child guidance rates by schools and electoral wards

those of the wards in which the schools were situated. FIGURE 17 shows the distribution of secondary schools with high, medium, and low delinquency rates against the background of the electoral wards.

Rank correlations between school and ward probation rates proved significant for the fifty-eight primary schools (tau = +0·39*), the twenty-seven secondary non-selective schools (tau = +0·46**), and the twelve secondary selective schools (tau = +0·45**). These associations were, however, insufficiently strong to account for the degree of variation in the school rates. It appeared probable that, for delinquency as for child guidance rate, the individual school had exercised an influence, independently of any neighbourhood effect.

The findings thus far did not exclude the possibility that the same *children* might have contributed to the distinctive rates both of their schools and of the neighbourhoods in which they resided. Secondary school children, in particular, by no means always attend schools in their own home localities. Some

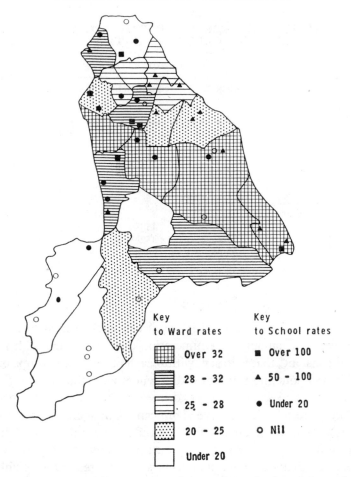

Key
to Ward rates

▦	Over 32
▤	28 - 32
▤	25 - 28
▦	20 - 25
☐	Under 20

Key
to School rates

■	Over 100
▲	50 - 100
●	Under 20
○	Nil

Fig. 17. Distribution of delinquency rates by secondary schools and electoral wards

high-rate schools could conceivably have had large numbers of pupils travelling in daily from high-rate neighbourhoods. To examine this question, we had to estimate school rates which were independent of the neighbourhood effect, and this was done by analysing the distribution of child guidance cases by school within each cluster of enumeration districts. TABLE 8.6 shows the referral rates for children *within each cluster* who were attending high-rate, medium-rate, and low-rate schools. In most cells of the table, the observed numbers of cases were found to differ from the numbers to be expected on a random basis (see APPENDIX C, TABLE 8b). The differences were significant in five of the seven clusters for primary school children, and in four of the seven clusters for secondary school children. It appears, in short, that the inter-school variation could not be explained simply as an effect of the neighbourhoods from which each school drew its pupils: rather, the schools made their own independent contribution to the pattern of child guidance referral.

TABLE 8.6
CHILD GUIDANCE RATE BY DISTRICT OF RESIDENCE OF
CHILDREN AND REFERRAL RATE FOR SCHOOL

E.D. CLUSTER	SCHOOL RATES			LEVEL OF SIGNIFICANCE
	High Ref.	Medium Ref.	Low Ref.	
Primary Schoolchildren				
1	47·4	44·5	20·4	NS
2	62·8	21·3	8·7	***
3	81·2	34·5	13·3	**
4	55·8	46·0	16·8	NS
5	78·9	30·0	—	***
6	52·5	38·8	15·0	***
7	81·8	25·2	19·7	**
Secondary Schoolchildren				
1	38·5	45·0	15·7	*
2	68·4	31·9	10·3	***
3	83·3	62·5	26·5	NS
4	73·2	42·1	12·6	***
5	30·5	25·9	36·1	NS
6	67·9	31·8	18·4	***
7	67·9	48·8	14·1	NS

The data on which TABLE 8.6 is based can also be used to examine the extent of variation among the enumeration-district clusters with the school effect held constant; that is to say, within each of the three groups of schools. When this was done, no significant differences were found among the high-referral schools (Chi-square = 0·51; d.f. = 2; p > 0·05). Differences among the medium-referral schools were significant (Chi-square = 7·56; d.f. = 2; p < 0·025), while those among the low-referral schools were of borderline significance (Chi-square = 4·84; d.f. = 2; p > 0·05 < 0·10). It seems probable, therefore, that although school factors contributed to the neighbourhood differences, they could not wholly account for them: a conclusion supported by the finding that inter-cluster differences in referral rates were significant among pre-school children (Chi-square = 26·20; d.f. = 6; p < 0·01).

It is clear that data based on a cross-sectional survey cannot be accepted as evidence for a *causal* hypothesis. In the present instance, no assessment could be made of the relative influence of the neighbourhood and of the school, since it could not be assumed that the selection of children for individual schools or for types of school (selective or non-selective) had not been influenced by their district of residence. It seems probable that in fact neighbourhood and school factors were interdependent, both directly in the allocation of school places, and indirectly through personal and family characteristics of the individual child. To separate out the respective contributions of neighbourhood and school would require, therefore, an anterospective study of a cohort of children followed up over a number of years from pre-school age.

The respective importance of neighbourhood and school in a *predictive* sense could, however, be examined by means of a multiple regression analysis in which both neighbourhood and school characteristics were employed as predictor variables. When such an analysis was carried out, using socio-demographic indices of the seven large district-clusters and features of the schools averaged for three large groups (see APPENDIX B3), the best predictor of child guidance referral for secondary-school children was found to be the school probation rate. The next three indices, in order of importance, were all ecological; namely, the proportion of persons living in shared households, the proportion of foreign-born residents, and the rate of migration. Together, these four variables accounted for nearly half the total variance in child guidance rates. The multiple regression analysis thus indicated that both the child's neighbourhood and his school could be regarded as important pre-dictors of his likelihood of being referred for child guidance.

SUMMARY

In order to examine the influence of the school on child guidance and delinquency rates, we collected data for all Local Education Authority schools in Croydon: a total of 100 schools, or 128 separate school departments. Apart from the child guidance survey material, the main sources of information were the Chief Education Officer, the Probation Service, and a special one-in-four sample of school health cards.

School child guidance rates varied among primary schools from 0 to 153, and among secondary schools from 0 to 82, per 10,000 children. Comparison of the sources of referral for children attending high-rate, medium-rate, and low-rate schools showed no trend to suggest that the over-all child guidance rates were simply a reflection of referral policy or habits within the schools.

Probation rates for the schools (which could be taken as a good index of total delinquency rates) also covered a wide range: among primary schools from 0 to 38, and among secondary schools from 0 to 152, per 10,000 children.

The two sets of rates showed parallel trends, schools with high child guidance rates having high probation rates, and vice-versa. Both differed as between the main types of school (primary, secondary selective, secondary non-selective, and special), and these differences appeared to be related to class-size, teacher turn-over, and proportion of immigrant children. Within each type of school, however, no predictive indices were found.

School child guidance rates were not affected by distance of the school from the Child Guidance Clinic, nor by the social character of the ward in which the school was situated. School probation rates did show a partial correlation with local ward rates, but this was insufficient to explain the ob-served pattern of variation. Examination of primary and secondary school rates separately, for children drawn from each of the larger clusters of enumeration districts, revealed a non-random distribution. In other words, correcting for the neighbourhood effect did not serve to cancel out the appa-rent effect of the school. Conversely, holding the school effect constant did not eliminate the neighbourhood differences.

Finally, a multiple regression analysis incorporating both neighbourhood and school indices as predictor variables showed that, for secondary school-children, the school probation rate was the best single predictor of child guidance referral, followed by three district variables.

All the evidence thus pointed to the conclusion that both neighbourhood and school were important determinants of child guidance referral and of delinquency, although on the basis of a cross-sectional survey it was not possible to assess the relative importance of their separate contributions.

CHAPTER IX

CHILD GUIDANCE AND THE GENERAL PRACTITIONER

SINCE the principal aim of the research project was to study environmental influences on child guidance rates, we could not ignore the part played by the general practitioners, who had been directly responsible for nearly half the survey referrals. It seems probable that the general practitioner exercised an influence on the referral pattern independently either of neighbourhood or of school. The general practice research cited in CHAPTER II suggested as much, and additional evidence was provided by the observation that the numbers of children in the survey referred by each Croydon doctor varied from 0 to 18 (see APPENDIX C, TABLE 9a). Further examination of the role of the general practitioner was thus firmly indicated.

MATERIAL AND METHOD

The first step was to compute a referral rate for each family doctor practising in Croydon during the survey period. Here, we encountered serious problems of method, the foremost being that of defining and enumerating the population at risk. Since the Local Executive Council kept no separate index of children registered with each practitioner, rates could not be estimated for the child population of individual practices. As a compromise, we computed two other rates, based respectively on the practitioner's total list-size (adults and children combined) and on the number of schoolchildren registered with each practice. For convenience, these will be referred to as the T- (total) and S- (schoolchildren) rates respectively. The T-rate must always be less than the S-rate, being based on a much larger denominator: adults and children as opposed to children only. Individual practitioners may have widely varying proportions of children among their patients; hence the S-rate was regarded both as a useful check on the T-rate and as a possible alternative to it. The S-rate was derived from data collected in the school health card survey, described in CHAPTER VIII.

THE POSTAL QUESTIONNAIRE SURVEY

For the T-rate, we had to estimate each doctor's average list-size over the survey period. As the Local Medical Committee could not supply information on individual doctors' lists, we had to rely on data provided by the doctors themselves. An item on list-size was included, therefore, in the postal questionnaire designed to investigate the practitioner's use of, and attitudes towards, child psychiatric services (see CHAPTER IV). The findings of this postal survey were required for estimation of the T-rate as well as in trying to explain individual variation. The questionnaire is set out in full in APPENDIX A3. At this point, its use in estimating and interpreting referral rates will be discussed only briefly.

1. ESTIMATION OF REFERRAL RATES

On the questionnaire, the doctor was asked to give his current list-size (in 1967, when the survey was undertaken) and, if applicable, his list-size in 1962, according to the groupings: less than 1,500; 1,500–2,000; 2,000–2,500; 2,500–3,000; over 3,000. The general practitioner can provide such estimates because he receives a quarterly return from the Local Executive Council.[1]

The responses were then scored by taking the mean value in each case; so that, for example, 2,500–3,000 was treated as 2,750. Under 1,500 was scored as 1,250, and over 3,000 as 3,250, the maximum list normally permitted under the National Health Service being 3,500. The number of patients in each practice at the mid-point of the survey period we estimated as the mean of the list-sizes for 1962 and 1967.

Each doctor working in a partnership or group-practice was also asked for the approximate size of the practice as a whole. We then calculated individual patient-loads based on the number of partners and checked each doctor's estimate against his partners' questionnaire responses. This we judged to be the most realistic approach, since junior partners may only have small patient lists, yet contribute their full share to the work of the practice.

The questionnaire also supplied a list of nineteen child psychiatric and child guidance clinics situated within ten miles of Croydon, and asked the doctor to say which he used 'always', 'usually', or 'occasionally'. If his reply was vague or unclear, we telephoned him and discussed the question until a clear picture emerged. This information was then used to apply a corrective weighting to the rates computed for the doctor from the number of children he had sent to Croydon Child Guidance Clinic.

From the questionnaire findings, together with those of the school health card survey, we computed two sets of referral rates as follows:

(i) *rates based on total list-size (T-rates)*

$$\text{G.P. referral rate} = \frac{n_1 \times 10{,}000}{p}$$

$$\text{Other referral rate} = \frac{n_2 \times 10{,}000}{p}$$

$$\text{Total referral rate} = \frac{(n_1 + n_2) \times 10{,}000}{p}$$

[1] Now the Family Practitioner Committee of the Area Health Authority.

where p = estimated list-size for adults and children, derived from the postal questionnaire;

n_1 = number of children referred by the practitioner;

n_2 = number of children on the practitioner's list referred by other agencies.

(ii) *rates based on number of school children registered with the doctor (S-rates)*

G.P. referral rate $= \dfrac{n_1 \times 10,000}{p}$

Other referral rate $= \dfrac{n_2 \times 10,000}{p}$

Total referral rate $= \dfrac{(n_1 + n_2) \times 10,000}{p}$

where p = number of Croydon schoolchildren registered with the G.P.

n_1 = number of Croydon schoolchildren referred by the practitioner;

n_2 = number of Croydon schoolchildren on the practitioner's list referred by other agencies.

2. INTERPRETATION OF REFERRAL RATES

The factors deciding a doctor's referral habits are complex and difficult to define. They may include his personal attributes: age, sex, intelligence, and personality. They may be partly a product of his medical training, his post-graduate experience, and the path by which he has reached general practice. His attitude towards maladjusted children may be affected by his own family and social background and by his religious beliefs. Finally, previous experience of referral to local agencies may have given him a firm opinion as to their usefulness.

In the present investigation, no comprehensive study of these factors was possible. We decided, therefore, to restrict the inquiry to two important areas: first, information was collected on certain basic characteristics of the doctors and of their practices. The main demographic data elicited by the questionnaire survey were the doctor's age and sex; his undergraduate medical school; the number of years he had spent in practice in Croydon; the size of his patient-list and whether he was single-handed, in partnership, or in group-practice. The relationship of each of these factors to the rate of psychiatric referral for children could then be examined.

Secondly, we attempted to measure the doctors' attitudes to child psychiatry and to the care of disturbed children. Strictly speaking, a formal attitude study was beyond the scope of our inquiry. The measurement of attitudes, involving construction and validation of standardized scales (Scott, 1968) presents many technical problems and is most successful where a single dimension is involved: an unlikely event in the present context. As a compromise, we decided to use a simple technique based on case-vignettes: a method previously employed in studying general practitioners' attitudes to adult psychiatry (Shepherd *et al.*, 1966).

The postal questionnaire contained eight short case-summaries, selected from the clinical material of an earlier study (Gath, 1968), and representing a series of childhood problems with which most general practitioners would be familiar. These comprised conduct disorders in an eight-year-old boy and in a fourteen-year-old girl; phobic fear of a dog; early childhood psychosis (autism); retarded school progress; transvestism; psychosomatic symptoms related to school attendance and persistent enuresis (see APPENDIX A3). They were selected to avoid over-emphasis on conduct disorder and to include some with a possible organic component. The doctor was asked to indicate on a list provided, his first choice of action and disposal for each case. As far as possible, the choices were standardized as follows:

1. Rejection of the case as a non-medical problem (O);
2. Medical treatment (usually medication) without regard to psychological or social factors (M);
3. Referral to a paediatrician (MR);
4. Social management, usually advice and counselling (S);
5. Referral to a specified social agency (SR);
6. Psychotherapy by the practitioner himself (P);
7. Referral to a child guidance or psychiatric clinic (PR).

The wording was modified to suit each case-history, and space was provided for any comments the doctor might wish to make.

The different forms of action could not be ranked on a linear scale. A number of factors influence such decisions, including the doctor's clinical experience and confidence as well as his interest in, or sympathy for, each type of case. The two scores eventually selected for analysis were:

(i) the PR score, based on the number of cases for which the doctor nominated psychiatric referral;
(ii) the C (Compound) score, based on the following system:

Response	No. of Points Scored
O	0
M	1
MR, S, or SR	2
P or PR	3

Each questionnaire was scored by one research worker and checked by another.

RESULTS

1. RESPONSE TO THE QUESTIONNAIRE SURVEY

We sent copies of the postal questionnaire to all 140 doctors practising in Croydon in 1967, and reminders enclosing extra copies to those who did not reply. Eventually, following second reminders, we received replies from 107 doctors (76·4 per cent). For the most part, examination of the factors influencing child guidance referral had to be limited to this group, although some information about the remaining doctors was available from the current Medical Directory.

On the basis of their questionnaire responses, we divided the 107 practitioners who had replied into four groups, as shown in TABLE 9.1. In most of the tables that follow, we are concerned with the eighty-three doctors comprising Groups A and B. The distinction between these two groups was necessary in considering the effect on child guidance rates of the practitioners' attitudes to specialist care, a question taken up later in the present chapter.

TABLE 9.1

GROUPING OF THE CROYDON PRACTITIONERS ON THE BASIS OF THEIR POSTAL QUESTIONNAIRE RESPONSES

GROUP	NO. OF G.P.S	CRITERIA FOR GROUPING	INCLUDED IN REFERRAL RATE
A	79	Using Croydon Child Guidance Clinic mainly or exclusively. In Croydon for 1–5 years of survey period.	Yes
B	4	As for A, but case-vignettes not fully completed.	Yes
C	11	As for A, but in Croydon for less than one year of survey period.	No
D	13	Mainly using other clinics.	No

2. THE PRACTITIONER'S LIST-SIZES

According to the method outlined above, the distribution of list-sizes for the Croydon doctors was as follows:

List-sizes	Proportion of Practitioners %
Under 1,500	4·6
1,500–2,000	13·1
2,000–2,500	26·2
2,500–3,000	27·1
Over 3,000	29·0
Total	100·0
No. of doctors	107

Exact comparison with national or regional figures was impossible, since official statistics do not use the same groupings. Broadly speaking, the Croydon lists appear to be larger than the national average; in 1963, for example, what are rather oddly described as 'unrestricted principals' (that is, doctors in full-time general practice) in England and Wales included 15 per cent with fewer than 1,600 patients and only 18 per cent with over 3,000 patients (Dept. of Health, 1969). Probably the Croydon statistics were fairly typical of the more densely-populated urban and metropolitan areas of the country.

As a check on the accuracy of the questionnaire responses, they were subsequently compared with the findings of an interview survey of Croydon practitioners, carried out as part of a separate inquiry two to three years later (Harwin et al., 1970). Of ninety doctors who took part in both surveys, 57·7 per cent reported the same approximate list-size on each occasion and 28·8 per cent a larger list-size on the second occasion. This finding is in keeping with the tendency for doctors established in general practice to increase their lists, partly through the death or retirement of local colleagues.

3. THE PRACTITIONERS' USE OF CHILD PSYCHIATRIC SERVICES

As anticipated, most of the practitioners reported that they used Croydon Child Guidance Clinic, either invariably or as a rule. The picture revealed by the questionnaire survey was roughly as follows: just over one-third sent children only to the Croydon Clinic; one-third used other clinics occasionally; one-fifth used other clinics equally with Croydon; about one doctor in twenty used other clinics mainly or exclusively. Finally, 6 per cent of the practitioners reported that they had sent *no* children for a psychiatric opinion during the survey period.

The effect of weighting the referral data to correct for the use of other clinics was to raise the T-rate from 5·7 to 6·2 per 10,000 population and the S-rate from 35·9 to 39·2 per 10,000 schoolchildren: an increase of about 8 per cent in each instance. The national rate for new referrals to child guidance in 1964 was 37 per 10,000 schoolchildren. The estimated rate for Croydon was thus slightly above the national average, suggesting that no substantial group of cases had been missed by the survey.

To cross-check the questionnaire responses against the records of the other eighteen clinics listed (not to mention those of psychiatrists in private practice) was beyond our resources. We made a partial check by extracting the names and referral agencies for all Croydon children seen during the survey period in the Maudsley Hospital Children's Department. This, the largest child psychiatric department in the southern half of the metropolis, is situated only three miles from the northern boundary of Croydon, and probably took the majority of outside referrals for the northern half of the borough. In fact, only forty-five Croydon children had been seen there: a number representing 4·3 per cent of those who went to the Croydon Clinic. This finding supported our belief that only a small proportion of medical referrals had been made to clinics outside Croydon.

A second check was made by comparing the rates of referral for three groups of doctors; namely, those who had used the Croydon Clinic exclusively, those who had used it mainly and those who had used it equally with other clinics. If the weightings given were correct, one would expect the estimated rates for these three groups to be similar. This proved to be the case, the mean values being 19·2, 20·4, and 21·7 per 10,000 at risk, respectively.

A more difficult problem was posed by the thirty-three doctors who had failed to complete and return their questionnaires, since for this group no corrective weights could be applied. Comparison of the unweighted rates for the respondent and non-respondent groups of doctors revealed that whereas on average the latter had referred fewer children to the Croydon clinic, the rates for children from their practices referred by other agencies were similar for the two groups. The data are summarized in TABLE 9.2.

TABLE 9.2

CHILD GUIDANCE REFERRAL RATES OF CROYDON SCHOOL-CHILDREN REGISTERED WITH TWO GROUPS OF PRACTITIONERS: THOSE WHO RETURNED THE POSTAL QUESTIONNAIRE AND THOSE WHO DID NOT

| | REFERRAL RATE PER 10,000 SCHOOLCHILDREN[1] | |
SOURCE OF REFERRAL	Children whose doctors (83) completed questionnaire[2]	Children whose doctors (33) did not complete questionnaire
Referral by the doctors themselves	17·7	10·6
Referral from other sources	18·3	16·1
Referral from all sources	36·0	26·7

[1] Unweighted rates.
[2] Excluding those practising in Croydon for less than one year in the survey period, and those who used mainly clinics outside the borough.

If we assume an equal ratio of the two types of referral for both groups of practices, the true rate for the non-respondent doctors can be estimated at about 15·5, suggesting that they had referred approximately one-third of their cases outside Croydon. In this event, the true child guidance rate (S-rate) for the borough should be estimated at 35·9, rather than 39·2, per 10,000 at risk.

As expected, both weighted referral rates showed wide variation among individual doctors, the T-rates ranging from 0 to 14 per 10,000 population and the S-rates from 0 to 179 per 10,000 schoolchildren. The two sets of rates were only partially correlated ($r = +0.74$): not a surprising finding, since they were computed from different samples and populations at risk. Probably the ratio of children to adults varied as between practices and in so doing affected the correspondence between the two rates.

4. PRACTITIONER REFERRALS AND THE NEIGHBOURHOOD EFFECT

As for the school data, it was important to gauge how much individual variation might simply reflect the neighbourhood effect; that is to say, how closely the doctors' referral rates were associated with the child guidance rates of the districts in which their practices were situated. We examined this question in five different ways, as follows:

(i) *Ratio of practitioner referrals to other referrals*

If doctors with high referral rates were working in practices with high child guidance rates, and many of their child patients were sent to the clinic by teachers, the courts, or other agencies, one could infer that high rates were characteristic of the child population, rather than of the doctor. Conversely, if the number of children picked out for child guidance by other agencies was small, an explanation of the doctor's high rate would have to be sought in his own referral habits rather than in his patient-population.

Statistical testing showed little association between the rates for doctors' referrals and other referrals, within each practice. Product–moment correlations were low both for the T-rate ($r = +0.24$) and for the S-rate ($r = -0.01$). Details are given in APPENDIX C, TABLES 9a and 9b.

(ii) *Practitioner referrals and the electoral ward*

The next step was to compare each doctor's referral rate with that of the electoral ward in which his practice surgery was situated. When this was done, again no clear association was found, product–moment correlations proving low both for the T-rate ($r = +0.07$) and for the S-rate ($r = +0.04$). Details are set out in APPENDIX C, TABLES 9a and 9b.

(iii) *Distance of the practice from the clinic*

Next, we located on a map of Croydon the surgery premises of each of the eighty-three doctors who had returned the questionnaire and for whom full information was available. Groups with high, medium, and low referral rates were found to be distributed with no relation to their distance from the Child Guidance Clinic. The point was confirmed by correlating referral rate with distance in miles, the results again proving low both for the T-rate ($r = +0.04$) and for the S-rate ($r = -0.21$). Whether a doctor had sent many or few children to the clinic seemed to have been little influenced by the distance involved.

(iv) *Referral rates for children and for adults*

In the course of the survey of adult psychiatric referral in Croydon, mentioned in CHAPTER VII, we computed rates for all general practitioners practising in the borough over the two-year period, 1967–8. A positive correlation was found between these rates and the same doctors' rates of child guidance referral in the present survey ($r = +0.50$). If, as the evidence suggests, both rates were largely independent of any neighbourhood effect, it seems probable that both represented a general tendency on the doctors' part to seek specialist help more or less frequently.

(v) *Analysis of variance of referral rates*

Finally, we carried out a three-way analysis of variance in which neighbourhood, school, and general practitioner were treated as main effects. This analysis had to be restricted to children attending Croydon Local Authority schools and registered with the eighty-three doctors who returned their questionnaires. The results, set out in APPENDIX B4, strongly suggested that the individual practitioners had exercised an influence on the overall referral pattern, independently both of neighbourhood and of school effects.

In summary, all the evidence indicates that the doctors' rate of child guidance referral was not simply a reflection of the neighbourhood in which he practised, but was related in some way to his own personal or professional characteristics; to the type of his practice or to his interactions with the children and their parents.

5. REFERRAL RATES AND CHARACTERISTICS OF THE PRACTITIONERS

(i) *Age and sex distribution*

TABLE 9.3 reveals no clear association between the doctor's age and his referral rate, other than that the small group of over-70 doctors had very low rates. Product–moment correlations were insignificant both for the T-rate ($r = -0.13$) and for the S-rate ($r = -0.16$).

TABLE 9.3

DISTRIBUTION AND MEAN CHILD GUIDANCE REFERRAL RATES OF THE PRACTITIONERS, BY AGE-GROUP

AGE IN YEARS	NO. OF G.P.S	MEAN REFERRAL RATE PER 10,000 POPULATION (T-rate)	MEAN REFERRAL RATE PER 10,000 SCHOOL-CHILDREN (S-rate)
30–39	15	3·5	20·6
40–49	32	3·4	21·0
50–59	18	3·2	19·8
60–69	14	3·1	20·4
70+	4	1·0	5·1
All G.P.s	83	3·3	20·3

The ten women doctors had higher referral rates than their male colleagues, the respective T-rates being 4·3 and 3·2 per 10,000 population, and the respective S-rates 29·8 and 19·2 per 10,000 schoolchildren. The latter finding suggests that the difference was not due merely to higher proportions of children on the female doctors' lists.

(ii) *Undergraduate medical school*

TABLE 9.4 shows that two-thirds of the practitioners had qualified at London medical schools; hence it seemed improbable that differences in their referral habits could be related to differences in basic medical education. The numbers involved were too small to permit comparison of individual medical schools.

TABLE 9.4

DISTRIBUTION AND MEAN REFERRAL RATES OF THE PRACTITIONERS, BY REGION OF UNDERGRADUATE MEDICAL SCHOOL

REGION OF MEDICAL SCHOOL	NO. OF G.P.s	MEAN REFERRAL RATE PER 10,000 POPULATION (T-rate)	MEAN REFERRAL RATE PER 10,000 SCHOOL-CHILDREN (S-rate)
London	53	2·9	19·7
English provinces	4	5·9	27·9
Wales	—	—	—
Scotland	11	3·1	19·9
Ireland	11	3·8	20·6
European	3	1·7	8·5
Other	1	10·6	38·4
All G.P.s	83	3·3	20·3

(iii) *Length of time in practice in Croydon*

The length of time each doctor had been in practice was discounted as a separate factor, because it was so highly correlated with his age (see TABLE 9.3). The length of time spent in practice in Croydon did, however, merit examination. The distribution is summarized in TABLE 9.5.

TABLE 9.5

DISTRIBUTION AND MEAN REFERRAL RATES OF THE PRACTITIONERS, BY DURATION OF PRACTICE IN CROYDON

NO. OF YEARS IN PRACTICE IN CROYDON	NO. OF G.P.s	MEAN REFERRAL RATE PER 10,000 POPULATION (T-rate)	MEAN REFERRAL RATE PER 10,000 SCHOOL-CHILDREN (S-rate)
Under 5	3	5·1	57·3
5–10	9	3·4	17·7
10–15	19	3·7	22·9
15–20	14	2·7	16·5
20 & over	30	3·1	20·1
Not known	8	3·1	17·1
All G.P.s	83	3·3	20·3

No linear trend is apparent in TABLE 9.5. The three doctors with the shortest time in local practice had the highest referral rates; otherwise this variable was not relevant. Product–moment correlations were low both for the T-rate ($r = -0.09$) and for the S-rate ($r = -0.10$).

(iv) *Size of doctor's list*

The number of registered patients on a doctor's list may influence his referral rate, though it would be difficult to predict in which direction. A practitioner with many patients might refer the more readily because of pressure of work; on the other hand, one with a small list might recognize the need for specialist care more often because of his greater opportunities to spend time with individual patients. It is, of course, possible that these opposing trends would cancel each other out; the absence of any statistical association would not show that such trends did not exist, but merely that the net result was unimportant in trying to explain referral rates. TABLE 9.6 examines this question in relation to child guidance referral by the Croydon practitioners.

TABLE 9.6

DISTRIBUTION AND MEAN REFERRAL RATES OF THE PRACTITIONERS BY SIZE OF THEIR PATIENT-LISTS

SIZE OF PATIENT-LIST	NO. OF G.P.s	MEAN REFERRAL RATE PER 10,000 POPULATION (T-rate)	MEAN REFERRAL RATE PER 10,000 SCHOOL-CHILDREN (S-rate)
Less than 1,500	3	1·6	9·2
1,500–2,000	9	4·6	24·8
2,000–2,500	20	3·7	20·2
2,500–3,000	24	2·5	20·1
Over 3,000	27	3·5	19·8
All G.P.s	83	3·3	20·3

Here again, no linear trend can be discerned. The three doctors with the smallest lists had abnormally low referral rates; otherwise list-size did not appear to be a relevant variable. Product–moment correlations were again low both for the T-rate ($r = -0·05$) and for the S-rate ($r = +0·02$).

(v) *Structure of the practice*

A number of features of a doctor's practice may bear on his referral habits. The postal questionnaire used in this inquiry, being deliberately restricted in scope, dealt with only one; namely, whether the doctor was single-handed or in partnership and, if the latter, the number of his partners. TABLE 9.7 indicates that this factor also failed to explain the variation in referral rates.

TABLE 9.7

DISTRIBUTION AND MEAN REFERRAL RATES OF THE PRACTITIONERS BY NUMBER OF PRACTICE PRINCIPALS

NO. OF PRINCIPALS	NO. OF G.P.s	MEAN REFERRAL RATE PER 10,000 POPULATION (T-rate)	MEAN REFERRAL RATE PER 10,000 SCHOOL-CHILDREN (S-rate)
Single-handed	21	1·9	17·9
Two partners	23	4·3	23·4
Three partners	33	3·6	19·4
Four partners	6	2·3	18·0
All G.P.s	83	3·3	20·3

6. REFERRAL RATES AND THE PRACTITIONERS' ATTITUDES

The effect on the doctors' referral rates of their attitudes to child psychiatry was examined in terms of their responses to the case-vignettes included in the postal questionnaire. Comment will be restricted to Group A ($n = 79$); that is, to practitioners who completed the questionnaire, including the case-vignettes, and for whom child guidance referral rates could be estimated. The distribution of responses for this group was as follows:

	%
Not a medical problem	1·7
Medication only	10·5
Referral to paediatrician	6·7
Advice and counselling	24·2
Referral to social agency	1·7
Psychotherapy by G.P.	22·6
Referral to Child Guidance Clinic	27·1
Not answered, or other	5·5
	100·0

Rejection of the problem as non-medical was an infrequent choice. The modal responses were as follows:

Child guidance referral: A (conduct disorder)
C (early childhood psychosis) and
H (conduct disorder)
Advice and counselling: B (dog phobia)
D (poor progress at school)
E (transvestism) and
F (psychosomatic disorder related to school attendance)
Medication only: G (enuresis)

The psychiatric referral (PR) scores were generally low, only fifteen of the seventy-nine doctors scoring more than three out of a possible eight. On the C scale, which was intended to measure how far the case-histories were perceived as 'psychiatric', all but three of the doctors were in the upper half of the possible range (12–24), the mean score being 18·5.

We subjected the practitioners' scores on the C scale to a principal components analysis which, as anticipated, showed no single dimension along which attitudes were being measured (see APPENDIX B5).

Correlation of the doctors' referral rates against the PR and C scores, calculated from their questionnaire responses, showed no important associations. Co-efficients of correlation with the PR score were +0·24 (T-rate) and +0·26 (S-rate); those with the C score were +0·18 (T-rate) and +0·23 (S-rate).

The data were further examined by dividing the doctors into four sub-groups, with high, medium-high, medium-low, and low referral rates respectively. No difference was found between the mean PR and C scores of these groups, as can be seen from TABLE 9.8. Correlations between the mean referral rates of the four sub-groups and their demographic indices were uniformly low.

TABLE 9.8

MEAN ATTITUDE SCORES OF PRACTITIONERS DIVIDED INTO FOUR GROUPS BY REFERRAL RATE

G.P. GROUP BY REFERRAL RATE	MEAN ATTITUDE SCORES	
	PR score	C score
High	2·5	18·4
Medium-high	2·6	18·1
Medium-low	2·1	19·0
Low	1·6	18·3
All G.P.s	2·2	18·5

Next, we divided the doctors according to the proportion of referrals from their practices for which they, as distinct from other agencies, had been responsible. Here again, no inter-group differences were found in the mean C score, the distribution being as follows:

Proportion of Referrals made by G.P. %	Mean Attitude Score (C score)
0–20	18·2
21–50	18·2
51–80	19·5
81–100	18·4

Finally, we made use of two ratings available from the complementary interview-survey of general practitioners in Croydon (Harwin et al., 1970), in the course of which both the practitioners' interest in psychiatric problems, and their satisfaction with local psychiatric services, had been assessed. Correlation of each of these indices with the doctors' child guidance referral rates were uniformly low, the highest coefficient being less than 0·1.

Thus, exhaustive attempts to explain the observed variation in referral rates among general practitioners, in terms of their personal attitudes, their types of practice, or their attitudes to children's problems, proved signally unrewarding. This failure may have been due to the use of unsatisfactory research instruments, or to the fact that our information about the practitioners was limited and incomplete. The possibility must also be borne in mind that many of the practitioners may have played a relatively passive role in the referral process, and that differences between their individual rates corresponded largely to differences in the social pressures acting upon them.

SUMMARY

Nearly half the cases in the child guidance sample had been referred by general practitioners. In order to examine the effect of individual variation among the practitioners, we calculated two referral rates for each: the T-rate (based on total list-size) and the S-rate (based on number of schoolchildren known to be registered with each doctor). The latter rate was computed from the school health card survey, described in CHAPTER VIII.

A postal questionnaire survey of Croydon doctors provided information about each regarding list-size; use of child psychiatric facilities; attitudes to psychological problems of children and certain personal characteristics. The responses indicated that over 90 per cent of child psychiatric referrals by Croydon practitioners were being made to the local Child Guidance Clinic. Indirect evidence suggested that those doctors who did not complete the questionnaire may have been referring a higher proportion of cases outside the borough; in which case, the true proportion sent to the Croydon Clinic could be estimated at about 86 per cent of the total.

No association was found, either between the doctors' own rates of referral and those for their patient-populations as a whole, or between the doctors' rates and those for the electoral wards in which their surgeries were situated. The distance of each surgery from the Child Guidance Clinic also appeared to bear no relation to the number of children sent there. These findings suggested that the doctors' referral habits had had an effect on the over-all pattern of child guidance utilization, independent of neighbourhood and school influences: a point confirmed by an analysis of variance in which the general practitioner was treated as a main effect.

All attempts to explain the pattern of variation among the practitioners were unsuccessful: individual referral rates could not be related to the doctor's age, medical school, length of time in practice in Croydon, size of list, type of practice, or attitudes to child psychological problems as revealed by the postal questionnaire survey. The only positive finding of this analysis was that the small group of women doctors had higher rates on average than their male colleagues.

The observation that practitioners' rates of psychiatric referral for children and for adults were positively correlated suggests that both may have been part of a more general underlying trend which remains to be defined. In the absence of any clear evidence that some characteristic of the doctor himself, or of his style of practice, is the main determinant, the possibility must be considered that varying attitudes and levels of demand for care among the patient-population (and, in the present instance, among parents) must be invoked to explain the referral patterns.

CHAPTER X

CONCLUSIONS

THE last three chapters have dealt with the research findings in relation to three distinct environmental factors: the neighbourhood, the school, and the family doctor. In the light of these findings, we can now review the hypotheses formulated at the outset of this inquiry (see p. 40).

1. Child-guidance and delinquency rates were found to vary widely among the wards and local districts of Croydon. As predicted, the two sets of rates co-varied and revealed similar patterns of association with demographic and socio-economic indices.

2. Child-guidance and delinquency rates also showed large differences as between the Croydon schools. Again as predicted, the two sets of rates co-varied and showed similar profiles when examined against a number of school indices.

3. Child-guidance rates were influenced by the referral habits of the local practitioners, who were responsible for sending nearly half the children seen at the clinic. Referral rates varied widely among the practitioners, and these differences could not be explained in terms of other environmental factors.

Broadly speaking, therefore, the research findings provided support for each of the principal hypotheses. Only the latter part of the third hypothesis, which stated that child guidance rates could be related to defined characteristics of the family doctors and their practices, could not be verified.

Before discussing possible implications, it is necessary, especially in view of the many problems of method encountered in this research, to consider how far the findings can be accepted as valid, and how far they can be extrapolated beyond the boundaries of the survey area.

EVALUATION OF THE SURVEY FINDINGS

The success of the investigation must be judged in terms of what it set out to achieve; not of any more ambitious aims which it was never intended to fulfil. We have repeatedly emphasized that no attempt was made to gauge the total extent of maladjustment, or of need for child-guidance services, in the local child-population, and that such an objective would have called for quite a different strategy. For purely practical reasons, the investigation had to be limited to a retrospective survey, based chiefly on second-hand information.

Most of the data were derived from the records of public agencies, or from official statistics collected at national or local level. Enumeration of these sources shows how much we had to depend upon the accuracy and completeness of administrative records and statistics:

(i) day-books and case-files of Croydon Child Guidance Clinic;

(ii) card-index and case-files of Croydon Children's Department;

(iii) card-index and case-files of Croydon Probation Service;

(iv) card-index of Croydon School Health Service;

(v) school-rolls and descriptive data on the local authority schools of Croydon, supplied by the Chief Education Officer;

(vi) data on the electoral wards and enumeration-districts of Croydon, extracted from the 1966 Census tables for England and Wales (10 per cent sample);

(vii) data on the Croydon family doctors and their practices, derived from a special questionnaire survey.

Items (i), (ii), and (iii) represent the sources from which were derived the *numerators* employed in estimating rates. Items (iv), (v), (vi), and (vii) each provided data for the estimation of base-populations; that is, for *denominators*. Items (v), (vi), and (vii) were also the sources for various indices against which the estimated rates were subsequently tested for correlation.

In relation to these sources of information, three principal types of error can be defined; namely, inaccuracies of data; incompleteness of data; errors arising from sampling-procedures.

1. ACCURACY OF THE DATA

Retrieval of the data was virtually complete, apart from the item on parental occupation, for children seen at the child guidance clinic; and fairly good even for the small group who had failed to attend. The survey sample tallied closely with the numbers recorded in the clinic's annual returns.

Basic data were also obtained for all children in the delinquency and probation samples. Here again, the numbers agreed closely with those given in the annual returns for Croydon; moreover, good agreement was found between the records of the Children's Department and those of the Probation Service. Compared with other reported delinquency samples, those drawn for the present inquiry were fairly typical in respect of age–sex composition, and in the type and frequency of known offences. To this extent, the data on juvenile delinquency could be deemed reliable.

The least rewarding aspect of the inquiry, and that subject to most doubts regarding its validity, was the study of general practitioners. Estimation of referral rates for the individual practitioners was based, first, on the survey of School Health Cards (see CHAPTER VIII); secondly, on the postal-questionnaire survey: each of these methods was of limited reliability. Though the school card-indices were complete and the basic demographic data invariably recorded, the family doctor's name was probably out-of-date in some instances, changes of registration under the N.H.S. not being noted routinely. The postal questionnaire on which we depended for most of our information about the doctors and their practices was completed and returned by only three-quarters of them; the extent to which this majority could be taken as representative was uncertain, though some indirect evidence suggested that the referral habits of the non-responding group differed from those of the majority (see CHAPTER IX).

2. COMPLETENESS OF THE DATA

The psychiatric-referral data were incomplete insofar as we could not count referrals to services outside Croydon, or to specialists in private practice. Indirect evidence suggested that the proportion of such cases was small, since:

(i) the local educational, health and social-service agencies routinely sent all cases for child guidance assessment or treatment to the Croydon clinic;

(ii) the postal-questionnaire survey indicated that the local practitioners made their referrals mostly to the Croydon clinic;

(iii) a check of the records of Maudsley Hospital Children's Department, the largest teaching clinic in the area, showed that only a small number of Croydon children had attended in the survey period;

(iv) no child psychiatrist had worked mainly in private practice in or near Croydon during that period; private referrals could have been made in any numbers only to specialists practising some miles away.

On the evidence, children seen at the Croydon clinic were thought to account for 90 per cent of referrals from within the borough. Even so, a loss of 10 per cent of cases, if they differed in some important respects from the remainder, could create a bias which would not be detectable in the survey analysis. Such bias could be avoided only with the help of a case-register, or record-linkage system, which would monitor all referrals to specialist agencies. To date, no ecological analysis of the kind described here has been carried out on the basis of a local or regional record-linkage system.

The data on juvenile delinquency were not subject to this type of inaccuracy, since the records of the Croydon Children's Department and Probation Service comprised, in effect, a case-register of delinquency for the borough: the names of all Croydon children brought before juvenile courts were routinely notified to these local agencies.

3. SAMPLING PROCEDURES

The child guidance sample could be taken as representative, in that all children seen at the local clinic were included in the sample and hence no technique of probability-sampling was employed. The same point applies to the probation sample, which also included all eligible cases. The main delinquency sample, on practical grounds, had to be restricted to every second child brought before the courts during the relevant period; however, the risk of serious bias arising in a 1-in-2 sample of over 2,000 cases can be regarded as slight.

These considerations do not exclude the possibility that our samples were in some respects atypical as a result of the choice of survey period. While no clear time-trends were observed in the rates for these years, it is entirely possible that patterns of child guidance referral, of delinquency, or of court-disposal have changed since 1962–6 and are no longer represented by our data. Only a replication of the study, in whole or in part, could establish the point.

Sampling errors may have affected the general practitioner rates which were based on a 1-in-4 sample of Croydon schoolchildren. Here again, in view of the large sample size (over 11,000), the danger of any major bias must be considered small.

Another possible source of error was the use of a base–population derived from a 1-in-10 Census sample. Although such samples are accurate enough for social-survey research in general (Office of Population, Censuses & Surveys, 1966; Gray and Gee, 1972), the numbers involved in some of our own computations—notably the cluster analysis and multiple-regression analyses, both based on enumeration-districts (see CHAPTERS VII and VIII)—were at times so small as to affect the value of the data. From this viewpoint, a national or regional survey would appear desirable, although the associated problems of data-collection and data-analysis would be formidable.

The fact that our study was confined to a single metropolitan borough must give rise to some doubt as to how widely the findings can be extrapolated. A review of the demographic, vital, child-health, and educational statistics for Croydon (see CHAPTER III) suggested that the borough is in many ways typical of Outer London, and hence that its population resembles that of a huge number of suburban dwellers. Errors could certainly arise if the findings were applied to populations in quite different types of environment; for example, in rural areas or in centres of heavy industry.

Lack of information prevents any detailed comparison of the clientele and mode of operation of Croydon Child Guidance Clinic with those of other clinics or of the child guidance service as a whole. No single clinic can be seen as representative, because local levels of provision and professional staffing ratios vary so greatly. From the data summarized in CHAPTER I, it appears that the Croydon clinic was fairly typical as regards its staffing provision, mode of functioning, and facilities for assessment and treatment; but that it dealt with higher-than-average proportions of medical referrals and of pre-school children, while the ratio of neurotic disorders to conduct disorders among the clientele was unusually high. In so far as these features may have affected the survey findings, they could be expected to diminish rather than to increase any association between child guidance and delinquency rates, or between child guidance rates and socio-economic indices. In short, the probability of confirming our initial hypotheses could be deemed higher for services with high proportions of school and social-agency referrals than for the medically-orientated Croydon service.

IMPLICATIONS FOR FUTURE RESEARCH

Causal research in child psychiatry has tended to concentrate on intra-psychic and intra-familial factors. As Danziger (1971) has remarked, 'it is an ironical fact that preoccupation with family influences appears to be most intense in societies where the importance of such influences is in sharp decline'.

The potential importance of sociological and ecological studies is indicated by the neighbourhood analysis outlined in CHAPTER VII, which showed that, in one urban area, child guidance rates were linked with such environmental indices as population-density, type of housing, and social-class distribution of the inhabitants: associations not to be explained in terms simply of the accessibility of treatment services.

The literature of child psychiatry contains very few published results to compare with these findings. The Isle of Wight survey (Rutter et al., 1970) found no difference between the housing conditions of maladjusted children and those of normal controls: perhaps because housing standards for the island-population as a whole compared favourably with those in most parts of Great Britain. A subsequent comparison between the Isle of Wight and an Inner London Borough (Rutter et al., 1975) demonstrated that social indices, such as overcrowding and the proportion of schoolchildren receiving free meals, were related to maladjustment rates and helped to explain disparities in prevalence between the two child-populations. The findings were thus in broad agreement with our own.

When one turns to the extensive literature on delinquency in urban areas, numerous parallels can be found: a number have already been cited in CHAPTER II (see, inter alia, Morris, 1957; Bagley, 1965; Power et al., 1967; Wallis and Maliphant, 1967). The ecological patterns delineated by these studies corresponds roughly to that shown by surveys of adult mental disorder in cities, where again concentrations have been found in areas of high population-density and low socio-economic status (Faris and Dunham, 1939; Hare, 1955; Häfner and Reimann, 1970). One can postulate that, in some measure, the same environmental factors are implicated in each instance; though how far by propagating deviant forms of behaviour, how far by differential migration, and how far by influencing case-recognition and the probability of contact with official agencies, is still far from clear.

Future research in child psychiatry might profitably pay more regard to the wider social environment of the child; to the pressing need to develop what Apley (1964) has called 'an ecology of childhood'. Such a shift of emphasis could help to bring the sub-specialty closer, not only to the socio-logical study of delinquency, but to the mainstream of child-health research and practice, where the moulding influence of geographical, cultural, and socio-economic factors has been recognized at least since the nineteenth century. It should not imply any slackening of interest in the family group: the causes of maladjustment and of delinquency are unlikely to be found exclusively either in the nuclear family or in the larger community, but rather to exist in both as part of a continuing, dynamic interaction that could be fully demonstrated only with the help of inter-generation studies. Modern child psychiatry is open to criticism, not for devoting too much attention to the family and the home, but only for neglecting that 'variable and complex environment that permeates to the growing child through the family' (Apley, 1964).

In this context, the first priority must be to ascertain if the distribution of cases reported in this study reflected the prevalence of child psychiatric disorders, as distinct from demand for a treatment-service. This question can be resolved only by means of field-surveys; in particular, by comparison of total incidence- and prevalence-rates, as gauged by standardized case-finding methods, between areas with contrasting social features and child guidance rates. Such studies will demand larger resources than were available for the present survey; they are essential, however, if the existing services are to be correctly evaluated and a rational approach to prevention is to be planned. This viewpoint has recently won acceptance from the official body of British psychiatry:

There are many areas where research is required, but priority should be given to studies which help the identification of high-risk groups in the population, so that child health services can be mobilized to meet needs for prevention and treatment (Royal College of Psychiatrists, 1974).

A second priority will be to develop more sensitive measures of the child's environment. It must be stressed that the demographic and social indices which we employed were not chosen from a wide range as being specially appropriate for our purposes; on the contrary, they represented simply what was available from the Census tables. There is an outstanding need for new and better social indices, partly to permit more accurate discrimination between defined areas, partly so that the variables most closely linked to disease and social pathology may be identified, and others of smaller import discarded from future analyses.

The lack of adequate statistical indicators is a general problem of research in urban ecology. Carlestam (1971) has itemized the 'likely partial causes' of mental disturbance and behavioural disorder, conditioned by the urban environment, as follows:

Size, density and growth rate of the city. Size, grouping and location of work places, dwellings, recreational areas (fatiguing trips). Organization and rhythm of the city (stress of urban life). Control of slums and segregation tendencies. Control of congestion and queuing. Degree of functional segmentation of areas, extent of services and facilities provided in residential areas. The individual's isolation and estrangement.

For no city are there statistical indicators adequate to translate these concepts into operational terms. Characteristics such as the grouping and location of dwellings, recreational facilities and services have obvious relevance to the problems of children's upbringing, as also have indices of *change* in the urban environment. Had it been feasible to do so, we should certainly have wanted to examine the effects of, for example, the relative proportions in each district of high-rise flats and of houses with gardens; the accessibility of parks, open spaces, and playgrounds; the numbers and distribution of youth-clubs, sports-clubs, and swimming-pools; the local pattern of church attendance; the stability of peer-relationships; the amount of contact with television, films, and other mass media; the density of traffic and the rate of traffic accidents. Only by a detailed, laborious screening of these and other possible factors will it be possible to identify and select those of heuristic value, and to discard the remainder from future analyses.

A third priority must be to refine the methods of statistical analysis. To begin with, the administrative areas and population units, for which statistical indices are available, may be too large and too heterogeneous to be satisfactory for ecological research. Ways must then be found of dividing them into smaller, more homogeneous entities, and if necessary of re-grouping them. The present investigation indicates one possible strategy for dealing with this problem; but there are others. The need for refinement also extends to statistical interpretation of the data. Hitherto, medical and social research workers have relied heavily on parametric statistics, despite the fact that the clinical and social variables under scrutiny are either of unknown distribution, or are known not to be normally distributed. It seems inevitable that non-parametric statistics will come to be employed more and more frequently in ecological research. Furthermore, there are special technical problems in the interpretation of areal data, which have received much attention from geographers, but have been largely ignored by medical and social investigators. Such are the problems of 'spatial auto-correlation' (Cliff and Ord, 1970), and of the need to weight values derived from areal units of varying size (Thomas and Anderson, 1965). Since the technical questions involved are beyond the competence of most medical and sociological workers, the need for close collaboration with geographers or survey statisticians must be recognized.

Doubtless in the future our attempts to measure the social milieu, and to analyse its effects on the individual, will seem as crude and clumsy as do the methods of seventeenth-century biology today. Yet economic pressures and common sense alike will dictate limits to the collection of social data for administrative purposes, and hence to the scope for purely ecological research.

For the testing of more sophisticated hypotheses, such as those implicit in Carlestam's list of 'likely partial causes', cited above, direct studies using comparisons with matched control-groups will be essential.

One research strategy with much to commend it is that of 'multi-level analysis', in which ecological correlations derived from aggregate data are linked with direct correlations derived from individual data (Welz, 1975). An example of the need for this kind of two-pronged assault is supplied by our data on socio-economic status. We wanted to know if the association with low socio-economic status suggested by our ecological findings reflected a characteristic of the individual children in our child guidance and delinquency samples. The evidence to hand suggested that it did not, but because the survey data on social class were inadequate, no firm conclusion could be reached. In more general terms, there is a need to establish whether the ecological correlates of child guidance referral and delinquency can be explained simply in terms of family characteristics; or whether the neighbourhood exercises an influence independently of the child's family and home environment. For this type of analysis, detailed information would be required about the nuclear-family group, as well as about the structure and characteristics of the local community.

A further topic for research is indicated by our findings in relation to the schools. Establishments of low status within the educational system were found to have high child-guidance and delinquency rates: whether this finding reflected a selective process or a greater exposure to risk for some children could not be decided on the evidence, though the inter-school variation was independent of neighbourhood effects. As in the study of Tower Hamlets (Power *et al.*, 1967), disparities between neighbouring schools were so large as to suggest that major factors must operate within the individual school.

The elucidation of this problem is too urgent for it to be neglected or set aside, either by the educational authorities or by the teaching profession. If it be established that the school exercises an independent influence on the risks of maladjustment and of delinquency, the nature of this influence must be explored by further research. Clegg and Megson (1968) have posed the problem succinctly:

How can a school make a bad child good? Why . . . do some schools which draw from a bad social area manage to steer clear of juvenile crime?

Acknowledging that the answers to their own questions are concerned with 'the somewhat indefinite and even mysterious qualities of tone and morale', these authors stressed the part played by the individual head teacher, and gave an illuminating account of the changes wrought in one school by the appointment of a new headmaster. During the next few years, the delinquency rate was markedly reduced, until '. . . a school which was certainly the most notorious in the County became the most respected'.

A comparison of schools in Manchester with low and high delinquency rates (Reade, 1971) showed that the head teachers in the two groups differed in their personalities and professional attitudes. Those working in the low-rate schools, who typically believed that much could be done to counteract an unfavourable home environment, had established contact with many of the parents and were aware both of the children's home backgrounds and of the parents' attitudes; they also appreciated the need for social support of problem families. In all these respects, they differed from their colleagues in the high-rate schools. While such observations by themselves cannot demonstrate causal relationships, they can serve as useful guidelines for antero-spective studies as and when these become feasible.

One relatively specific connection between delinquency and the school environment has been suggested by the Isle of Wight survey team (Rutter and Yule, 1970). Emphasizing the strong association between reading retardation and anti-social behaviour, they put forward the hypothesis that deviant conduct may arise as a maladaptive response to scholastic failure, and that 'the schools with the lowest rates of crime are the ones which are most successful in treating reading backwardness'. The testing of this hypothesis clearly merits high priority in future research.

In more general terms, the role of the school in determining children's behavioural patterns has major implications for preventive psychiatry as well as for the educational system. This is especially true if, in the present state of our society, the prospects for improving bad schools are better than those for improving bad neighbourhoods (Scott, 1974).

CHILD PSYCHIATRIC SERVICES: A POSTSCRIPT

Discussion of the scope for applied research leads on naturally to a consideration of the planning of psychiatric and related services for children. It must be said at once that research-findings, whether from the present investigation or from other published work, cannot yet provide a rational basis for such planning: the gaps in established knowledge are too wide. At the beginning of this project, we accepted, as a general principle governing health-care research, the importance of distinguishing clearly between *need*, *demand*, and *utilization*, as these concepts apply to defined populations. Our findings represent a measure of service-utilization and, less directly, of demand, since the number of children investigated or treated at the Child Guidance Clinic was virtually equal to the number who were referred there.[1] Of the need for specialist care—the only firm, scientific basis for service-planning—they can give no estimate. Nor can they tell us if observed variations in the level of demand, as between neighbourhoods and schools, corresponded to variations in the level of need; though the correlations with

[1] This is not to say that the *potential* demand was not greater than the number of referrals might suggest; nor, indeed, that the *actual* demand might not have been greatly increased by some such change in service-provision as, for example, a reduction of waiting-times.

delinquency and probation rates suggested that this was indeed the case. It may be added that, while the indications for specialist referral and treatment remain so ill-defined, not even accurate prevalence and incidence data could answer these questions.

Under the circumstances, no firm conclusions can be drawn as to the correct deployment of child guidance facilities. Nevertheless, it would be unrealistic to discuss prospects and priorities in applied research without reference to the possible implications for services or, for that matter, without some awareness that the existing services are subject to criticism and that the need for change is being widely canvassed.

The child guidance movement, not for the first time, is under attack. Much of the dissatisfaction can be attributed to those longstanding inter-professional rivalries and tensions to which child-guidance services, by reason of their tripartite structure, have always been prone. Some of the more forceful criticism, however, has come from outside observers who have become convinced that child guidance as a movement has 'gradually lost the momentum of its preventive approach and, at least until quite recently, also lost its major commitment to a community perspective' (Sabshin, 1966). In Great Britain, this view has been reinforced by a growing belief that the hitherto-fragmented child health services must somehow be integrated into an effectively-working whole (Chamberlain, 1972).

The case for a radical change in the structure and organization of children's services has been cogently summarized by Rehin (1972), who has argued that the traditional child guidance centre, with its inter-disciplinary team, actually tends to perpetuate deficiencies in the services provided by general practitioners, teachers, school psychologists, and social workers. The very existence of such a facility, in his opinion, encourages these primary care givers to abdicate responsibility. If child guidance were to be more preventively orientated, and to collaborate more effectively with doctors, teachers, and welfare workers, the situation could be transformed.

The remedy proposed by Rehin is nothing short of the abolition of child-guidance services as at present constituted, together with the abandonment of such concepts as 'child guidance', 'child psychiatry', and 'psychiatric social work'. Clinic personnel should be dispersed to their respective departments: health, educational, and social-service. Child psychiatrists should become family psychiatrists, working more closely with obstetricians and paediatricians, and taking clinical responsibility for the care of disturbed families; they should, for instance, share with paediatricians the care of mentally retarded children, whether in hospital or in the community. The family psychiatrist should act as advocate, consultant, and counsellor in community health services, since 'only by unifying psychiatry and concentrating attention on the family and its members throughout the life-cycle will psychiatry learn to be preventive'.

Similarly, educational psychologists should have increased scope for counselling, preventive work, and advocacy in the schools. Psychiatric social workers should move back into the local social-service departments, some possibly to be seconded to hospital or community medical services in a reorganized National Health Service:

The resolution of the child guidance predicament . . . would reduce myth, ambiguity and contradiction; there would emerge a stronger, more preventive psychiatry, a concentrated and more school- and community-involved educational psychology, and a more autonomous and confident family social service (Rehin, 1972).

Such a sweeping set of proposals has undoubted appeal. It is clearly desirable that the responsibilities of family doctors, school-teachers, and social workers for the welfare of the family and the emotional health of the child should be emphasized, and that these responsibilities should be taken into account during professional training. There is, however, a danger of seeking facile solutions to problems that are intrinsically difficult and complex. Rehin's critique, which is unsupported by factual data, has at times—as in the passage quoted above—an inspirational ring that fails to carry conviction. It may be that in recent years we have seen too many changes in our health and social services fail to bring about the promised improvements. In the light of this experience, any suggestions that a new broom should be taken to the child guidance services will be received with mixed feelings.

There can be little doubt that changes are being contemplated. In 1973, the Departments of Education and of Health published a joint memorandum on the future of child guidance, based on three major premises:

. . . that there are many more children with behaviour, emotional or learning difficulties than was previously assumed; secondly, that a high proportion of these difficulties arise at pre-school age; and thirdly, that there are frequently related family problems which also need to be tackled at the same time (Depts. of Education and Health, 1973).

Because of the growing demand for children's services and the probability that resources will continue to be scarce, the memorandum urged a fresh look at child guidance, to find new ways of bringing help to large numbers of children and their families. More flexible patterns of providing assistance should be developed, so as to ensure that professional skills are used to the best advantage. Future child guidance services should enjoy a larger consultative and preventive function; they should be concerned not only with specialist assessment and treatment but also with counselling of parents, general practitioners, health visitors, social workers, and the staff of residential homes. By these means, many problems could be assessed and dealt with at an earlier stage than is permitted by formal case referral. Instead of a highly specialized service operating within a narrow framework, a network of services, each with its own resources and functions, could be developed so as to facilitate joint action in various combinations. Each service would work independently but would have working arrangements for child guidance with other services in the network. To foster this approach, each service would nominate staff-members to take part in joint activities, on either a sessional or an occasional basis.

The official memorandum thus adopts, or coincides with, some of the views expressed by Rehin, though without going so far as to propose the abolition of child psychiatry or dismantling of the tripartite team.

Commenting on these proposals, the Royal College of Psychiatrists (1974a) argued more positively for retention of the specialist team, on the grounds that effective working-teams are built up with difficulty and should not be arbitrarily disrupted. Predictably, the Royal College memorandum couched the issue in medical terms: recommending, for example, that all child guidance clinics, whatever their provenance, should in future become the responsibility of health authorities. It criticized sharply the official distinction between child psychiatry as a hospital-based specialty and child guidance as a community service, arguing that to perpetuate a distinction based largely on geographical site or administrative convenience would be divisive and retrograde, and could lead to a two-tier service.

According to this viewpoint, child guidance clinics and child psychiatry units in hospitals deal for the most part with similar problems and should be seen as complementary. At present many child guidance clinics are isolated from hospital practice and hence from modern developments in paediatrics and child health practice. Conversely, hospital units tend to concentrate on in-patient care and intramural contacts, at the expense of community services. Unnecessary duplication of work may result, while the flow of information and the effective use of common resources are impeded.

To overcome such defects, the Royal College urged that all psychiatrists working with children and adolescents should be employed in the National Health Service, but should hold both hospital and community appointments, so as to bring the two arms of the service together. A second memorandum expressed concern lest the notion of a service based on the district general hospital should hamper development. With the expected reduction in hospital building programmes, the creation of the new units could be postponed indefinitely; whereas they could be sited outside the hospitals just as effectively and much more cheaply (Royal College of Psychiatrists, 1974b).

Thus the debate continues, with weighty arguments conflicting and no agreement in sight. Our research findings, though not directly concerned with service problems, have some relevance. They suggest that child guidance clinics are dealing to a large extent with disorders caused or conditioned by the social environment; that whatever new pattern of services evolves should be strongly orientated towards the community, and that in service-planning some regard should be paid to the distribution of disorders in the child population. It would, however, be naïve to suppose that traditional-type clinics, situated in areas of high social need, would provide a satisfactory solution. A policy of selective referral and treatment could easily perpetuate the *status quo ante*, and ensure that the great majority of disturbed children—in particular, those with early symptoms—would continue to lack skilled attention. The basic question of secondary preventive care would remain; namely, how to achieve and maintain effective collaboration between the specialist team and those primary care-givers who are in direct contact with children at risk.

In the absence of evaluative research, no firm answer can be given to this question. Some tentative suggestions can be derived from an appraisal of the existing services and, in particular, of the handful of experiments, scattered and unco-ordinated, which are being conducted up and down the country. Two areas of development are of special interest in connection with our survey findings: the school and general medical practice.

1. DEVELOPMENT IN THE EDUCATIONAL SERVICES

There can be no doubt that the school system represents one of the major 'pick-up points' for child psychiatric disorders. Its significance in this respect is all the greater because many parents of delinquent, aggressive, or socially-disturbed children either fail to recognize the disturbance or refuse to accept that special care is necessary (Rutter *et al.*, 1970). A high proportion of parents whose children have been referred fail to co-operate with the child guidance clinic (Cartwright, 1972). The school may, therefore, in many instances offer a more promising therapeutic milieu than the clinic.

Some educational authorities have already built up active treatment-services within the school system. The number of sessions worked by child psychiatrists for the Inner London Education Authority (I.L.E.A.) surpasses 1,100 each year in the day-schools for maladjusted children and 1,300 in the boarding-schools (Tait, 1972). Yet there is a growing awareness that even this level of provision is wholly inadequate, and that a further expansion of special-school programmes is not the answer. In the words of Whitmore (1974):

For twenty years we have worked with the programme announced by the Underwood Committee: an attack on the problems of maladjustment by the establishment of child guidance services and the special schools ... let us stop planning and expanding services on the ostrich-like principle that generic labels attached to groups of children identify the needs of each child and the professional service responsible for meeting them ... The attack on the problems of maladjustment through inco-ordinated programmes of more special schools, more community homes and more child guidance clinics needs now to be called off.

If the dimensions of the problem are such that no foreseeable expansion of special schools can suffice, the only hope must reside in the management of most disturbed children within the ordinary schools: a policy which will require much closer liaison between schools and specialist teams, as well as improved facilities within the schools themselves.

One form of liaison is the provision of counselling services to the schools by child guidance teams, with regular case-conferences in which teachers can participate (Skynner, 1974; Harris and O'Shaughnessy, 1967). As yet, only a minority of child guidance services have plans to develop counselling services of this kind (Parfit, 1974).

A second possible growth-point is the renewed interest in behaviour problems being shown by educational psychologists, some of whom are clearly determined to extend their activities into the fields of counselling and of therapy (Caspari and Osborne, 1971; Parfit, 1974). The supply of educational psychologists remains, however, well below the target of one to 10,000 schoolchildren set by the Summerfield Report (Dept. of Education, 1968), so that their scope for therapeutic activity must remain limited.

Finally, there are increasing opportunities for teachers to acquire special skills in counselling work and to apply these within their own schools. A number of university courses designed to train experienced teachers as school counsellors have been set up in the past ten years and appear to be flourishing. A one-year diploma course in the education of maladjusted children, which includes practical experience in a child guidance clinic, is given by the Institute of Education of London University. The potential scope and value of counselling in the schools emerges from the account by one graduate teacher of her five years' experience of running such a service in a girls' secondary school (Jones, 1970).

Each of these shoots may flourish, though it is still too soon to judge their prospects. Each will grow only if the soil is healthy; and here the general level of school provision will be crucial. Seriously disturbed children can be dealt with only in small classes; their management will require high teacher-pupil ratios and extra classrooms, to say nothing of school counsellors or social workers who can visit the homes and maintain regular contacts with the parents. These questions cannot be divorced from the central economic issue:

Concern about the best way of using specialist resources should not divert attention from the fact that the overwhelming need is for more money to be spent on the ordinary educational needs of schools in depressed areas (Lancet, 1974).

While changes in the educational system afford the best hope for coping with maladjustment among schoolchildren, much will depend on intervention in the pre-school years. Here, a central role must be played, especially in socially-disorganized areas, by nursery schools and play-groups. But even if the supply of buildings and of trained staff were adequate, attendance at such centres would never be general; many of the children in greatest need would remain unidentified. A complementary approach is required, and it may be to hand in the primary medical-care team.

2. DEVELOPMENT OF THE PRIMARY HEALTH TEAM

One of the more significant changes in medical care, during recent years, has been the rapid growth of primary care teams based on general practice.

Over the past two decades, the number of single-handed practitioners in Great Britain has declined steadily, with a corresponding increase in group practice. This change has been accompanied by a large-scale redeployment of district nurses and health visitors; so that, for example, 70 per cent of the latter were attached in general practice by 1973 (Clark, 1974). Over the same period, the number of local authority health centres, in which general practitioners, nurses, and social workers can form effective teams, has increased sharply: by 1972, some 400 had opened or were under construction (Royal College of General Practitioners, 1973).

This spread of teamwork has special significance for psychiatric services. A recent W.H.O. report concluded, on the basis of evidence from European countries, that 'the primary care team is the keystone of community psychiatry' (W.H.O., 1973). If this assertion be correct, co-operation with such teams must be a matter of importance for all mental health professionals (Brook and Cooper, 1975).

Liaison between primary care and child guidance teams is a case in point. The general practitioner is often consulted about children showing behavioural or developmental abnormality. Where once he could offer no facilities other than specialist referral for the most severe or intractable cases, now increasingly he can call on other team-members to assess the family situation and to support the parents. The health visitor pays routine visits to families with young children, and is nowadays trained to recognize emotional disorders. Social workers attached in general practice also encounter a wide range of psycho-social problems, many at an earlier stage than those coming to social service departments. Direct links with the child guidance team would extend and improve the services these primary care-givers can provide.

Neither of the possible lines of development outlined here offers any assurance of rapid, substantial improvement in the care of maladjusted children. Experimental schemes have yet to be evaluated, and their wider applicability to be gauged. Those which show promise must be viewed against the sombre background of contemporary urban life. Schools in many of our big cities are suffering from acute staff shortages, as well as from chronically inadequate buildings and equipment. Educationists are increasingly concerned, less with achieving higher standards than with preventing a major breakdown of the system. Metropolitan general practice presents an almost-equally discouraging spectacle. In one London Borough (not Croydon), a survey found predominantly

... ageing, single-handed doctors, many of them trained in central European or Mediterranean countries, working in isolation from inadequate premises and by-passed by many of the innovations in the delivery of medical care. Many of the features of practice in the Borough appeared characteristic of metropolitan general practice (Sidel, Jefferys, and Mansfield, 1972).

It must also be borne in mind that, whatever their working conditions, teachers and medical practitioners alike are resistant to change in their professional habits and attitudes. All in all, few people conversant with the state of our schools, or familiar with general practice, would feel sanguine about these agencies taking over from specialist services the care of most severely-disturbed children.

The importance of 'primary care' in this field may be, therefore, less as an alternative to specialist care than as a supplement: as a means whereby skilled help can be extended to a greatly-increased clientele and at the same time can become more preventively orientated. Collaboration with primary care-givers offers the child guidance team a chance to build up both screening and support systems in the community, and in doing so to take the maximum advantage of existing resources under the Welfare State. Only in this way can we begin to face what Eisenberg (1973) has called 'the greatest unmet challenge in child psychiatry and paediatrics': the failure of children to attain their full genetic potential as a result of combined biological and social insult.

Provided advance into the preventive field can be conducted with hard-headed realism, and its results carefully monitored and assessed by means of evaluative research, there are no good grounds to fear that the child guidance service will be fragmented, or that its therapeutic skills will be dissipated. On the contrary, there is every reason to hope that they will be greatly reinforced.

APPENDIX A
Research Instruments

APPENDIX A1

Item Sheet used in Compiling Child Guidance Sample

SER. NO.

1	2	3	4

SURNAME   OTHER NAMES   SEX   AGE (at first
                                      (1) Male   attendance)
                                      (2) Female

5		6	7

ADDRESS   DISTRICT
                                       REF.

8

SCHOOL   SCHOOL
                                       REF.

9	10

OCCUPATION   OCCUP.
OF FATHER   CLASS

11

G.P.   ADDRESS   G.P. REF.

12	13	14

REFERRING (1) G.P.   (5) Parents   YEAR OF
AGENCY   (2) School Health (6) Infant Welfare Clinics INDEX
          (3) Teacher   (7) Hospital Physician   REFERRAL
          (4) Children's Dept. (8) Other

15		16

DIAGNOSTIC (1) Organic   (5) Conduct disorder
CATEGORY   (2) Mental subnormality (6) Mixed Neurosis/Conduct disorder
           (3) Psychosis   (7) Other
           (4) Neurosis

                            SPECIFY:

17

APPENDIX A2

Item Sheet used in Compiling Total Delinquency Sample

| NAME: | Serial No. | 1,2,3,4 | | | | |

Remanded in custody:	YES NO	Sex	5			
		No. of offences: { Before Survey Period	6		
		During Survey Period	7		

FIRST OFFENCE

	Age	8,9
ADDRESS:		10,11
	Court	12
	Offence	13
	Court action	14
SCHOOL: (& type)		15,16,17

SECOND OFFENCE

	Age	18,19
ADDRESS:		20,21
	Court	22
	Offence	23
	Court action	24
SCHOOL: (& type)		25,26,27

THIRD OFFENCE

	Age	28,29
ADDRESS:		30,31
	Court	32
	Offence	33
	Court action	34
SCHOOL: (& type)		35,36,37

NAME :

FOURTH OFFENCE

Age	38,39	
	40,41	
Court	42	
Offence	43	
Court action	44	

ADDRESS :

SCHOOL : (& type)   45,46,47

FIFTH OFFENCE

Age	48,49	
	50,51	
Court	52	
Offence	53	
Court action	54	

ADDRESS :

SCHOOL : (& type)   55,56,57

SIXTH OFFENCE

Age	58,59	
	60,61	
Court	62	
Offence	63	
Court action	64	

ADDRESS :

SCHOOL : (& type)   65,66,67

No. of further
offences   68

APPENDIX A3

Postal Questionnaire sent to 140 Croydon General Practitioners

QUESTIONNAIRE ON CHILD PSYCHIATRY IN GENERAL PRACTICE

This questionnaire contains three sections, which are listed below. Most of the questions can be answered by a tick or a cross, and each section can be completed quite quickly. It is necessary in evaluating the results that all the questions be answered.

It goes without saying that there are no right or wrong answers, and that what we are interested in is your personal opinion. Wherever you find statements ambiguous, or the alternatives listed are inadequate, please add any comments you think necessary.

Part I—Case Histories
Part II—Use of Child Psychiatric Services
Part III—Your Practice and Yourself

PART I—CASE HISTORIES

In this section you will find eight case-vignettes. Beneath each is listed a number of alternative ways of assessing and dealing with the case. The alternatives represent assessments made *at the initial consultation*.

Please indicate for each case the *one* alternative which you think would correspond to your own assessment. If you find it necessary to ring more than one alternative for any case, please indicate which you consider to be of greatest single importance.

A. An 8-year-old boy is brought to you by his mother because, since her husband deserted her two years ago, the boy has been lying, stealing, fighting with other children, and behaving spitefully towards his brothers and sisters. The mother is very anxious and seems unable to control the child.

1. I should not regard this as a medical problem.

2. In the first instance I should treat expectantly, e.g. by prescribing a sedative or other medication.

3. I should advise the mother on methods of discipline, and try to make the boy understand that he must improve his behaviour.

4. I should try to enlist the help of the Children's Department or other social agency. (*Please specify.*)

5. I should refer the boy to a paediatrician.

6. I should spend some time with the boy and his mother, trying to bring out the underlying emotional difficulties; if indicated, I should continue with psychotherapy for the child and/or parent.

7. I should refer the boy to a Child Guidance Clinic.

COMMENTS

B. A 6-year-old boy is brought to you by his mother because he has recently become terrified of dogs. On one occasion he was nearly run over in the street when he ran blindly away from a dog. He appears to be a sturdy, healthy boy in other respects.

1. I should not regard this as a medical problem.

2. In the first instance I should treat expectantly, e.g. by prescribing a sedative or other medication.

3. I should regard this as a case for firm reassurance and positive advice. (I should probably give the boy and his mother some explanation and instruction on a simple level, and assure them that with patience all would be well.)

4. I should refer the boy to a paediatrician.

5. I should spend some time with the boy and his parent, trying to bring out the underlying emotional difficulties; if indicated, I should continue with psychotherapy for the child and/or parent.

6. I should refer the boy to a Child Guidance Clinic.

COMMENTS

C. A 3-year-old girl is brought to you by her parents who say that she seems to live in a world of her own. She spends all her time playing on her own, but becomes very tense and frightened at times for no clear reason. When seen in the surgery, the girl completely ignores you.

    1. I should not regard this as a medical problem.
    2. In the first instance I should treat expectantly, e.g. by prescribing medication.
    3. I should regard this as a case for reassurance and positive advice (e.g. I should advise the parents to encourage the child to play with other children, or I should recommend a play group).
    4. I should refer the child to a paediatrician.
    5. I should spend some time with the parents and child, trying to bring out the underlying emotional difficulties. If indicated, I should continue with psychotherapy for the child and/or parents.
    6. I should refer the girl to a Child Guidance Clinic.

COMMENTS

D. An 11-year-old boy is brought to you by his parents with a letter from his school-teacher saying that he is making poor progress at school, although he is in a class of younger boys. The teacher adds that he seems to be slow in all his responses, but quite well behaved. Physical examination is negative.

    1. I should not regard this as a medical problem.
    2. I should advise the parents to accept the child's limitations, and to avoid showing excessive concern.
    3. I should advise the parents to seek extra tuition via the school or privately.
    4. I should refer the boy to a paediatrician.
    5. I should spend some time with the boy and his parents, trying to bring out the underlying emotional difficulties; if indicated, I should continue with psychotherapy for the child and/or parents.
    6. I should refer the boy to a Child Guidance Clinic.

COMMENTS

E. The parents of a 13-year-old boy ask for your help because recently they found him in his room wearing his mother's underwear. In other respects the parents think of him as a normal boy.

1. I should not regard this as a medical problem.

2. In the first instance I should treat expectantly, e.g. by prescribing medication.

3. I should regard this as a case for firm reassurance and positive advice (e.g. I should probably tell the parents that many adolescent boys pass through a similar phase and grow out of it, and that their son would almost certainly do likewise).

4. I should refer the boy to a paediatrician.

5. I should spend some time with the boy and his parents, trying to bring out the underlying emotional difficulties; if indicated, I should continue with psychotherapy for the boy and/or parents.

6. I should refer the boy to a Child Guidance Clinic.

COMMENTS

F. A 12-year-old girl with a disturbed home background has recently had many absences from school because of complaints of headache, abdominal pain, and nausea. She is said to be free from these symptoms at weekends. Physical examination reveals no abnormality.

1. I should not regard this as a medical problem.

2. In the first instance I should treat expectantly, e.g. by prescribing medication.

3. I should regard this as a case for firm reassurance and positive advice (e.g. I should counsel the mother on how she should handle the problem; in addition I might get in touch with the School Head Mistress to ensure proper management of the girl at school).

4. I should refer the girl to a paediatrician.

5. I should spend some time with the girl and her parents, trying to bring out the underlying emotional difficulties; if indicated, I should continue with psychotherapy for the girl and/or parents.

6. I should refer the girl to a Child Guidance Clinic.

COMMENTS

G. A boy of 8 has started wetting the bed every night, having previously been dry. Physical examination is negative and the urine is normal. He is said to be timid and solitary.

1. I should not regard this as a medical problem.
2. In the first instance I should treat expectantly, e.g. by prescribing medication.
3. I should regard this as a case for firm reassurance and positive advice (e.g. that many children pass through a similar phase, and that he will almost certainly grow out of it).
4. I should refer the boy to a paediatrician.
5. I should spend some time with the boy and his parents, trying to bring out the underlying emotional difficulties; if indicated, I should continue with psychotherapy for the child and/or parents.
6. I should refer the boy to a Child Guidance Clinic.

COMMENTS

H. A 14-year-old adopted girl is brought to you by her adoptive parents because for the past twelve months she has been rebellious and disobedient. She has been absconding from home and boasting to her friends of promiscuity.

1. I should not regard this as a medical problem.
2. In the first instance I should treat expectantly, e.g. by prescribing medication.
3. I should refer the child to the Probation Service, or other social agency. (Please specify.)
4. I should advise the parents on methods of discipline, and try to make the girl understand that she must improve her behaviour.
5. I should refer the girl to a paediatrician.
6. I should spend some time with the girl and her parents, trying to bring out the underlying emotional difficulties; if indicated, I should continue with psychotherapy for the child and/or parents.
7. I should refer the girl to a Child Guidance Clinic.

COMMENTS

PART II—USE OF CHILD PSYCHIATRIC SERVICES

Would you please indicate in the Table below the Child Guidance Clinics to which you have referred children in the last five years, approximately.

	Always	Usually	Occasionally
Croydon Child Guidance Clinic			
Brixton Child Guidance Unit			
Mitcham Child Guidance Clinic			
Sutton Child Guidance Clinic			
The Belgrave Hospital Child Guidance Clinic			
Bromley Hospital Psychiatric Department			
Children's Hospital, Sydenham Road			
Farnborough Hospital			
Carshalton, Fountain, and Queen Mary's Hospital Group Clinic			
Chipstead Child Guidance Clinic			
Redhill Child Psychiatry Clinic or Redhill Child Guidance Clinic			
Maudsley Hospital, Children's and Adolescents' Department			
London Undergraduate Teaching Hospital, e.g., Westminster Guy's St. Thomas' St. George's			
Hospital for Sick Children, Gt. Ormond Street, Dept. of Psychological Medicine			
Tavistock Clinic			
Other (specify)			
Private			

This page has been left blank so that you can make any comments you think relevant about the treatment and management of disturbed children and child psychiatric services under the N.H.S.

PART III—YOUR PRACTICE AND YOURSELF

The information requested below would be of great help in evaluating the questionnaire, and we should be greatly obliged to you for answering the questions. All information given will be treated as *strictly confidential*.

1. Please state your age.

2. Please state your medical qualifications and the years in which they were obtained.

3. What was your Medical School and Teaching Hospital?

4. Have you had any special training

    (a) in paediatrics   YES   NO
    (b) in psychiatry (adult or child)   YES   NO

    IF YES please give details

5. Please state how long you have been in practice continuously in Croydon:

Under 3 years   ....

3 to 6 years   ....

6 years & over   ....

6. Please indicate, by means of ticks in the appropriate squares, the approximate size of *your own* N.H.S. list *now* and, if applicable, in 1962.

No. of Patients	Now	1962
less than 1,500		
1,500–2,000		
2,000–2,500		
2,500–3,000		
Over 3,000		

7. Are you single handed   ....

   or in partnership?   ....

   If the latter, please state:

   (a) how many partners you have   ....
   (b) the approximate size of the *total practice*
       list at present   ....

APPENDIX B

Statistical Procedures

APPENDIX B1

Computation of Rates

1.1 *Electoral Ward rates for Child Guidance referral: method used in weighting for changes in the Borough Boundary*

Five new electoral wards were added to the Borough of Croydon on 1 April 1965, in the fourth year of the five-year survey period.

The uncorrected numbers of referrals for these five wards during the quinquennium were:

Ward	62	63	64	65	66
Sanderstead North	9	10	9	5	6
Purley	—	3	2	6	10
Coulsdon East	—	—	—	5	7
Sanderstead & Selsdon	5	4	9	12	11
Woodcote & Coulsdon West	1	—	1	5	7

In calculating child guidance referral rates for these wards, the following weightings were applied:

Sanderstead North: Before 1965, three of the seven polling districts were in Croydon. From inspection of the figures it was assumed that there had been no change in the ward referral policy during the five years, and no weighting was applied.

Purley: Before 1965, one of the six polling districts was in Croydon. In the two years 1965 and 1966 there were six and ten referrals. The figure used for the five year period was $\frac{6 + 10}{2} \times 5 = 40$.

The three remaining wards: These were wholly outside Croydon before 1965. In each case the figure used was the sum of the referrals for the two years 1965 and 1966, multiplied by 5/2:

Coulsdon East:	$(5 + 7) \times 5/2 = 30$
Sanderstead & Selsdon:	$(12 + 11) \times 5/2 = 57.5$
Woodcote & Coulsdon West:	$(5 + 7) \times 5/2 = 30.$

1.2 *Weighting of School Rates for changes in the Borough Boundary*

Twenty-six schools were situated in the five Electoral Wards added to the Borough of Croydon in 1965. No children attending three of these schools had been referred in the survey period. Children from a further seven schools had been referred throughout the period; it was therefore assumed that the boundary changes had not affected these schools, and hence no weightings were applied. Children attending the remaining sixteen schools had been referred only in the last two years of the survey period. The referrals from these schools were accordingly weighted by a factor of 5/2. The effects of this weighting procedure are shown in the Table over:

	NO. OF CHILD GUIDANCE REFERRALS IN SURVEY PERIOD	
	Raw No.	*Weighted No.*
Primary Schools	469	490
Secondary Selective	52	56·5
Secondary Non-selective	205	223
	726	769·5

APPENDIX B2

Cluster Analysis of Enumeration Districts

2.1 Technique of cluster analysis

Cluster analysis is a method of constructing groups or clusters of individual units such that the members within any one cluster are similar to each other in respect of certain defined characteristics. The purpose of the analysis is to divide a hetero-geneous set of data into homogeneous groups, in order to simplify description, to suggest a scheme for classification, or to test a hypothesis.

Several techniques of cluster analysis have been described (Everitt, 1972). Most operate on a matrix of between individual similarity coefficients, similarity being assessed by such measures as correlation coefficients and Euclidean distance. They then attempt to maximize some criterion of cluster homogeneity such as between cluster to within cluster variance.

The method has a wide variety of applications. In the medical field it has been used as a way of deriving syndromes and, in recent years, of classifying psychiatric illness (Pilowsky et al., 1969; Paykel, 1971). Patients are rated on a variety of clinical items and the item-scores for individual patients are then submitted to cluster analysis, which groups those patients having similar profiles. In the field of epidemiology, cluster analysis may be employed to amalgamate small population units, defined in terms of demographic and social variables, so as to obtain larger, relatively homogeneous groups. Because the clusters are homogeneous, they provide a sensitive method of examining inter-relationships between the variables used to define the cluster and any dependent variable which may be under scrutiny.

Two technical problems of this type of procedure require some mention: the first concerns the question of standardization of the data; the second the time taken on the computer. According to Fleiss and Zubin (1969), standardization to give zero means and unit variance can lead to weakening of the inter-group differences on those variables which are the best discriminators. The amount of computer-time required by most cluster analysis techniques can be a practical difficulty, par-ticularly since it increases greatly with increase in the number of variables.

Both problems can be overcome by first performing a principal components analysis; if a satisfactory solution is obtained, the first few principal component scores for each individual can then be used as the input for the clustering technique. This method was adopted in the present study.

A further point concerns the number of clusters required. Some programmes start with one group and run on until computer time expires or a defined criterion is fulfilled. The criteria used to determine the optimum number of clusters are as follows:

(a) The average within-group density (A.W.G.D.) should be maximized. The A.W.G.D. is given by the number of points falling within a cube of specified dimensions, centred at a mean vector;

(b) The within-group variation divided by between-group variation should be minimized.

In some methods the starting-point is to choose two mean vectors which are as far apart as possible. Observations are allocated to the mean vector to which they are nearest, those which are very deviant being excluded as *outliers*. As observations are added to a group, the mean vector is adjusted; this process is continued until all individuals have been assigned. The process is then repeated, starting with the final two mean vectors, the observations being re-introduced at random and re-allocated until a new solution is reached. This process is repeated until a stable solution for the mean vectors is reached. The A.W.G.D. is calculated for every solution, and the optimum cluster solution is that which gives a maximum A.W.G.D.

If a solution is required for more than two clusters, the procedure starts with x points such that the total distance between them is at a maximum.

In the present study, the 1966 10 per cent sample census was used to obtain estimates of the number of persons aged under 16 resident within each enumeration district of the study area. These constituted the populations at risk upon which referral rates to child guidance were to be calculated. Both the populations at risk within each enumeration district and the number likely to be referred from such a unit were very small, so that to obtain reliable estimates of referral rate it was necessary to combine sets of enumeration districts, thus forming larger units of the population. As the association between the socio-demographic characteristics of an area and the referral rate which it produced were to be examined, it was desirable that the enumeration districts making up each area should have similar socio-demographic characteristics. The socio-demographic profile of each enumeration district was calculated and this formed the basic input for the cluster analysis. The method of cluster analysis was then employed to form clusters of enumeration districts, the districts within any given cluster being alike in respect of their socio-demographic indices. The socio-demographic profile of each cluster was derived from the profiles of its constituent enumeration districts.

2.2 *Composition of the Clusters*

Of the total of 453 enumeration districts, fourteen were discarded from the cluster analysis because they were residential institutions, and ten because they were non-residential areas. Only eleven of the 1,061 child guidance referrals were lost as a result of these omissions.

Forty-eight districts with very small populations were not entered individually in the analysis, but were merged, seventeen being amalgamated to form seven larger units and thirty-one being added to larger districts. The criteria for merging were as follows: (i) geographically contiguous wherever possible; (ii) matched in proportions of Social Classes IV and V within 10 percentage points; (iii) matched on proportion of owner-occupiers within 20 percentage points.

Thus, the total number of individual units included in the analysis was reduced from 453 to 388. These 388 enumeration districts were grouped into clusters as follows:

7 Clusters

Cluster No.	No. of Enumeration Districts
1	34
2	130
3	39
4	16
5	31
6	107
7	31
	388

22 Clusters

Thirteen districts were excluded as 'outliers' during the computer analysis. The remaining 375 were grouped initially into twenty-four clusters, but, since two of these each contained only three districts, it was decided to omit them. The total number of districts in the remaining twenty-two clusters was therefore 369, grouped as follows:

Cluster No.	No. of Enumeration Districts
01	34
02	7
03	7
04	15
05	6
06	10
07	13
08	9
09	21
10	29
11	34
12	8
13	37
14	6
15	41
16	31
17	10
18	5
19	10
20	8
21	22
22	6
	369

The number of clusters chosen as providing a suitable basis for the ecological analysis was determined by a compromise between the mathematically-best solution $\left(\text{i.e., the solution which minimized } \frac{\text{within-cluster variation}}{\text{between-cluster variation}}\right)$ and a solution providing the optimum size of cluster. The twenty-two-cluster solution was chosen as the basis for inter-correlations because it gave a larger sample-size; the seven-cluster solution for multivariate analyses in which each cluster would have to be sub-divided on the basis of school and G.P. categories, so preventing the units of analysis from becoming too small. Comparison of the inter-correlations obtained using the twenty-two- and seven-cluster solutions showed a high degree of similarity, so that their alternative use in this way was thought to be justifiable.

2.3 Socio-demographic Rank Order of seven Clusters of Enumeration Districts

This rank order was arrived at by first placing the seven clusters in rank order for each of the four socio-demographic indices which showed the higher correlations with child guidance rates; viz: (a) Proportion in Social Classes I and II; (b) Proportion in Social Classes IV and V; (c) Proportion of Owner-Occupiers and (d) Density of Population, (b) and (d) being inverted. The result was as follows:

Rank Order of Clusters

(a) S.C. I & II	(b) S.C. IV & V	(c) Propn. Owner-Occupiers	(d) Density of Population
2	2	2	2
3	3	5	6
6	6	6	3
5	5	3	1
7	4	7	5
4	1	1	7
1	7	4	4

By giving a score of 1 for first place, 2 for second place etc., the following total scores were arrived at:

$$\text{Cluster } 1: \quad 7 + 6 + 6 + 4 = 23$$
$$2: \quad 1 + 1 + 1 + 1 = 4$$
$$3: \quad 2 + 2 + 4 + 3 = 11$$
$$4: \quad 6 + 5 + 7 + 7 = 25$$
$$5: \quad 4 + 4 + 2 + 5 = 15$$
$$6: \quad 3 + 3 + 3 + 2 = 11$$
$$7: \quad 5 + 7 + 5 + 6 = 23$$

resulting in a rank order of:

Cluster 2
3 & 6
5
1 & 7
4

In order to rank the two tied pairs, use was made of the only other index which correlated significantly with the child guidance rate; namely, Proportion Renting from the Local Authority. As a result, the final ranking, in descending order of social conditions, was as follows:

Cluster 2
6
3
5
7
1
4

APPENDIX B3

Multiple Regression Analysis

3.1 *Regression of Child Guidance and Delinquency Rates on Socio-demographic Indices*

A series of scatter-diagrams, in which child guidance rates were plotted against individual socio-demographic indices for the twenty-two clusters, showed widely differing patterns of association (see FIGURES 18–21). Whereas, for example, the social-class composition and density of population produced relatively steep regression slopes, that for the proportion of owner-occupiers was almost horizontal.

Regression coefficients provided a mathematical expression of the findings, which indicated that the three factors most strongly predictive for the child guidance rate were, in descending order:

(i) density of population;
(ii) proportion of persons in Social Classes IV and V;
(iii) proportion of persons in Social Classes I and II.

Scatter diagrams in which delinquency rates were plotted against the socio-demographic indices of the twenty-two clusters also showed varying patterns of association (see FIGURES 22–25).

The values obtained by regressing the delinquency rate on the main socio-demographic variables differed somewhat from those for child guidance. Here, the best predictors proved to be, in descending order:

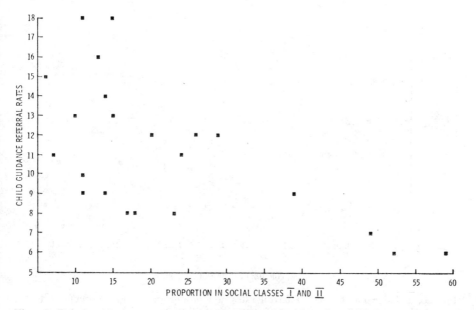

Fig. 18. Relationship between referral rates and social classes I and II for 22 clusters of enumeration districts

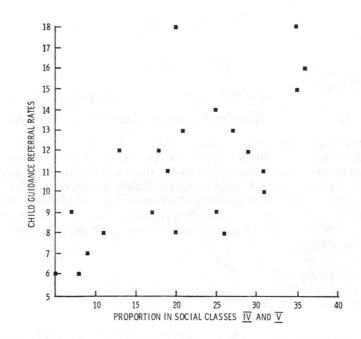

Fig. 19. Relationship between referral rates and social classes IV and V for 22 clusters of enumeration districts

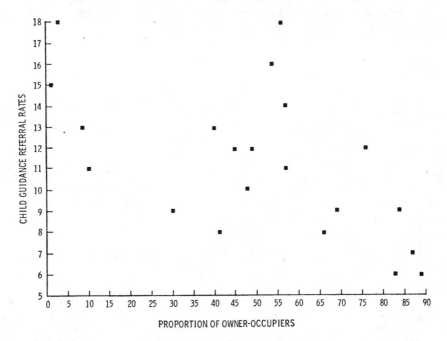

Fig. 20. Relationship between referrral rates and proportion of owner-occupiers for 22 clusters of enumeration districts

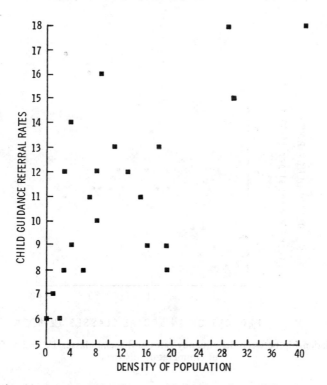

Fig. 21. Relationship between referral rates and density of population for 22 clusters of enumeration districts

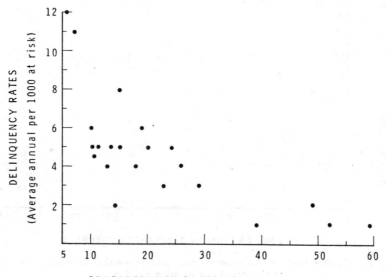

Fig. 22. Relationship between delinquency rates and social classes I and II for 22 clusters of enumeration districts

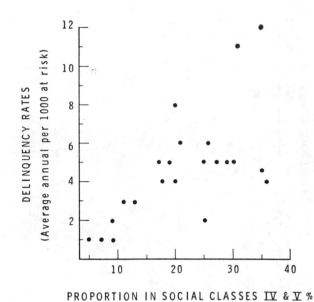

Fig. 23. Relationship between delinquency rates and social classes IV and V for 22 clusters of enumeration districts

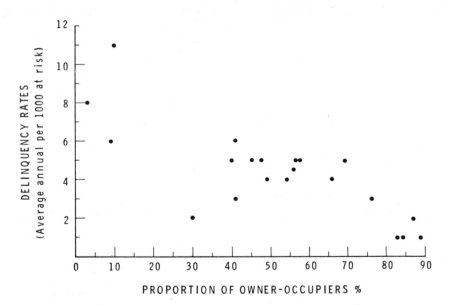

Fig. 24. Relationship between delinquency rates and proportion of owner-occupiers for 22 clusters of enumeration districts

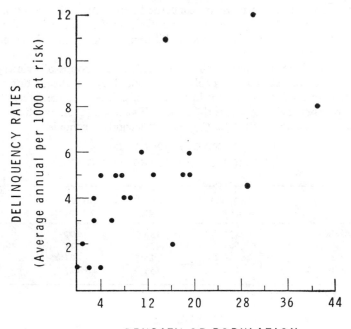

Fig. 25. Relationship between delinquency rates and density of population for 22 clusters of enumeration districts

(i) proportion of persons in owner-occupied dwellings;
(ii) Proportion living in dwellings rented from the local authority;
(iii) proportion in Social Classes I and II.

As a generalization, one can say that indices relating to the social-class composition of the population, the predominant type of housing and the density of population, have predictive value both for child guidance and for delinquency rate.

3.2 Grouping of the Schools for Multiple Regression Analysis

For the purpose of this analysis, we decided to use the two indices which correlated most highly with school child guidance rates; namely, the proportion of immigrant children and the proportion of known delinquents (probation cases) in each school. Since the schools could also be divided into primary and secondary, the problem was to devise a means of dividing ninety-seven schools (the three special schools being excluded) by proportion of immigrants, proportion of delinquents, and principal type of school, into a manageable number of units.

The first step was to standardize the scores for probation rates and proportion of immigrants so that a constant change in child guidance rate was produced by one unit change in the weighted proportion of immigrants and one unit change in the weighted proportion of probation cases. The weights were chosen by re-scaling the proportions of immigrants and of probation cases so as to give the same regression slope with the child guidance rate. These two axes were used to define areas within which there was a relatively constant level of exposure to the joint influence of the two variables. The observations contained within these areas constituted groups defined by x units of exposure to the joint influence of the two variables in question.

It must be emphasized that we are concerned here only with *prediction*, and not with a causal relationship: we do not know if either the proportion of immigrant children, or the proportion of delinquent children, has any causal influence on the child guidance rate.

On the basis of the distribution thus obtained, three groups of primary schools and three groups of secondary schools were defined. A significant difference was found between each of these groups in the rate of child-guidance referral, a steady increase in rate being shown across the groups. TABLE 3.2 (a) shows the distribution for primary schools and TABLE 3.2 (b) that for secondary schools.

TABLE 3.2 (a)
GROUPING OF PRIMARY SCHOOLS
(*n* = 58)

	GROUP I 0–1 units	GROUP II 1–9 units	GROUP III 9+ units	TOTAL
No. of referrals	131·5	158·5	200	490
Popn. at risk	8,665	8,472	9,523	26,660
Ref. rate per 1,000	15·2	18·7	21·0	
Expected no. of refs.	158	155	177	490

Chi sq. = 8·1; d.f. = 2; P < 0·02.

TABLE 3.2 (b)
GROUPING OF SECONDARY SCHOOLS
(SELECTIVE AND NON-SELECTIVE)
(*n* = 39)

	GROUP I 0–1 units	GROUP II 1–12 units	GROUP III 12+ units	TOTAL
No. of referrals	54	73	138	265
Popn. at risk	5,203	6,044	7,373	18,620
Ref. rate per 1,000	10·4	12·1	18·7	
Expected no. of refs.	74	86	105	265

Chi sq. = 21·0; d.f. = 2; P < 0·001.

3.3 *Multiple Regression Analysis: Technique and Results*

A multiple regression analysis was now undertaken, to examine the respective contributions of the various socio-demographic and school variables mentioned in B3.1 and B3.2. The population at risk was divided into twenty-one basic units, each of which was defined in terms of two variables, viz:

(1) Cluster of enumeration districts: a seven cluster solution was chosen as this combined an acceptably high homogeneity coefficient with an adequate number of persons within each cluster.

(2) School group: primary and secondary schools were classified separately on the basis of proportion of immigrants attending the school and the delinquency rate for the school. Three groups were used for primary and secondary schools separately (see APPENDIX B3.2).

Each of the twenty-one basic units of the population was thus relatively homogeneous in terms of the variables used to define it. The values of the predictor variables and the child guidance rates were calculated for each of the basic population units.

The multiple regression analysis was undertaken for primary and secondary schools separately; in each case the intercorrelation between the predictor variables and child guidance referral rates were all fairly low.

		Primary Schools	*Secondary Schools*
VARIABLE	1 Proportion of foreign-born residents	0·168	0·001
	2 Rate of migration	0·068	0·394
	3 Proportion of Social Class I & II	−0·209	−0·020
	4 Proportion of Social Class IV & V	0·211	0·138
	5 Proportion of owner-occupiers	−0·179	−0·187
	6 Proportion renting from Local Authority	0·137	0·037
	7 Density of population	0·189	0·011
	8 Proportion sharing households	0·064	0·396
	9 School probation rate	0·043	0·422
	10 Proportion of immigrant children in school	0·029	0·499

A stepwise multiple regression only produced a significant result for the secondary schools, the values for the regression coefficients being:

		Multiple Regression Coefficient (secondary schools)
VARIABLE	1 Proportion of foreign-born residents	−1·1033
	2 Rate of migration	0·3784
	8 Proportion sharing households	0·5877
	9 School probation rate	20·0426

The regression was significant at the 5 per cent level.

The multiple correlation coefficient was $R = 0·687$, giving $R^2 = 47·20$ per cent. Since the predictor variables had widely different standard deviations, standardized betas were calculated.

		Std. Deviation
VARIABLE	1 Proportion of foreign-born residents	−0·4312
	2 Rate of migration	0·2017
	8 Proportion sharing households	0·5425
	9 School probation rate	0·4218

$$(\beta \text{ std.} = \beta \text{ unstd.} \cdot \frac{\text{std deviation of predictor variable}}{\text{std deviation of dependent variable}}$$

where β unstd. is the unadjusted regression coefficient of the appropriate predictor variable).

If the predictor variables are uncorrelated, then a one standard deviation change in the predictor variable produces a change equal to its standardized β in the dependent variable. Thus for secondary schools, as the school probation and supervision rate increases by one standard deviation the child guidance referral rate increases by 0·4218 of its standard deviation. The standardized βs allow the relative importance of each of the predictor variables to be assessed in terms of the effect which they have on the dependent variable.

The results for secondary schools show that the child guidance rate decreases as the percentage of foreign-born in an area increases, but that the rate increases with an increase in the percentage of persons sharing or in the migration rate. Increases in the school probation rate also tend to increase the child guidance rate.

In order to examine the combined effect of neighbourhood, school, and general practitioner, two further multiple regression analyses were carried out. The same predictor variables were used for the neighbourhood and school variables, the additional variable, general practitioner, being defined on the basis of the ratio of the practitioner's own referrals to referrals from within their practices by other agencies.

This defined three groups of general practitioners, so dividing the population at risk into sixty-three basic units (there being seven clusters, three school groups, and three groups of G.P.s). The multiple regression analyses were repeated for primary and secondary schools separately. The intercorrelations between predictor variables and child guidance referral rate were:

			Primary Schools	Secondary Schools
VARIABLE	1	Proportion of foreign-born residents	−0·170	0·083
	2	Rate of migration	−0·003	0·218
	3	Proportion of Social Class I & II	0·018	0·020
	4	Proportion of Social Class IV & V	0·005	0·073
	5	Proportion of owner-occupiers	−0·143	−0·032
	6	Proportion renting from Local Authority	0·108	−0·114
	7	Density of population	0·132	−0·016
	8	Proportion sharing households	0·044	0·289
	9	School probation rate	0·187	0·244
	10	Proportion of immigrant children in school	0·213	0·241
	12	G.P. groups	0·020	−0·180

The solution of the stepwise multiple regression analysis produced the following values for the regression coefficients:

Multiple Regression Coefficients			Primary Schools	Secondary Schools
VARIABLE	1	Proportion of foreign-born residents	−0·0158	−0·0117
	7	Density of population	0·0032	−0·0015
	8	Proportion sharing households	0·0051	0·0111
	9	School probation rate	−16·49	0·2882
	10	Proportion of immigrant children in school	0·1507	
	12	G.P. groups		−0·0029

Multiple correlation coefficient	$(R) =$	0·422	0·443
	$R^2 =$	17·81%	19·62%

Both solutions were significant at the 5 per cent level.

Standardized βs			Primary Schools	Secondary Schools
VARIABLE	1	Proportion of foreign-born residents	−0·3376	−0·1840
	7	Density of population	0·1157	−0·03988
	8	Proportion sharing households	0·2564	0·4107
	9	School probation rate	−1·932	0·2442
	10	Proportion of immigrant children in school	2·131	—
	12	G.P. groups	—	−0·1803

The results for primary schools show that the predictor variables having the greatest effect are the proportion of immigrants within a school and then the probation rate for that school. Once account has been taken of the proportion of immigrants in the school, the probation rate has a negative relationship to child guidance referral rate. The two indices of overcrowding both operate to increase the child guidance rate while the proportion of foreign born persons acts in the opposite direction.

The secondary schools show a different pattern of relationships between the predictor and dependent variables. The proportion sharing households and the school delinquency rate have a positive relationship with the child guidance rate while the percentage of foreign born and the influence of the general practitioner show a negative relationship.

Comparison of the results for secondary schools with and without general practitioner shows that three variables were consistently associated with the child guidance rate, viz: the percentage of foreign-born, the proportion sharing households, and the school probation rate.

APPENDIX B4

Analysis of Variance

The relative importance of three major variables thought to be related to referral to child guidance (viz: characteristics of the neighbourhood, the school, and the general practitioner) were investigated by undertaking a three-way analysis of variance. Each of the major variables was treated as a main effect.

The three major variables were divided, as in the multiple regression analysis, into:

(1) Seven clusters of enumeration districts, each cluster being made up of enumeration districts having similar socio-economic characteristics. This constituted the neighbourhood variable.

(2) Three groups of schools, defined within primary and secondary schools separately, on the joint basis of the proportion of immigrants within the school and the probation rate for the school.

(3) Four groups of general practitioners, the groups being formed on the basis of the ratio of the practitioner's own referrals to referral from within his practice by other agencies.

The results of the analysis for primary schools were:

Source of Variation	DF	SS	MS	F	5% critical value
Between school groups	2	1837	918·6	0·5734	3·26
Between clusters	6	7323	1220·5	0·7619	2·36
Between G.P. groups	3	5544	1848·2	1·1538	2·87
School × cluster interaction	12	10574	1256·1	0·7841	2·03
School × G.P. interaction	6	14962	2493·7	1·5568	2·36
Cluster × G.P. interaction	18	21332	1185·1	0·7398	1·90
Residual	36	57667	1601·8		
Total	83	123739			

Although none of the effects was significant, differences between groups of practitioners accounted for a higher proportion of the total variation than any other single factor. The fairly high school × G.P. interaction indicates that differences between practitioner groups do not remain constant over school groups, i.e., the relative effect of each practitioner group changes when different school groups are considered.

The findings for secondary schools showed a somewhat different pattern:

Source of Variation	DF	SS	MS	F	5% critical value
Between school groups	2	8030	4015·1	3·095	3·26
Between clusters	6	8807	1467·8	1·132	2·36
Between G.P. groups	3	8548	2849·4	2·197	2·87
School × cluster interaction	12	13870	1155·9	0·891	2·03
School × G.P. interaction	6	11198	1866·3	1·439	2·36
Cluster × G.P. interaction	18	30179	1676·6	1·293	1·90
Residual	36	46691	1297·0		
Total	83	127323			

None of the effects was significant. Differences between school groups and between practitioner groups were the two factors accounting for most of the variation. Interaction between these two main effects appeared to be present, indicating that they did not operate independently of each other.

While the general practitioners had a separate effect on the referral rates both for primary- and for secondary-school children, the schools themselves appeared to have a separate effect only on the rate for secondary-school children.

APPENDIX B5

Principal Components Analysis

Principal components analysis is a technique whereby a set of intercorrelated variables $(x_1, x_2 \ldots x_k)$ are transformed to a set of uncorrelated variables $(z_1, z_2 \ldots z_k)$ each of which is a linear combination of $x_1, x_2 \ldots x_k$. It has been utilized in the field of attitude-research as a means of assessing the number of dimensions underlying an attitude scale. A general explanation of the technique as a standard method of analysis has been given by Blalock (1972).

An analysis of this type was carried out on the responses of the individual practitioners to the individual case-vignettes described in CHAPTER IX, in order to ascertain to what extent the resulting attitude-scores ('Scale C') were measuring a single dimension. In the event, the first three components accounted respectively for 25 per cent, 15 per cent, and 12 per cent of the total variance in the practitioners' scores: a firm indication that there was no single dimension, corresponding to a latent attitude-factor, which would serve to explain the broad pattern of the responses.

APPENDIX C

Tables

APPENDIX C

TABLE 6a
TOTAL DELINQUENCY SAMPLE:
TYPE OF OFFENCE AT SUCCESSIVE COURT APPEARANCES

TYPE OF OFFENCE	COURT APPEARANCES						
	1st	2nd	3rd	4th	5th	6th	7th
BOYS							
Offence against property	427	109	39	13	9	3	1
Taking and driving away	95	39	15	8	1	1	1
Driving offence	262	57	17	8	4	2	1
Offence against person—sexual	6	1	2	—	—	—	—
Offence against person—other than sexual	36	8	8	2	2	—	1
Education Act offences	39	11	3	1	—	—	—
Care and protection cases	31	3	—	—	1	—	—
Breach of Probation or Supervision Order	10	18	13	4	1	1	—
Other	6	4	—	2	—	—	—
Total	912	250	97	38	18	7	4
GIRLS							
Offence against property	74	11	2	1			
Taking and driving away	2	—	—	—			
Driving offence	2	—	—	—			
Offence against person—sexual	2	—	—	—			
Offence against person—other than sexual	1	2	1	—			
Education Act offences	30	3	—	1			
Care and protection cases	62	3	1	—			
Breach of Probation or Supervision Order	6	14	4	1			
Other	3	—	—	—			
Total	182	33	8	3			

TABLE 6b
TOTAL DELINQUENCY SAMPLE:
COURT ACTION AT SUCCESSIVE COURT APPEARANCES

COURT ACTION	COURT APPEARANCES						
	1st	2nd	3rd	4th	5th	6th	7th
BOYS							
Conditional discharge	189	35	19	2	4	2	—
Fine	463	90	28	14	4	3	—
Probation Order	122	60	16	5	4	—	—
Supervision Order	58	11	3	2	1	—	—
Attendance Centre	44	26	6	—	—	1	—
Detention Centre	3	4	5	4	2	—	3
Approved School	27	24	16	11	1	—	—
Borstal	—	—	4	—	2	—	1
Other	2	—	—	—	—	—	—
Not known	4	—	—	—	—	1	—
Total	912	250	97	38	18	7	4
GIRLS							
Conditional discharge	25	3	3	—			
Fine	37	3	—	—			
Probation Order	31	6	2	—			
Supervision Order	83	12	—	—			
Attendance Centre	—	—	—	—			
Detention Centre	—	—	—	—			
Approved School	5	9	3	3			
Borstal	—	—	—	—			
Other	1	—	—	—			
Not known	—	—	—	—			
Total	182	33	8	3			

TABLE 7a
CHILD GUIDANCE REFERRAL RATES FOR ELECTORAL WARDS BY SEX (AVERAGE ANNUAL RATES PER 10,000 CHILDREN AT RISK)

WARD	BOYS			GIRLS			BOTH SEXES		
	Popn. 0–16 1966 Census	No. of Refs.	Rate	Popn. 0–16 1966 Census	No. of Refs.	Rate	Popn. 0–16 1966 Census	No. of Refs.	Rate
Central	1066	31	58·2	1234	21	34·0	2300	52	45·2
Shirley	2846	63	44·3	2938	43	29·3	5784	106	36·6
New Addington	4678	95	40·6	4302	55	25·6	8980	150	33·4
Broad Green	1588	34	42·8	1706	19	22·3	3294	53	32·2
Norbury	1666	31	37·2	1764	21	23·8	3430	52	30·3
Whitehorse Manor	1906	32	33·6	1968	24	24·4	3874	56	28·9
Sanderstead & Selsdon	2022	24	33·2	2022	17	23·8	4044	41	28·4[1]
Waddon	1966	38	38·7	1878	16	17·0	3844	54	28·1
Thornton Heath	1560	30	38·5	1818	17	18·7	3378	47	27·8
South Norwood	1870	34	36·4	1904	18	18·9	3774	52	27·6
Bensham Manor	1573	25	31·8	1607	17	21·2	3180	42	26·4
Woodside	2054	33	32·1	1950	19	19·5	4004	52	26·0
Addiscombe	1668	21	25·2	1578	19	24·1	3246	40	24·6
West Thornton	1800	28	31·1	1696	12	14·2	3496	40	22·9
East	2092	24	22·9	1870	19	20·3	3962	43	21·7
Purley	2200	16	27·3	1804	5	11·1	4004	21	20·0[1]
Sanderstead North	2356	27	22·9	2266	18	15·9	4622	45	19·5
Upper Norwood	1642	21	25·6	1910	12	12·6	3552	33	18·6
Woodcote & Coulsdon West	1746	9	21·8	2078	5	10·6	3824	14	15·7[1]
Coulsdon East	1956	7	17·9	2088	5	12·0	4044	12	14·8[1]

[1] Rates weighted for changes in Borough Boundary—see APPENDIX B 1.1.

TABLE 7b
DELINQUENCY RATES FOR TOTAL OFFENDERS, TOTAL OFFENCES, AND PROBATION/SUPERVISION, BY ELECTORAL WARD, SHOWING RANK ORDER

WARD	POPN. AGED 0–16	ESTIMATED NO. OF OFFENDERS[1]	AV. ANN. RATE PER 10,000	ESTIMATED NO. OF OFFENCES[1]	AV. ANN. RATE PER 10,000	NO. OF PROB/SUP. ORDERS	AV. ANN. RATE PER 10,000
Broad Green	3294	168	102·0 (1)	254	154·2 (1)	57	34·6 (1)
Norbury	3430	158	92·1 (2)	242	141·1 (2)	25	14·6 (11)
New Addington	8980	388	86·4 (3)	554	123·4 (4)	108	24·0 (3)
Waddon	3844	160	83·2 (4)	246	128·0 (3)	50	26·0 (2)
East	3962	156	78·7 (5)	200	101·0 (6)	34	17·2 (5)
Thornton Heath	3378	124	73·4 (6)	170	100·6 (7)	28	16·6 (7)
Whitehorse Manor	3874	138	71·2 (7)	198	102·2 (5)	33	17·0 (6)
Central	2300	76	66·1 (8)	110	95·6 (8)	20	17·4 (4)
Woodside	4004	128	63·9 (9)	188	93·9 (9)	30	15·0 (10)
South Norwood	3774	110	58·3 (10)	140	74·2 (11)	20	10·6 (12)
Addiscombe	3246	82	50·5 (11)	94	57·9 (14)	15	9·2 (13)
Shirley	5784	142	49·1 (12)	216	74·7 (10)	45	15·6 (9)
West Thornton	3496	78	44·6 (13)	126	72·1 (12)	13	7·4 (14)
Bensham Manor	3180	70	44·0 (14)	104	65·4 (13)	25	15·7 (8)
Upper Norwood	3552	70	39·4 (15)	100	56·3 (15)	12	6·8 (15)
Sanderstead North	4622	64	27·7 (16)	74	32·0 (16)	11	4·8 (16)
Woodcote & Coulsdon West	3824	22	11·5 (17)	24	12·6 (18)	—	—
Purley	4004	22	11·0 (18)	26	13·0 (17)	—	—
Sanderstead & Selsdon	4044	14	6·9 (19)	16	7·9 (20)	—	—
Coulsdon East	4044	14	6·9 (19)	18	8·9 (19)	—	—

[1] No. in sample × 2.

TABLE 7c
CHILD GUIDANCE REFERRAL RATES FOR 7 AND 22 CLUSTERS OF ENUMERATION DISTRICTS

CLUSTER NO.	POPULATION AGED 0–19 1966 CENSUS (10% SAMPLE)	NO. OF REFERRALS	AVERAGE ANNUAL RATE PER 10,000 AT RISK
7 CLUSTERS			
1	1289	167	25·9
2	3055	221	14·5
3	801	108	27·0
4	760	119	31·3
5	594	69	23·2
6	2200	236	21·5
7	715	70	19·6
22 CLUSTERS			
01	856	50	11·7
02	300	45	30·0
03	180	15	16·7
04	305	30	19·7
05	124	20	32·3
06	519	69	26·6
07	274	35	25·5
08	216	29	26·8
09	381	46	24·1
10	712	56	15·7
11	698	59	16·9
12	442	81	36·6
13	758	67	17·7
14	106	19	35·8
15	729	102	28·0
16	750	44	11·7
17	211	20	19·0
18	147	12	16·3
19	195	22	22·6
20	175	21	24·0
21	737	82	22·2
22	134	12	17·9

TABLE 7d

DELINQUENCY RATES FOR 7 AND 22 CLUSTERS OF ENUMERATION DISTRICTS—PERSONS AND OFFENCES

CLUSTER NO.	POPULATION AGED 0–19 1966 CENSUS (10% SAMPLE)	ESTIMATED NO. OF DELIN- QUENTS[1]	AVERAGE ANNUAL RATE PER 10,000 AT RISK	ESTIMATED NO. OF OFFENCES[1]	AVERAGE ANNUAL RATE PER 10,000 AT RISK
7 CLUSTERS					
1	1289	600	93·1	904	140·3
2	3055	256	16·8	330	21·6
3	801	152	38·0	214	53·4
4	760	348	91·6	522	137·4
5	594	126	42·4	178	59·9
6	2200	510	46·4	706	64·2
7	715	164	45·9	208	58·2
22 CLUSTERS					
01	856	54	12·6	74	17·3
02	300	180	120·0	290	193·3
03	180	58	64·4	70	77·8
04	305	82	53·8	106	69·5
05	124	26	42·0	36	58·1
06	519	168	64·7	238	91·7
07	274	60	43·8	74	54·0
08	216	56	51·8	96	88·9
09	381	62	32·5	96	50·4
10	712	58	16·3	84	23·6
11	698	152	43·6	192	55·0
12	442	186	84·2	270	122·2
13	758	72	19·0	84	22·2
14	106	24	45·3	38	71·7
15	729	182	49·9	216	59·3
16	750	60	16·0	70	18·7
17	211	24	22·7	28	26·5
18	147	24	32·6	36	49·0
19	195	52	53·3	88	90·3
20	175	42	48·0	68	77·7
21	737	398	108·0	608	165·0
22	134	36	53·7	58	86·6

[1] No. in sample × 2.

TABLE 7e

RANK ORDERING OF 7 AND 22 CLUSTERS OF ENUMERATION
DISTRICTS—CHILD GUIDANCE REFERRAL, TOTAL OFFENDERS,
TOTAL OFFENCES

CLUSTER NO.	CHILD GUIDANCE REFERRAL		TOTAL DELINQUENCY OFFENDERS		TOTAL DELINQUENCY OFFENCES	
	Rate	Rank Order	Rate	Rank Order	Rate	Rank Order
7 CLUSTERS						
4	31·3	1	91·6	2	137·4	2
3	27·0	2	38·0	6	53·4	6
1	25·9	3	93·1	1	140·3	1
5	23·2	4	42·4	5	59·9	4
6	21·5	5	46·4	3	64·2	3
7	19·6	6	45·9	4	58·2	5
2	14·5	7	14·8	7	21·6	7
22 CLUSTERS						
12	36·6	1	84·2	3	122·2	3
14	35·8	2	45·3	12	71·7	10
05	32·3	3	42·0	15	58·1	13
02	30·0	4	120·0	1	193·3	1
15	28·0	5	49·9	10	59·3	12
08	26·8	6	51·8	9	88·9	6
06	26·6	7	64·7	4	91·7	4
07	25·5	8	43·8	13	54·0	15
09	24·1	9	32·5	17	50·4	16
20	24·0	10	48·0	11	77·7	9
19	22·6	11	53·3	8	90·3	5
21	22·2	12	108·0	2	165·0	2
04	19·7	13	53·8	6	69·5	11
17	19·0	14	22·7	18	26·5	18
22	17·9	15	53·7	7	86·6	7
13	17·7	16	19·0	19	22·2	20
11	16·9	17	43·6	14	55·0	14
03	16·7	18	64·4	5	77·8	8
18	16·3	19	32·6	16	49·0	17
10	15·7	20	16·3	20	23·6	19
01	11·7	21	12·6	22	17·3	22
16	11·7	22	16·0	21	18·7	21

TABLE 7f

CHILD GUIDANCE AND DELINQUENCY RATES : CORRELATIONS WITH WARD SOCIAL INDICES

(No. of Wards = 20)

| SOCIAL INDICES | CORRELATIONS WITH CHILD GUIDANCE RATES | | | CORRELATIONS WITH DELINQUENCY RATES | | | | | |
| | | | | Offenders | | | Offences | | |
	Pearson	Kendall	Spearman	Pearson	Kendall	Spearman	Pearson	Kendall	Spearman
Proportion in Social Classes I & II	−0·34	−0·33*	−0·43	−0·75***	−0·54***	−0·71**	−0·74***	−0·52**	−0·69**
Proportion in Social Classes IV & V	+0·37	+0·33*	+0·44	+0·72***	+0·53**	+0·70**	+0·72***	+0·50**	+0·68**
Proportion of owner-occupiers	−0·62**	−0·48**	−0·62**	−0·70***	−0·54***	−0·71**	−0·69***	−0·53**	−0·70**
Proportion renting from Local Authority	—	+0·34*	+0·47*	—	+0·37*	+0·53*	—	+0·40*	+0·58*
Proportion sharing households	+0·16	+0·03	+0·04	+0·24	+0·10	+0·14	+0·19	+0·07	+0·11
Density of population[1]	+0·41	+0·21	+0·29	+0·35	+0·21	+0·32	+0·30	+0·17	+0·26
Proportion of foreign born	+0·06	+0·01	+0·04	+0·13	+0·12	+0·10	+0·12	+0·09	+0·09
Rate of migration[2]	−0·22	−0·09	−0·07	−0·50*	−0·25	−0·35	−0·51*	−0·24	−0·33

[1] Percentage of persons in private households living more than one to a room.
[2] Number of persons entering or leaving during survey period, as a proportion of at-risk population.

TABLE 7g
CORRELATIONS OF CHILD GUIDANCE RATES WITH DEMOGRAPHIC AND SOCIO-ECONOMIC INDICES FOR (a) 20 ELECTORAL WARDS AND (b) 22 CLUSTERS OF ENUMERATION DISTRICTS

SOCIAL INDICES	CORRELATIONS WITH CHILD GUIDANCE RATE					
	20 Electoral Wards			22 Clusters of E.D.s		
	Pearson	Kendall	Spearman	Pearson	Kendall	Spearman
Proportion in Social Classes I & II	−0·34	−0·33*	−0·43	−0·65**	−0·43**	−0·60**
Proportion in Social Classes IV & V	+0·37	+0·33*	+0·44	+0·67**	+0·50**	+0·65**
Proportion of owner-occupiers	−0·62**	−0·43**	−0·62**	−0·57**	−0·36*	−0·52*
Proportion renting from Local Authority	—	+0·34*	+0·47*	+0·43*	+0·32*	+0·41*
Proportion sharing households	+0·16	+0·03	+0·04	+0·01	+0·07	+0·07
Density of population[1]	+0·41	+0·21	+0·29	+0·68**	+0·44**	+0·60**
Proportion of foreign born	+0·06	+0·01	+0·04	+0·28	−0·03	−0·05
Rate of migration[2]	−0·22	−0·09	−0·07	−0·10	−0·03	−0·07

[1] Percentage of persons in private households living more than one to a room.
[2] Number of persons entering or leaving during survey period, as a proportion of at-risk population.

TABLE 7h
CORRELATIONS OF DELINQUENCY RATES WITH DEMOGRAPHIC AND SOCIO-ECONOMIC INDICES FOR (a) 20 ELECTORAL WARDS AND (b) 22 CLUSTERS OF ENUMERATION DISTRICTS

SOCIAL INDICES	CORRELATIONS WITH DELINQUENCY RATE (OFFENDERS)]					
	20 Electoral Wards			22 Clusters of E.D.s		
	Pearson	Kendall	Spearman	Pearson	Kendall	Spearman
Proportion in Social Classes I & II	−0·75***	−0·54***	−0·71**	−0·71***	−0·61***	−0·75***
Proportion in Social Classes IV & V	+0·72***	+0·53**	+0·70**	+0·63**	+0·44**	+0·61**
Proportion of owner-occupiers	−0·70***	−0·54***	−0·71**	−0·82***	−0·56***	−0·73***
Proportion renting from Local Authority	—	+0·37*	+0·53*	+0·78***	+0·42**	+0·59**
Proportion sharing households	+0·24	+0·10	+0·14	−0·13	−0·10	−0·17
Density of population[1]	+0·35	+0·21	+0·32	+0·66**	+0·55***	+0·73***
Proportion of foreign born	+0·13	+0·12	+0·10	—	−0·12	−0·26
Rate of migration[2]	−0·50*	−0·25	−0·35	−0·26	−0·12	−0·18

[1] Percentage of persons in private households living more than one to a room.
[2] Number of persons entering or leaving during survey period, as a proportion of at-risk population.

TABLE 8a
CHILD GUIDANCE REFERRAL AND PROBATION/SUPERVISION RATES FOR SCHOOLS

	NO. ON REGISTER AT MID-PERIOD 1962–6	CHILD GUIDANCE REFERRAL		PROBATION/SUPERVISION ORDERS	
		No. of Referrals	Average Annual Rate per 10,000 at Risk[1]	No. of Orders	Average Annual Rate per 10,000 at Risk
PRIMARY SCHOOLS					
Infants only	120	7	116·7	—	—
	94	3	64·2	—	—
	221	3	27·1	2	18·1
	166	2	24·1	—	—
	137	1	14·6	—	—
Juniors only	333	6	36·1	6	36·1
Infants and Juniors	262	20	153·0	5	38·2
	128	2	78·1[1]	—	—
	680	25	73·5	3	8·8
	488	16	65·6	1	4·1
	650	21	64·6	—	—
	752	23	61·2	—	—
	462	14	60·7	1	4·3
	613	16	52·2	—	—
	848	22	51·9	—	—
	272	7	51·6	—	—
	412	10	48·5	—	—
	680	16	47·1	—	—
	916	21	45·8	—	—
	228	5	43·9	—	—
	364	8	43·9	—	—
	735	16	43·6	3	8·2
	559	12	42·9	—	—
	285	6	42·1	—	—
	612	12	39·2	1	3·3
	723	14	38·7	2	5·5
	130	1	38·5[1]	—	—
	786	15	38·2	5	12·7
	946	18	38·0	3	6·3
	879	16	36·4	1	2·3
	841	15	35·7	3	7·1
	283	5	35·3	—	—
	515	9	35·0	—	—
	442	3	33·9[1]	—	—
	1125	19	33·8	3	5·3
	341	2	29·3[1]	—	—
	536	7	26·1	—	—
	232	3	25·9	—	—
	817	10	24·5	2	4·9
	372	4	21·5	—	—
	474	5	21·1	—	—
	237	1	21·1[1]	—	—
	194	2	20·6	—	—
	532	5	18·8	—	—
	266	1	18·8[1]	—	—
	428	4	18·7	1	4·7
	435	4	18·4	1	4·6
	327	3	18·3	1	6·1

TABLE 8a—cont.

	NO. ON REGISTER AT MID-PERIOD 1962–6	CHILD GUIDANCE REFERRAL		PROBATION/SUPERVISION ORDERS	
		No. of Referrals	Average Annual Rate per 10,000 at Risk[1]	No. of Orders	Average Annual Rate per 10,000 at Risk
Infants and Juniors—contd.	287	2	13.9	—	—
	386	1	12.9[1]	—	—
	456	1	11.0[1]	—	—
	501	1	10.0[1]	—	—
	580	1	8.6[1]	—	—
	307	1	6.5	—	—
	398	1	5.0	2	10.1
	418	1	4.8	—	—
	260	0	0.0	—	—
	296	0	0.0	—	—
Mean Rate: Primary Schools			36.6		3.4
SELECTIVE SECONDARY SCHOOLS					
Boys' Schools	612	10	32.7	2	6.5
	296	4	27.1	10	67.6
	604	2	16.6[1]	—	—
	407	3	14.7	2	9.8
	827	4	9.7	2	4.8
Girls' Schools	568	11	38.7	—	—
	540	4	14.8	—	—
	566	4	14.1	—	—
	567	1	8.8[1]	—	—
Mixed Schools	501	5	20.0	—	—
	330	2	12.1	4	24.2
	657	2	5.9	1	3.0
Mean Rate: Selective Secondary Schools			17.4		6.5
NON-SELECTIVE SECONDARY SCHOOLS					
Boys' Schools	534	14	52.4	38	142.3
	538	14	52.0	41	152.4
	635	15	47.2	19	59.8
	419	8	38.2	28	133.7
	622	8	25.7	43	138.3
	377	2	10.6	11	58.4
Girls' Schools	343	14	81.7	5	29.2
	193	7	72.7	—	—
	287	7	48.8	15	104.5
	619	14	45.2	18	58.2
	489	7	28.7	4	16.4
	489	6	24.6	6	24.5
	593	7	23.6	19	64.1
	414	2	9.7	5	24.2
Mixed Schools	230	3	65.2[1]	—	—
	255	7	54.9	13	102.0
	424	11	51.9	11	51.9
	572	13	45.5	19	66.4
	598	5	41.8[1]	—	—
	597	11	36.9	26	87.1
	347	6	34.6	13	74.9

TABLE 8a—cont.

	NO. ON REGISTER AT MID-PERIOD 1962-6	CHILD GUIDANCE REFERRAL		PROBATION/SUPERVISION ORDERS	
		No. of Referrals	Average Annual Rate per 10,000 at Risk[1]	No. of Orders	Average Annual Rate per 10,000 at Risk
Mixed Schools— contd.	397	6	30·2	2	10·1
	585	8	27·3	15	51·3
	484	6	24·8	1	4·1
	695	3	21·6[1]	—	—
	303	1	16·5[1]	—	—
	229	0	0·0	—	—
Mean Rate: Non-Selective Secondary Schools			36·4		57·4
SPECIAL SCHOOLS					
	17	3	363·6	—	—
	210	15	142·8	12	114·3
	192	12	125·3	2	20·8
Mean Rate: Special Schools			143·5		67·0

[1] Schools weighted for length of time using Croydon services.

TABLE 8b

SCHOOLCHILDREN REFERRED TO CHILD GUIDANCE: OBSERVED AND EXPECTED NUMBERS BY DISTRICT OF RESIDENCE AND REFERRAL RATE FOR SCHOOL

	E.D. CLUSTER						
	1	2	3	4	5	6	7
PRIMARY SCHOOLS							
High Referring:							
Population	2404	2452	616	1076	380	1752	220
Observed refs.	57	77	25	30	15	46	9
Expected refs.	52·7	37·4	14·6	24·8	6·8	32·4	3·5
Medium Referring:							
Population	988	1596	812	1088	1132	2832	1112
Observed refs.	22	17	14	25	17	55	14
Expected refs.	21·7	24·3	19·3	25·0	20·1	52·4	17·7
Low Referring:							
Population	392	2976	300	356	288	1468	304
Observed refs.	4	13	2	3	0	11	3
Expected refs.	8·6	45·3	7·1	8·2	5·1	27·2	4·8
Total Population	3784	7024	1728	2520	1800	6052	1636
Total refs.	83	107	41	58	32	112	26
Chi Square (d.f. = 2)	2·87 n.s	68·39***	13·00**	4·50 n.s	15·93***	15·73***	10·26**

TABLE 8b—cont.

SECONDARY SCHOOLS

High Referring:							
Population	416	380	264	164	328	884	324
Observed refs.	8	13	11	6	5	30	11
Expected refs.	6·8	4·3	6·8	2·1	4·6	15·7	7·3
Medium Referring:							
Population	1200	1380	288	760	348	1132	328
Observed refs.	27	22	9	16	3	18	8
Expected refs.	19·6	15·5	7·5	9·7	4·8	20·1	7·4
Low Referring:							
Population	1020	2520	452	1592	332	1412	284
Observed refs.	8	13	6	10	6	13	2
Expected refs.	16·6	28·3	11·7	20·2	4·6	25·1	6·4
Total Population	2836	4280	1004	2516	1008	3428	936
Total refs.	43	48	26	32	14	61	21
Chi Square (d.f. = 2)	7·64*	29·24***	5·78 n.s	16·86***	1·17 n.s	19·37***	5·08 n.s

TABLE 9a

GENERAL PRACTICE REFERRAL RATES IN RELATION TO ELECTORAL WARD RATES BASED ON TOTAL LIST SIZE—T RATE

(Figures in brackets represent Rank Order of G.P. Referral Rate)

ELECTORAL WARD IN RANK ORDER OF C.G. RATE	CODE NO. OF G.P.	G.P. REFERRALS		OTHER AGENCY REFS.	
		No. of Refs.	Av. Ann. Rate per 10,000	No. of Refs.	Av. Ann. Rate per 10,000
Central—45·2	98	8	6·2 (12)	5	3·9
	81	2^1	4·6 (24)	2	2·3
	88	4^1	3·1 (36)	3	1·8
	87	2	1·6 (53)	2	1·6
	109	2	1·5 (56)	1	0·8
	105	—	0·0 (83)	1	1·6
Shirley—36·6	39	12	7·3 (5)	2	1·2
	8	11	6·7 (9)	2	1·2
	58	8	5·3 (16)	11	7·3
	18	5	3·6 (33)	6	4·3
	31	5	2·9 (40)	11	6·3
New Addington—33·4	68	18	10·6 (3)	15	8·8
	61	7	7·0 (8)	9	9·0
	24	4	4·0 (28)	6	6·0
	13	4	2·3 (44)	10	5·7
	103	1	0·6 (75)	3	1·7
Broad Green—32·2	12	9	6·0 (13)	4	2·7
	74	2	1·8 (51)	3	2·7
	92	—	0·0 (83)	2	1·5
Norbury—30·3	142	1^1	6·7 (9)	—	0·0
	37	5	3·1 (36)	5	3·1
	78	3	2·7 (42)	2	1·8
Whitehorse—28·9	44	11	6·7 (9)	6	3·6
	82	8	4·9 (23)	8	4·9
	30	7	4·2 (27)	11	6·7
	80	1	1·5 (56)	—	0·0
	75	2	1·2 (63)	1	0·6
	47	2	1·2 (68)	12	7·3
Sanderstead and Selsdon—28·4	91	2^1	2·2 (46)	—	0·0
	5	—	0·0 (83)	4	2·5
	143	—	0·0 (83)	1	1·3
Waddon—28·1	15	14	13·7 (1)	4	3·9
	40	9	5·8 (14)	6	3·9
	111	2	3·2 (34)	—	0·0
	59	2	2·3 (44)	4	4·6
	7	1	0·6 (74)	3	1·9
Thornton Heath—27·8	34	8	7·1 (7)	1	0·9
	35	7	5·1 (19)	4	2·9
	117	1^1	1·5 (59)	7	5·1

TABLE 9a—cont.

ELECTORAL WARD IN RANK ORDER OF C.G. RATE	CODE NO. OF G.P.	G.P. REFERRALS		OTHER AGENCY REFS.	
		No. of Refs.	Av. Ann. Rate per 10,000	No. of Refs.	Av. Ann. Rate per 10,000
South Norwood—27·6	57	3[1]	7·3 (5)	9	14·6
	42	6	4·4 (25)	4	2·9
	77	1[1]	1·6 (53)	4	3·2
	33	2	1·2 (63)	2	1·2
	126	—	0·0 (83)	4	3·8
	161	—	0·0 (83)	—	0·0
Bensham Manor—26·4	43	4	2·9 (39)	3	2·2
	95	2	1·8 (51)	2	1·8
	23	2	1·2 (63)	4	2·5
Woodside—26·0	25	4	4·0 (28)	5	5·0
	56	6	3·8 (31)	3	1·9
	93	6	3·8 (31)	2	1·3
	55	3	1·9 (50)	3	1·9
	107	—	0·0 (83)	5	3·9
Addiscombe—24·6	73	3[1]	5·3 (16)	2	1·8
	69	6	5·0 (20)	3	2·5
	119	1	0·9 (70)	4	3·6
West Thornton—22·9	86	5[1]	8·0 (4)	3	2·4
	129	2[1]	5·6 (15)	1[1]	2·8
	26	6	5·0 (20)	4	3·3
	112	3[1]	4·0 (28)	1[1]	1·3
	114	4	2·9 (40)	3	2·1
	36	2	2·2 (46)	5	5·6
	65	2	1·5 (56)	5	3·8
	14	2	1·4 (61)	5	3·6
	79	2	1·4 (61)	2	1·4
East—21·7	67	5	5·3 (18)	2	2·1
	127	2[1]	3·1 (36)	2	1·5
	63	3	2·2 (46)	2	1·5
	118	2	2·0 (49)	2	2·0
	16	2	1·6 (53)	7	5·6
	32	2	1·1 (69)	13	7·4
	49	1	0·8 (73)	3	2·4
Purley—20·0	116	2	1·2 (63)	1	0·6
	157	—	0·0 (83)	—	0·0
Sanderstead North—19·5	2	3[1]	5·0 (20)	2	2·0
	83	2[1]	4·3 (26)	5	4·3
	10	4	3·2 (34)	1	0·8
	146	1	0·9 (71)	—	0·0
Upper Norwood—18·6		—		—	
Woodcote and Coulsdon West—15·7	133	5[1]	12·1 (2)	—	0·0
	101	1[1]	2·4 (43)	1	1·2
	124	1	1·5 (59)	—	0·0
	137	1[1]	1 2 (63)	1	0·6
	106	1	0·9	2	1·8
Coulsdon East—14·8		—		—	

[1] Weights given to these referrals.

TABLE 9b

GENERAL PRACTICE REFERRAL RATES IN RELATION TO ELECTORAL WARD RATES BASED ON NUMBER OF REGISTERED SCHOOLCHILDREN—S RATE

(Figures in brackets represent Rank Order of G.P. Referral Rate)

ELECTORAL WARD IN RANK ORDER OF C.G. RATE	CODE NO. OF G.P.	G.P. REFERRALS		OTHER AGENCY REFS.	
		No. of Refs.	Av. Ann. Rate per 10,000	No. of Refs.	Av. Ann. Rate per 10,000
Central—45·2	98	5	61·4 (4)	4	49·1
	88	4[1]	52·1 (7)	2	20·8
	109	2	24·5 (26)	—	0·0
	87	1	12·3 (56)	1	12·3
	81	—	0·0 (83)	3	39·5
	105	—	0·0 (83)	1	166·7
Shirley—36·6	39	8	30·8 (18)	2	7·7
	18	4	29·4 (19)	6	44·1
	8	7	26·9 (23)	1	3·9
	58	6	23·1 (28)	8	30·8
	31	4	9·3 (63)	8	18·6
New Addington—33·4	68	16	38·4 (13)	11	26·4
	61	5	24·3 (27)	4	19·4
	24	4	19·4 (39)	5	24·3
	13	4	9·3 (63)	10	23·3
	103	1	2·9 (69)	2	5·8
Broad Green—32·2	12	7	74·9 (3)	3	32·1
	74	2	14·7 (50)	3	22·1
	92	—	0·0 (83)	2	21·4
Norbury—30·3	142	1[1]	178·6 (1)	—	0·0
	78	2	35·7 (14)	1	17·9
	37	4	18·7 (40)	3	14·0
Whitehorse—28·9	44	6	22·4 (29)	5	18·7
	82	5	18·7 (41)	5	18·7
	30	5	14·4 (51)	8	23·1
	75	2	14·1 (53)	1	7·1
	47	2	5·8 (67)	9	26·0
	80	—	0·0 (83)	—	0·0
tead and Selsdon—28·4	91	1[1]	11·3 (57)	—	0·0
	5	—	0·0 (83)	2	13·1
	143	—	0·0 (83)	—	0·0
Waddon—28·1	15	6	57·7 (5)	4	38·5
	40	7	49·3 (9)	6	42·3
	111	1	26·3 (24)	—	0·0
	59	2	20·0 (37)	4	40·0
	7	1	6·9 (66)	2	13·9
Thornton Heath—27·8	35	7	45·8 (11)	—	0·0
	34	7	44·3 (12)	—	0·0
	117	1[1]	13·1 (55)	6	39·2

TABLE 9b—cont.

ELECTORAL WARD IN RANK ORDER OF C.G. RATE	CODE NO. OF G.P.	G.P. REFERRALS		OTHER AGENCY REFS.	
		No. of Refs.	Av. Ann. Rate per 10,000	No. of Refs.	Av. Ann. Rate per 10,000
South Norwood—27·6	57	3[1]	47·2 (10)	9	70·9
	42	4	28·4 (20)	3	21·3
	33	2	10·2 (60)	2	10·2
	77	1[1]	9·2 (65)	3	13·7
	126	—	0·0 (83)	3	23·6
	161	—	0·0 (83)	—	0·0
Bensham Manor—26·4	43	4	21·3 (30)	2	10·6
	23	2	17·5 (44)	3	26·3
	95	1	9·6 (61)	2	19·2
Woodside—26·0	56	5	27·0 (21)	2	10·8
	93	5	27·0 (21)	3	16·2
	55	3	16·2 (47)	3	16·2
	25	2	14·1 (53)	4	28·2
	107	—	0·0 (83)	5	44·4
Addiscombe—24·6	69	6	57·7 (5)	—	0·0
	73	1[1]	22·0 (30)	1	11·0
	119	—	0·0 (83)	2	19·2
West Thornton—22·9	86	4[1]	52·0 (8)	—	0·0
	129	1[1]	20·9 (32)	1[1]	20·9
	112	2[1]	20·4 (34)	1[1]	10·2
	26	3	18·4 (42)	3	18·4
	36	2	16·7 (46)	4	33·5
	114	3	16·0 (48)	3	16·0
	65	2	15·8 (49)	4	31·6
	14	2	10·6 (58)	1	5·3
	79	—	0·0 (83)	3	16·0
East—21·7	127	2[1]	35·6 (15)	2	17·8
	67	2	20·2 (35)	1	10·1
	118	2	20·2 (35)	2	20·2
	16	2	17·8 (43)	5	44·4
	63	2	14·2 (52)	2	14·2
	32	2	4·8 (68)	12	28·8
	49	—	0·0 (83)	1	11·0
Purley—20·0	116	1	9·4 (62)	1	9·4
	157	—	0·0 (83)	—	0·0
Sanderstead North—19·5	10	3	33·0 (16)	—	0·0
	2	2[1]	20·5 (33)	3	20·5
	146	1	17·2 (45)	—	0·0
	83	—	0·0 (83)	7	92·1
Upper Norwood—18·6		—		—	
Woodcote and Coulsdon West—15·7	133	4[1]	103·9 (2)	—	0·0
	124	1[1]	31·3 (17)	—	0·0
	101	1[1]	26·0 (25)	—	0·0
	137	1[1]	20·0 (37)	1	10·0
	106	1	10·3 (59)	2	20·6
Coulsdon East—14·8		—		—	

[1] Weights given to these referrals.

REFERENCES

ANDERSON, F. W. and DEAN, H. C. (1956) Some aspects of child guidance intake policy and practice, *Public Health Monograph No. 42*, Washington D.C., U.S. Dept. of Health, Education and Welfare.

ANDERSON, J. CORBET (1882) *A Short Chronicle concerning the Parish of Croydon*, Republished 1970, S.R. Publications Ltd., Croydon.

APLEY, J. (1964) An ecology of childhood, *Lancet*, 2, 1–4.

ASUNI, T. (1963) Maladjustment and delinquency: a comparison of two samples, *J. child Psychol. Psychiat.*, 4, 219–28.

BAGLEY, C. R. (1965) Juvenile delinquency in Exeter: an ecological and comparative study, *Urban Studies*, 2, 33–50.

BALDWIN, J. A. (1968) Psychiatric illness from birth to maturity: an epidemiological study, *Acta psychiat. scand.*, 44, 313–33.

BARBOUR, R. F. and BEEDELL, C. (1955) Follow-up of a child guidance population, *J. ment. Sci.*, 101, 794–809.

BEACH, FLETCHER (1898) Insanity in children, *J. ment. Sci.*, 44, 459–74.

BEERS, C. W. (1948) *A Mind that Found Itself*. An autobiography (7th edition). New York.

BELSON, W. A. (1968) The extent of stealing by London boys and some of its origins, L.S.E., *Survey Research Centre Reprint Series No. 39*, London.

BLACKER, C. P. (1946) *Neurosis and the Mental Health Service*, London.

BLALOCK, H. M. (1972) *Social Statistics* (2nd edition), New York.

BRANDON, S. (1960) *An epidemiological study of maladjustment in childhood*, unpublished M.D. thesis, Univ. of Durham.

BREMER, J. (1951) A social psychiatric investigation of a small community in Northern Norway, *Acta psychiat. scand.*, *Suppl. 62*.

BROOK, P. and COOPER, B. (1975) Community mental health care: primary team and specialist services, *J. Roy. Coll. Gen. Practit.*, 25, 93–110.

BUCKLE, D. and LEBOVICI, S. (1960) *Child Guidance Centres*, Geneva.

BURT, C. (1925) *The Young Delinquent*, London.

CAMERON, K. (1955) Diagnostic categories in child psychiatry, *Brit. J. med. Psychol.*, 28, 67–71.

CARLESTAM, G. (1971) The individual, the city and stress, In *Society, Stress and Disease*, Vol. 1, *The Psychosocial Environment and Psychosomatic Diseases*. Ed., Levi, L., London.

CARTWRIGHT, A. (1972) *Report of an enquiry into roles of the services for maladjusted children*, unpublished.

CASPARI, I. E. and OSBORNE, E. L. (1971) *The neighbourhood schools' service of the Tavistock Clinic*, Unpublished MS. London, Tavistock Centre.

CHAMBERLAIN, R. N. (1972) Children in the integrated N.H.S., *Lancet*, 2, 963–5.

CLARK, J. (1974) The role of the health visitor, In *The Health Team in Action*. London.

CLEGG, A. and MEGSON, B. (1968) *Children in Distress*, Harmondsworth, Middlesex.

CLIFF, A. D. and ORD, K. (1970) Spatial auto-correlation: a review of existing and new measures with applications, *Economic Geography*, 46, 269–92.

COCHRANE, A. L. (1972) *Effectiveness and Efficiency: random reflections on health services*, The Rock Carling Fellowship Lecture, 1971, London.

COOPER, B. (1964) General practitioners' attitudes to psychiatry, *De Medicina Tuenda*, **1**, 43–8.

CROSSE, G. (1972) Personal communication.

DANZIGER, K. (1971) *Socialization*, Harmondsworth, Middlesex, p. 113.

DARWIN, C. (1877) Biographical sketch of an infant, *Mind*, **11**, pp. 877 f.

DAVIE, R., BUTLER, N., and GOLDSTEIN, H. (1972) From birth to 7, *2nd Report of the National Child Development Study (1958 cohort)*, London.

DEPT. OF EDUCATION AND SCIENCE (1968) *Psychologists in Education Services* (Summerfield Report), London.

DEPT. OF EDUCATION AND SCIENCE (1969) *The Health of the School Child*, Report of the Chief Medical Officer for the years 1966–8, London.

DEPT. OF HEALTH AND SOCIAL SECURITY (1969) *Digest of Health Statistics for England and Wales*, London.

DEPT. OF HEALTH AND SOCIAL SECURITY (1971) *The Nottingham Psychiatric Case Register Findings*, 1962–1969, Statistical Report Series No. 13, London.

DEPT. OF HEALTH AND SOCIAL SECURITY (1973) *Health and Personal Social Services Statistics for England and Wales*, 1972, London.

DEPTS. OF EDUCATION AND HEALTH (1973) Draft circular on Child Guidance.

DOUGLAS, J. W. B. and BLOMFIELD, J. M. (1958) *Children under Five*, London.

DOUGLAS, J. W. B., ROSS, J. M., HAMMOND, W. A., and MULLIGAN, D. G. (1966) Delinquency and social class, *Brit. J. Criminol.*, **6**, 294–302.

EISENBERG, L. (1961) The strategic deployment of the child psychiatrist in preventive psychiatry, *J. Child Psychol. Psychiat.*, **2**, 229–41.

EISENBERG, L. (1973) The future of psychiatry, *Lancet*, **2**, 1371–5.

EISNER, V. and TZUYEMURA, H. (1960) Interactions of juveniles with the law, *Public Health Reports, Vol. 80*, Washington, D.C., U.S. Dept. of Health, Education and Welfare.

EMMINGHAUS, H. (1887) Die psychische Störungen des Kindesalters, supplement 2 to Gerhardt's *Handbuch d. Kinderkrankheiten*, Tübingen.

EVERITT, B. S. (1972) Cluster analysis: a brief discussion of some of the problems, *Brit. J. Psychiat.*, **120**, 143–5.

FARIS, R. E. L. and DUNHAM, H. W. (1939) *Mental Disorder in Urban Areas*, Chicago.

FLEISS, J. L. and ZUBIN, J. (1969) On the methods and theory of clustering, *Multivariate Behavioural Research*, **4**, 235–50.

GATH, D. (1968) Child guidance and the general practitioner, *J. child Psychol. Psychiat.*, **9**, 213–27.

GINOT, H. G. and LEBO, D. (1963) Ecology of service, *J. consult. Psychol.*, **27**, 450–52.

GOLD, M. (1970) *Delinquent Behaviour in an American City*, Belmont, California.

GRAY, P. G. and GEE, F. A. (1972) *A quality check on the 1966 10% sample Census of England and Wales*, Office of Population, Censuses and Surveys, Survey Division (S.S. 391), London.

GREATER LONDON COUNCIL (1969) *Annual Abstract of Greater London Statistics*, vol. 2, 1967, Publication 222.

GUTHRIE, L. G. (1907) *Functional Nervous Disorders in Childhood*, London.

HÄFNER, H. and REIMANN, H. (1970) Spatial distribution of mental disorders in Mannheim, 1965, In *Psychiatric Epidemiology*, ed. Hare, E. H. and Wing, J. K., London.

HARE, E. H. (1955) Mental illness and social class in Bristol, *Brit. J. prev. soc. Med.*, **9**, 191–95.

HARE, E. H. (1956) Mental illness and social conditions in Bristol, *J. ment. Sci.*, **102**, 349–57.

HARE, E. H. (1968) *Triennial Statistical Report, 1964–6*, Bethlem Royal Hospital and the Maudsley Hospital.

HARRIS, M. and O'SHAUGHNESSY, E. (1967) *Consultation project in a comprehensive school*, unpublished MS, London, Tavistock Centre.

HARWIN, B. G., COOPER, B., EASTWOOD, M. R., and GOLDBERG, D. P. (1970) Prospects for social work in general practice, *Lancet*, **2**, 559–61.

HENDERSON, P. (1968) Changing patterns of disease and disability in schoolchildren in England and Wales, *Brit. med. J.*, **2**, 259–63.

HOLLINGSHEAD, A. B. and REDLICH, F. C. (1958) *Social Class and Mental Illness*, New York.

HOPKINS, P. and COOPER, B. (1969) Psychiatric referral from a general practice, *Brit. J. Psychiat.*, **115**, 1163–74.

HOWELLS, J. G. (1965) Organisation of Child Psychiatric Services, In *Modern Perspectives in Child Psychiatry*. Ed., Howells, J. G., Edinburgh.

HUNT, R. G. (1961) Age, sex and service patterns in a child guidance clinic, *J. child Psychol. Psychiat.*, **2**, 185–92.

IRELAND, W. (1898) *The Mental Affections of Children*, London.

JONES, A. (1970) *School Counselling in Practice*, London.

KAESER, A. C. and COOPER, B. (1971) The psychiatric patient, the general practitioner and the out-patient clinic: an operational study and a review, *Psychol. Med.*, **1**, 312–25.

KANNER, L. (1959) The thirty-third Maudsley lecture: Trends in Child Psychiatry, *J. ment. Sci.*, **105**, 581–93.

KEIR, G. (1952) A history of child guidance, *Brit. J. educ. Psychol.*, **22**, 5–29.

KELLETT, J. and MEZEY, A. G. (1970) Attitudes to psychiatry in the general hospital, *Brit. med. J.*, **4**, 106–8.

KENDALL, M. G. (Chairman) (1962) *Towards a Measure of Medical Care: operational research in the health services*, Symposium, sponsored by Nuffield Provincial Hospitals Trust, held at Magdalen College, Oxford, Dec. 1960. London.

KESSEL, N. (1963) Who ought to see a psychiatrist?, *Lancet*, **1**, 1092–4.

KOLVIN, I. (1973) Evaluation of psychiatric services for children in England & Wales, In *Roots of Evaluation*: the epidemiological basis for planning psychiatric services, Ed., Wing, J. K. & Häfner, H., London.

LANCET (1974) Editorial: Deviance in the classroom, **2**, 268–9.

LANDONI, G., PENNING, R., MERIUS, G., and BETTSCHART, W. (1973) Étude de la clientèle d'un service de guidance infantile: considérations statistiques et épidémiologiques, *Soc. Psychiat.*, **8**, 1–15.

LANGDON DOWN, J. (1887) *Mental Affections of Childhood and Youth*, London.

LANGFORD, W. S. (1964) Reflections on classification in child psychiatry as related to the activities of the Committee in Child Psychiatry of the Group for the Advancement of Psychiatry, *Diagnostic Classification in Child Psychiatry*, ed., Jenkins, R. L. and Cole, J. O., *Amer. Psychiat. Assoc., Psychiat. Res. Report No. 18*.

LANGNER, T. S. and MICHAEL, S. T. (1963) *Life Stress and Mental Health: the Midtown Manhattan Study*, New York.

LAPOUSE, R. and MONK, M. A. (1958) An epidemiological study of behaviour characteristics in children, *Amer. J. publ. Health*, **48**, 1134–44.

LAPOUSE, R. and MONK, M. A. (1964) Behaviour deviations in a representative sample of children: variation by sex, age, race, social class and family size, *Amer. J. Orthopsychiat.*, **34**, 436–46.

LEIGHTON, D. C., HARDING, J. S., MACKLIN, D. B., MacMILLAN, A. M., and LEIGHTON, A. H. (1963) The Character of Danger. Psychiatric symptoms in selected communities, *The Stirling County Study of Psychiatric Disorder and Sociocultural Environment*, Vol. III, New York.

LEVY, D. M. (1968) Beginnings of the child guidance movement, *Amer. J. Orthopsychiat.*, **38**, 799–804.

LEVY, L. and ROWITZ, L. (1970) The spatial distribution of treated mental disorders in Chicago, *Soc. Psychiat.*, **5**, 1–11.

MAAS, H. S. (1955) *Socio-cultural factors in psychiatric clinic services for children*, Smith College Studies in Social Work, Smith College, Northampton, Mass.

MACLACHLAN, G. (Ed.) (1962) *Towards a Measure of Medical Care*: operational research in the health services, Symposium, sponsored by Nuffield Provincial Hospitals Trust, held at Magdalen College, Oxford, Dec. 1960. London.

MANHEIMER, MARCEL (1899) *Les Troubles Mentaux de l'Enfance: Précis de Psychiatrie Infantile*, Paris.

MATTHEW, G. K. (1971) Measuring need and evaluating services, In MacLachlan, G. (ed.), *Portfolio for Health*, The role and programme of the D.H.H.S. in health service research, *Problems and Progress in Medical Care*, 6th series, London.

MAUDSLEY, HENRY (1879) *The Pathology of Mind*, London.

MILLER, A. D. (1968) Impressions of Soviet psychiatry: the child mental health care system, *Amer. J. Psychiat.*, **125**, 660–65.

MINISTRY OF EDUCATION (1955) Report of the Committee on Maladjusted Children (Underwood Report), London.

MOREAU DE TOURS, PAUL (1888) *La Folie chez les Enfants*, Paris (Review in *J. ment. Sci.*, 1891, **37**, 264).

MORRIS, T. (1957) *The Criminal Area: a Study in Social Ecology*, London.

MOWBRAY, R. M., BLAIR, W., JUBB, L. G., and CLARKE, A. (1961) The general practitioner's attitude to psychiatry, *Scot. med. J.*, **6**, 314–21.

MUGGERIDGE, M. (1966) *Tread Softly for you tread on my Jokes*, London.

MULLIGAN, D. G. (1964) *Some correlates of maladjustment in a national sample of schoolchildren*, Ph.D. thesis, Univ. of London.

MULLIGAN, D. G., DOUGLAS, J. W. B., HAMMOND, W. A., and TIZARD, J. (1963) Delinquency and symptoms of maladjustment: the findings of a longitudinal study, *Proc. roy. Soc. Med.*, **56**, 1083–6.

OFFICE OF POPULATION, CENSUSES AND SURVEYS. Sample Census, 1966, England and Wales, County Reports, General explanatory notes, London.

OXFORD (City of) EDUCATION COMMITTEE (1969) Report of the Principal School Medical Officer.

PALMAI, G., STOREY, P. B., and BRISCOE, O. (1967) Social class and the young offender, *Brit. J. Psychiat.*, **113**, 1073–82.

PARFIT, J. (1974) Child guidance in the community, *Spotlight No. 5*, National Children's Bureau, London.

PAYKEL, E. S. (1971) Classification of depressed patients: a cluster-analysis-derived grouping, *Brit. J. Psychiat.*, **118**, 275.

PILOWSKY, I., LEVINE, S., and BOULTON, D. M. (1969) The classification of depression by numerical taxonomy, *Brit. J. Psychiat.*, **115**, 937–45.

POWER, M. J., ALDERSON, M. R., PHILLIPSON, C. M., SHOENBERG, E., and MORRIS, J. N. (1967) Delinquent schools?, *New Society*, 19th October, p. 542.

PRINGLE, M. L. K. (1965) *Deprivation and Education*, London.

RABKIN, L. Y. and LYTTLE, C. (1966) Further information on the ecology of service, *J. consult. Psychol.*, **30**, 146–50.

RACHFORD, B. K. (1905) *Neurotic Disorders of Childhood*, New York.

RAWNSLEY, K. and LOUDON, J. B. (1962) Factors influencing the referral of patients to psychiatrists by general practitioners, *Brit. J. prev. soc. Med.*, **16**, 174–81.

READE, A. W. (1971) *Indications arising from a study of high and low delinquency rate schools*, Unpublished.

✗ REHIN, G. F. (1972) Child guidance at the end of the road, *Social Work Today*, **2**, No. 24, 21–4.

REID, R. S. (1968) *Report on Croydon School Psychological Service*, 1967–8, Confidential report to Croydon Schools Sub-committee, Unpublished.

ROACH, J. L., GURSLIN, O. and HUNT, R. G. (1958) Some social-psychological characteristics of a child guidance case-load, *J. consult. Psychol.*, **22**, 183–6.

ROBINS, L. N. (1966) *Deviant Children Grown Up*, Baltimore.

ROLLINS, N. (1973) *Child Psychiatry in the Soviet Union*, Harvard Univ. Press.

ROYAL COLLEGE OF GENERAL PRACTITIONERS (1973) Present state and future needs of general practice (3rd edition), *Reports from General Practice No. 16*, London, Journal of the College of General Practitioners.

ROYAL COLLEGE OF PSYCHIATRISTS (1974) Memorandum of evidence to the Committee on Child Health Services, In *News and Notes: Supplement to Brit. J. Psychiat.*, July, 1–2.

ROYAL COLLEGE OF PSYCHIATRISTS (1974a) Child guidance: comments on D.E.S./ D.H.S.S. Circular, In *News and Notes: Supplement to Brit. J. Psychiat.*, Jan., 10–11.

ROYAL COLLEGE OF PSYCHIATRISTS (1974b) Child psychiatric services: comments on the D.H.S.S. Document, In *News and Notes: Supplement to Brit. J. Psychiat.*, June, 1–3.

RUSKIN, John (1899) *Praeterita: Autobiography*, Reprinted, with Introduction by Sir Kenneth Clark, 1949, London.

RUTTER, M. (1965) Classification and categorization in child psychiatry, *J. Child Psychol. Psychiat.*, **6**, 71–83.

RUTTER, M., COX, A., TUPLING, C., BERGER, M., and YULE, W. (1975) Attainment and adjustment in two geographical areas. 1. The prevalence of psychiatric disorder, *Brit. J. Psychiat.*, **126**, 493–509.

RUTTER, M., SHAFFER, D., and SHEPHERD, M. (1973) An evaluation of the proposal for multi-axial classification of child psychiatric disorders, *Psychol. Med.*, **3**, 244–50.

RUTTER, M., TIZARD, J., and WHITMORE, K. (Eds.) (1970) *Education, Health and Behaviour*, London.

RUTTER, M. and YULE, W. (1970) Reading retardation and anti-social behaviour: the nature of the association, In *Education, Health and Behaviour*, op. cit., London, p. 253.

SABSHIN, M. (1966) Theoretical models in community and social psychiatry, In *Community Psychiatry*, ed. Roberts, L. M., Halleck, S. L., and Loeb, M. B., Madison, Wisconsin.

SAINSBURY, P. (1955) *Suicide in London*, Maudsley Monograph No. 1. London.

SAVITZ, L. (1962) Delinquency and migration, In *The Sociology of Crime and Delinquency*, ed., Wolfgang, M. E. *et al.*, New York.

SCHWARZ, E. E. (Ed.) (1950) *Children and Youth at the Mid-Century: a Chart Book*, Washington D.C., U.S. Federal Security Agency.

SCOTT, P. D. (1974) Personal communication.

SCOTT, W. A. (1968) Attitude measurement, In *The Handbook of Social Psychology* (2nd edition, Vol. 2), Ed., Lindzey, G. and Aronson, E., Massachusetts.

SEEBOHM COMMITTEE (1968) Report of the Committee on Local Authority and Allied Personal Social Services, Cmnd. 3703, London.

SHAW, C. R. and McKAY, H. D. (1942) *Juvenile Delinquency and Urban Areas*, Chicago.

SHEPHERD, M., COOPER, B., BROWN, A. C., and KALTON, G. W. (1966) *Psychiatric Illness in General Practice*, London.

SHEPHERD, M., OPPENHEIM, A. N., and MITCHELL, S. (1966a) The definition and outcome of deviant behaviour in childhood, *Proc. roy. Soc. Med.*, **59**, 379–82.

SHEPHERD, M., OPPENHEIM, A. N., and MITCHELL, S. (1971) *Childhood Behaviour and Mental Health*, London.

SIDEL, V. W., JEFFERYS, M., and MANSFIELD, P. J. (1972) General practice in the London Borough of Camden, *J. roy. Coll. Gen. Practit.*, **22**, *Suppl.* 3.

SKYNNER, A. C. R. (1974) Boundaries, *Social Work Today*, **5**, 290–4.

SMITHER, B. S. (1970) Church and charity, In *Croydon: the Story of a Hundred Years*, ed. Gent, J. B., Croydon Natural History and Scientific Society.

SPENCE, J., WALTON, W. S., MILLER, F. J. W., and COURT, S. D. M. (1954) *A Thousand Families in Newcastle upon Tyne*, London.

SPENCER, H. (1855) *Principles of Psychology*, **1**, 293.

STEVENS, S. (1955) *An ecological study of child guidance intake*, Thesis to Smith College School for Social Work, 1953.

STOTT, D. H. (1959) *Second interim report of the Glasgow survey of boys put on probation during 1957*, Glasgow.

TAIT, F. G. (1972) Gaps in medical education: the disturbed child, *Proc. roy. Soc. Med.*, **65**, 101–4.

TERRIS, M. (1965) Use of hospital admissions in epidemiological studies of mental disease, *Arch. gen. Psychiat.*, **12**, 420–6.

THOMAS, E. N. and ANDERSON, D. L. (1965) Additional comments on weighting values in correlation analysis of areal data, *Annals of the Association of American Geographers*, **55**, 492–505.

TIMMS, N. W. (1968) Child guidance service: a pilot study, In *Problems and Progress in Medical Care* (3rd series), ed., MacLachlan, G., London.

TIZARD, J. (1966) Mental subnormality and child psychiatry, *J. child Psychol. Psychiat.*, **7**, 1–15.

ULLMAN, C. A. (1952) Identification of maladjusted school children, *Public Health Monograph No. 7*, Washington D.C., U.S. Dept. of Health, Education and Welfare.

UNESCO (1956) Psychological services for schools, *Unesco Institute for Education Publications No. 3*, ed., Wall, W. D., Hamburg.

WALK, A. (1964) The pre-history of child psychiatry, *Brit. J. Psychiat.*, **110**, 754–67.

WALLIS, C. P. and MALIPHANT, R. (1967) Delinquent areas in the County of London: ecological factors, *Brit. J. Criminol.*, **1**, 250–84.

WELZ, R. (1975) Probleme der Anwendung von Kollektiv- und Individualdaten im Rahmen der psychiatrisch-epidemiologischen Forschung, *Social Psychiat.*, **10**, 189–98.

WEST, D. J. (1967) *The Young Offender*, Harmondsworth, Middlesex.

WEST, D. J. and FARRINGTON, D. P. (1973) *Who Becomes Delinquent?*, London.

WHITLOCK, F. A. (1973) Suicide in England and Wales, 1959–63. Part 2: London, *Psychol. Med.*, **3**, 411–20.

WHITMORE, K. (1974) *The contribution of child guidance to the community*, Talk given to the 30th Child Guidance Inter-Clinic Conference, 1974.

WING, J. K. (1973) Principles of evaluation, In *Roots of Evaluation*: the epidemiological basis for planning psychiatric services, Ed., Wing, J. K. and Häfner, H.,
London.

WITMER, H. L. (1933) The outcome of treatment in a child guidance clinic, *Smith
College Studies in Social Work*, **III**, 339–99.

WOLFF, S. (1967) Behavioural characteristics of primary school children referred to
a psychiatric department, *Brit. J. Psychiat.*, **113**, 885–93.

WORLD HEALTH ORGANIZATION (1973) *Psychiatry and Primary Medical Care*,
Report of a working group, Regional Office for Europe, Copenhagen.

INDEXES

Index of Subjects

Analysis of variance, 42, 101, *154–5*
Anthropometric laboratory, 4
At-risk registers, 34
Attitudes of general practitioners, 23–4,
  95–6, 103–5
Attitudes of parents, 23

Biographical Sketch of an Infant, 3
Bucks. Child Health Survey, 15, 21, 23

Child Guidance Council, 6
Child Guidance Demonstration Clinics,
  5, 6
Cambridge Study in Delinquent Development, 18
Census of England and Wales, 1966 (10 %
  sample), 46, 66, 68, 70, 108, 110, 112
Census office, 68
Chicago survey of mental disorders, xiii
Child guidance,
  international comparisons of, 10–12
  psychoanalytic influence on, 5, 11
Child guidance clientele,
  comparisons with normal and with
    maladjusted children, 21–2
  delinquent behaviour in, 59–61
  diagnostic distribution of, 49
  features of, 8–10
  sex ratio in, 22, 47
  social class distribution of, 50–1
Child guidance clinics, 2, 6, 36–8
  survey of six English, *7–10*, 13, 21, 22,
    47, 49
Child guidance referral rates, 1–2, 25
  attitudinal factors of, 23–4
  clinical factors of, 20–2
  comparison with adult psychiatric
    rates, 76
  demographic factors of, 22
  determinants of, 19–26
  ecology of, 61
  effect of distance on, 72–3
  effect of social class on, 73–4
  in Croydon, 46
  interactional model of, 20
  nosocomial factors of, 24–6

selective bias in, 26
sex ratio in, 47
sources of, 48
(*see also* School rates)
Child guidance service in Vaud, 11
Child psychiatric disorders,
  frequency of treated cases, 1, 24–5
  in an Inner London Borough, 14
  on Isle of Wight, 14
  prevalence of, 14–15
  regional and local differences in, 24–5
  social correlates of, 16
Child psychiatric services, organization
  of, 115–22
Child psychiatry,
  diagnostic categories in, 9, 45–6
  in the U.S.S.R., 12, 13
Cluster analysis of enumeration districts,
  64, 69, 110, *141–4*
Commonwealth Fund, 5, 6
Conduct disorders, 9, 45, 110
  and delinquent behaviour, 60–1
  frequency among child guidance
    clients, 49
  and referring agency, 52
  and social class, 51
Counselling in schools, 119–20
Correlation coefficients, 66
Croydon, London Borough of, 27–39
  Chief Education Officer, 41, 42, 44,
    78, 79, 91, 108
  Child Guidance Clinic, *36–8*, 39, 40,
    42, 44, 47, 52, 61, 64, 71, 72, 77, 81,
    87, 91, 94, 106, 108, 109, 110, 115
  rate of referral to, 46, 52
  child health, 34, 110
  Children's Department, 41, 55, 56, 61,
    108, 109
  electoral wards, 63–4
  enumeration districts, 68–71
  Guild of Social Service, 30
  history of, 28–30
  Juvenile Court, 54, 55
  Local Education Authority, 35, 37, 78,
    80, 81, 86
  Local Medical Committee, 93

Croydon—*contd.*
  Medical Advisory Committee, 46
  Medical Officer of Health, 41
  modern development of, 30–2
  Probation service, 41, 55, 56, 61, 83, 91, 108, 109
  school health service, 79, 108
  school psychological service, 36, 37–8, 39, 78
  schools, 34–5, 78–80
  statistics of, 32–6
  vital statistics of, 32–3, 110

Delinquency, juvenile
  ecological correlates of, 17
  in Croydon, 54–62
  in London Boroughs, 18
  influence of schools on, 18–19, 83–7
  maladjustment and, xii, 40, 54, 59–61
  number of offences, 57–8
  self-reporting of, 18
  sex ratio in, 56–7
  surveys of, 17
  types of offence, 58–9
  urban ecology of, 17
Department of Education and Science, 78–9, 117
Department of Health, 117
Diagnostic classification, 9, 45–6, 49–50, 51–2
  and social indices, 75

East London Child Guidance Clinic, 6
Edinburgh study of child guidance attenders, 21
Education Acts, 30, 80
Electoral ward rates,
  for child guidance, 63–4, 70
  for delinquency, 64–6, 71
Enumeration districts, 68–71
  clusters of, 69–71, 72, 142–4
Evaluation of services, xi

Family Welfare Association, 29

General practitioners, *93–106*, 117
  attitudes to child psychiatry, 95–6
  questionnaire survey of, 93–105
  use of child psychiatric services, 98–9
Glasgow survey of probation, xii
Greater London Boroughs, 27, 38
  statistics for, 32–5
Guy's Hospital, 6

Health visitors,
  case-reporting by, 22
  in primary care teams, 121

Heilpädagogik movement, 3
Historical background of child psychiatry, 2–6
Home Office, 54
Hypotheses, working 40, 107

Inner London Borough, survey of, 16, 111
Inner London Education Authority (I.L.E.A.), 34, 37, 119
Institute of Education, London University, 120
International Classification of Diseases, 45
Isle of Wight survey, 14, 15, 16, 21, 23, 111, 115

Jewish Health Organization, 6
Judge Baker Foundation, Boston, 5
Juvenile Psychopathic Institute, Chicago, 4

Local Executive Council, 41, 93, 94

Maladjustment, xii
  groups at high risk for, 15
  in child population, 14–16
  relation to delinquency, xii
  social class and, 22
  social correlates of, 16
Maudsley Hospital Children's Department, 9, 10, 23, 38, 109
Medical Research Council, study of delinquency, 19
Mental illness,
  ecological correlates of, 16
  surveys of, 16–17
Moray House Verbal Reasoning Test, 78, 86
Morbidity among children, changing trends, 36
Multi-level analysis, 114
Multiple regression analysis, 42, 69, 90–1, 92, 110, *145–53*

National Child Development Study, 25
National Health Service (N.H.S.), 1, 6, 10, 11, 12, 14, 22, 37, 94, 117, 118
Neighbourhood, as unit of,
  analysis, xii, 40, 42, 68, 111
  influence on child guidance referral, 63–4, 90–1, 92
  influence on delinquency rates, 64–6, 92
Neurotic disorders in childhood, 9, 45, 110
  frequency among child guidance attenders, 49

impairment and chronicity in, 21
and referring agency, 52
and social class, 51
New Addington, 31, 45, 63, 65, 83
New Machiavelli, The, 28
Nosocomial factors, 24–6

Parent and teacher questionnaires, 14–15
Pathology of mind, 3
Philanthropy, influence of, 5
Primary health care team, 120–2
Probation rates,
  of Croydon schools, 85
  and school characteristics, 85–7, 91
  (*see also* Delinquency)
Psychiatrists in child guidance service, 1,
  6, 7, 10, 11, 25, 37, 39, 116, 118
Psychologists, educational, in child guid-
  ance service, 6, 7, 10, 11, 25, 37,
  38, 39, 116–17
Public Health Act of 1848, 29

Questionnaire on child psychiatry in
  general practice, 128–36
Questionnaire responses, principal components analysis of, 104, 156

Referrals to child psychiatric services, 1
  by general practitioners, 23–4, 48
Referral rates, 95
  and attitudes of general practitioners,
  103–5
  and characteristics of general practitioners, 101–3
  in relation to neighbourhood, 99–101
Research,
  epidemiological, xi
  operational, xi
Royal College of Psychiatrists, 118

School Health Service, 30, 36
School rates for child guidance, 81–3,
  91, 114
  association with electoral ward rates,
  87–8
  and characteristics of schools, 85–7
  within clusters of enumeration districts,
  89–90
School rates for delinquency, 83–5, 91,
  114

Schools,
  as units of analysis, xii, 40, 42
  as 'pick-up points', 119
  counselling services in, 120
  influence on delinquency, 19, 26
  influence on maladjustment, 19
  of exceptional difficulty, 86
Seebohm Committee, 8
Social class,
  distribution of child guidance clients,
  22, 50–1
  and diagnostic category, 51
  and referring agency, 51
  influence on child guidance referral,
  73–5
Social disorganization, areas of, 17
Social workers,
  in child guidance services, 6, 7, 10, 11,
  25, 37, 39
  in primary care teams, 121
  sessions, 7
Socio-demographic indices,
  and diagnostic categories, 75
  of electoral wards, 66–7, 84
  of enumeration-district clusters, 70–1,
  72
Sources of referral to child guidance and
  child psychiatry, 8, 10
Soviet Union, child psychiatry in, 11–12,
  13
Spatial auto-correlation, 113
State of Illinois, 19
Suicide rates of London Boroughs, 18
Summerfield Report, 8, 25, 120

Tavistock Clinic, 6
Tower Hamlets, London Borough of, 19,
  114

Underwood Committee, 14, 119
Underwood Report, 8

Wandle, River, 28
Warlingham Park Hospital, 36
Welfare State, 122
West End Hospital for Nervous Dis-
  orders, 3
W.H.O. Working Party Report, 121

Young Delinquent, The, 4

Index of Names

Addams, J., 5
Apley, J., 111

Beach, F., 3
Beers, C. W., 5
Binet, A., 4
Blalock, H. M., 156
Brandon, S., 15
Bremer, J., 15
Burt, C., 4

Cameron, K., 45
Carlestam, G., 112, 114
Clegg, A., 114

Danziger, K., 111
Darwin, C., 3
Dewey, W., 5
Dummer, Mr. and Mrs., 5

Eisenberg, L., 14, 122

Fleiss, J. L., 141

Galton, F., 4
Gath, D. H., 23

Hare, E. H., 47, 68
Healy, W., 4
Henderson, P., 36
Howells, J. G., 47

Kanner, L., 2, 5
Keir, G., 2, 4
Kessel, N., 19

Langdon Down, J., 3
Levy, D. M., 4–5

Matthew, G. K., 14
Maudsley, H., 3
Megson, B., 114
Meyer, A., 5
Miller, E., 6
Moodie, W., 6
Morris, T., 30

Pringle, M. L. K., 15

Rees, T. P., 36
Rehin, G. F., 116, 117, 118
Ruskin, J., 28
Rutter, M. L., xii

Sanctis, S. de, 3
Seguin, E., 2, 3
Spencer, H., 3
Stevens, S., 19
Strachey, Mrs. St. Loe, 5
Sully, J., 4

Timms, N. W., 7, 9, 10, 13, 21, 22, 47, 49, 50
Tizard, J., xi, xii

Voisin, F., 2, 3

Walk, A., 2
Wells, H. G., 28
Whitmore, K., 119
Wing, J. K., xi
Witmer, H., 4

Zubin, J., 141

XB 2120670 8